DICKENS

DICKENS

The Orphan Condition

Baruch Hochman
and Ilja Wachs

Madison • Teaneck
Fairleigh Dickinson University Press
London: Associated University Presses

© 1999 by Associated University Presses, Inc.

All rights reserved. Authorization to photocopy items for internal or personal use, or the internal or personal use of specific clients, is granted by the copyright owner, provided that a base fee of $10.00, plus eight cents per page, per copy is paid directly to the Copyright Clearance Center, 222 Rosewood Drive, Danvers, Massachusetts 01923. [0-8386-3775-2/99 $10.00+8¢ pp, pc.]

Associated University Presses
440 Forsgate Drive
Cranbury, NJ 08512

Associated University Presses
16 Barter Street
London WC1A 2AH, England

Associated University Presses
P.O. Box 338, Port Credit
Mississauga, Ontario
Canada L5G 4L8

The paper used in this publication meets the requirements of the American National Standard for Permanence of Paper for Printed Library Materials Z39.48-1984.

Library of Congress Cataloging-in-Publication Data

Hochman, Baruch, 1930–
   Dickens : the orphan condition / Baruch Hochman and Ilja Wachs.
     p.   cm.
   Includes bibliographical references (p.   ) and index.
        ISBN 0-8386-3775-2 (alk. paper : acid-free paper)
   1. Dickens, Charles, 1812–1870—Characters—Orphans. 2. Orphans in literature. I. Wachs, Ilja, 1931– . II. Title.
PR4592.O76H63   1999
823'.8—dc21   98-2876
                                                                                                                  CIP

PRINTED IN THE UNITED STATES OF AMERICA

Contents

Preface

1. Introduction	11
2. *Oliver Twist*	32
3. *David Copperfield*	55
4. *Bleak House*	86
5. *Little Dorrit*	127
6. *Great Expectations*	166
7. A Bibliographic Overview	201
References	218
Index	221

To Our Children

Josh and Katti
Mike and Benjy

Preface

This book is the spillover of more than four decades of exuberant conversation about literature, as well as the precipitate of almost ten years of concerted work on Dickens and on the book itself. Its salient oddity is its intense collaborative nature. It is a weave of discourse generated, together and apart, by its authors, so that there is no simple way to follow the convention of designating this or that chapter as the work of either one of us. Most of it was first talked through and then formulated out of notes and drafts that grew out of the spume of talk and the spate of jottings that accompanied the talk. All of it is earnestly *meant,* though much of it emerges out of both sides of both our mouths. Taken all in all, it nonetheless seems to us a coherent discourse, whose essential argument we heartily affirm, even when we differ on details of argument or formulation.

The one place where there is a serious divergence of opinion is in the chapter on *Great Expectations,* where Ilja Wachs—whose contribution to our understanding of the novel is at least as great as his partner's—has deep reservations about the notion that the entire narrative may be read as Pip's fantasy and about the impugning of Dickens's insight that is implied by it.

Many friends are to be thanked for their very varied contributions to our work. Eynel Wardi is to be thanked for the somewhat soul-shattering insight that *Great Expectations* may in fact be thought of as Pip's fantasy, and that Pip may be taken to be responsible for having polished Magwitch off as an act of orphan vengeance. She first come up with that idea some fifteen years ago in a Hebrew University M.A. seminar on Dickens and then developed it in a chapter of her master's thesis. She has also helped, editorially, to purge the chapter in which the notion is argued of its more abrasive edges, and has helped us understand the anger in the narrative voice of *Little Dorrit.* John Landau has also lent keen insight to the honing of the *Expectations* chapter. Gili Talmor read it closely as well, and pointed to flaws in its construction.

Ruth Ginsburg, for her part, enriched our consciousness of the orphan and feminist aspects of our argument in the course of a long conversation. So has Talia Trainin. Murray Baumgarten read a very early draft of the *Bleak House* chapter. So did Francis Baudry. Joshua Adler had interesting things to say about the "death of God" in relation to our orphan theme. Fred Kaplan responded constructively to an early exposition of our abandonment theme.

We are also grateful to the many students whose interest in Dickens has been a source of new ideas and to the many colleagues whose discourses contributed significantly to our sense of literature and life.

Without Barbara Hochman's endless patience in listening to tentative arguments and then combing over the text of many of the chapters for loose ends, tangled arguments, and jangled syntax, the book would still suffer from greater dishevelment than it does.

We would like to thank Martin Green for his generous editorial responsiveness, and Noa Sandbank for a careful scrutiny of the manuscript for scriptorial errors. Thanks are due to Gadia Zrihan for swift and accurate help with proofreading and indexing.

Acknowledgment is due for sabbatical and paid released time from The Hebrew University in Jerusalem and Sara Lawrence College, time that has facilitated the writing of this book. The Hebrew University is to be thanked for student assistance in research.

1
Introduction

ORPHANS AND ORPHANHOOD ARE EVERYWHERE IN DICKENS. OLIVER Twist, Little Nell, David Copperfield, Esther Summerson, Amy Dorrit, Pip, and a host of other Dickens characters are all orphaned, and their plight as orphans is a powerful emphasis in the novels that depict them. However complex the plot of a Dickens novel, however florid its rhetoric, however urgent its moral statement, the orphan condition, with its pain and its pathos, is always close to the center of its concerns.

So deep is Dickens's imaginative implication in the challenges of the orphan condition that we come to feel that his ultimate loyalty is to the abandoned child. Indeed, the development of his work is toward an evermore fierce critique of the world from within the perspective of that child, or of the adult who cannot separate from that child. Again and again, and with ever greater explicitness, the novels scrutinize, from the position of the abandoned child, the implications of embodying oneself in the concrete roles available in the world and of fulfilling oneself in terms of the attitudes and ideologies that define that world. As a result, Dickens's fiction questions all the forms that give shape to the self—status, work, citizenship, marriage, parenthood, and property—and it does so from the subjective vantage point of what may be termed the orphan imagination.

The shape of Dickens's novels is determined by this perspective, as is the texture of the world represented in the novels. Their moral passion and their hectic urgency are also a derivative of the orphan imagination. Indeed, it is the unresolvable tension between the conflicting impulses of the orphan state that feeds his inexhaustible inventiveness. The taproot of Dickens's art may be said to be the clash between the orphan's wish to accommodate to the received world and the fury-driven compulsion to obtain restitution for its abandonment.

Because of its close identification with the conflict-ridden consciousness of the abandoned child, all of Dickens's art is transformative of reality. Dickens does not so much seek to reproduce reality as to constitute it imaginatively. His fiction has as the condition for its creativity a tenuousness in the boundary line between fantasy and reality; it draws upon the magical consciousness of the wounded child and uses the magically omnipotent power of fantasy to ward off the disintegration threatened by the experience of powerlessness that is caused by abandonment. Even at its most horrendous, the world becomes tolerable for Dickens only when it has been reprocessed and repossessed by the imagination—only when the concerns of the abandoned child have been incorporated in such a way as to give it meaning.

The depth of Dickens's identification with the orphan experience should not, of course, obscure the real-world targets of his critique of society. Dickens was deeply concerned with corrupt political and judicial systems, with social neglect and abuse, and with inefficient and dehumanizing bureaucracies. Yet both the energy and the figuration of his assault upon the evils of his society spring largely from his capacity for not only empathizing with the orphan condition, but also for transforming it into an image of the human condition. The ripest and richest of Dickens's works judge the world in terms of a vision that never leaves the orphan perspective behind.

No novelist exhibits a more intense hatred of falsehood, a keener scent for the inauthentic and the hypocritical in adult experience. The critical thrust of the novels ordinarily takes the form of an interminable process of hunting for and unmasking fraudulent claims to moral integrity. Dickens's radical distrust of false forms of being and the related craving for forms of life that can be absolutely trusted derives from the experience of the child whose world suddenly collapses because of its abandonment—the child who interprets its abandonment as a betrayal of the promise of constant love.

In placing orphans at the center of his actions, Dickens carries to an extreme a tendency of the English novel itself. Moll Flanders and Tom Jones, Dorothea Brooke, Pendennis, Becky Sharp, Jude the Obscure are all orphans, and much has been said about why such figures are central to the tradition Dickens belongs to. Critics have referred the ubiquitous presence of orphans in British fiction to its concern with the realities of social life and to the interest that follows from it, in figures that must evolve an identity and a place in a world where social mobility becomes an evermore urgent challenge. Indeed, Nina Auerbach has suggested that the orphan's lack of antecedents provides novelists of different periods with a plasticity that provides them with the opportunity to dramatize their notions of identity and of the ways of shaping it (403). Others relate the preoccupation with orphans to the harsh conditions of life in the world, where disease was far more likely to carry off the parents of young children with alarming suddenness and where anxiety about survival pervaded the reader's imagination. For some time now, readers have been suggesting that the "death of God" made for the suspension of a deep-rooted and reassuring fantasy of sheltering under the wings of an all-powerful cosmic parent.

All these reasons hold for Dickens as much or as little as they do for other novelists of his time. None of them, however, adequately explains the depth of his involvement in the orphan condition, and none of them interrogates that involvement for all it is worth. Dickens does not merely mine an available vein of the nineteenth-century novelistic imagination; rather, he brings to it a unique charge of imaginative energy, and he channels that energy in ways that are decisive for the shape and substance of his work.

What we mean by "the orphan condition" is both obvious and elusive. Orphans lack parents or, at best, one of their parents. In the extreme, as with Oliver Twist or Pip, they are born into a violent and assaultive world and are reared without the sheltering presence of parents. Oliver lives in perpetual danger of being dropped into the fire, of being battered or cannibalized by the other children at the baby farm, and of being slowly starved to death on the meager gruel that constitutes his daily fare. Pip enjoys the advantages of a home and of surrogate parents, but his tale bears witness to a pervasive sense of abuse. Though he is assured of his daily bread, his life is full of tormenting terror and suffocating guilt.

Again and again, Dickens returns to scenes of deprivation and brutalization reminiscent of Oliver's life in the workhouse and Pip's experience with Mrs. Joe. Dotheboys Hall is a machine for repression and torment; Nicholas Nickleby's experience there bears home on us the torment it inflicts on its inmates. Paul Dombey's life at school highlights his plight as a motherless child. David Copperfield's initial experience at Salem House is a suitable concomitant of his emotional battering by the Murdstones.

The conditions of abuse and exposedness in the institutions that Dickens pillories serve to foreground the sorts of deprivation to which he is profoundly sensitive. Yet these conditions do not wholly define the orphan condition. Amidst the ostentatious opulence of her home, Florence Dombey suffers the deadening chill of relentless rejection. For Esther Summerson, not only is there rejection, but the inculcation of guilt for her very existence. Arthur Clennam, who does not even know that he has lost his real mother, is subjected to an analogous emotional battering within what he takes to be an intact family.

In this sense, the orphan condition is not essentially the objective state of growing up without one's real parents, or even of being bruised and battered by wicked stepparents and brutal, exploitative institutions. It is, rather, a state of mind that besets the orphan child and the adult whom that child eventually becomes, but that also, ultimately, informs some part of everyone's imagination. Loss is a primary condition of human life; orphanhood is the ultimate reach of our ineluctable sense of loss. This, we suggest, explains much of Dickens's continuing power over his readers. Much of Dickens's magic lies in his gift of rendering our universal experience of loss and of our need to contend with this experience. In the phrase he has Joe utter to Pip, life is a series of "partings welded together" (*Great Expectations*, 246), and it necessarily entails a struggle with the danger of their coming apart.

The orphan condition entails a profound sense of having been rejected and abandoned. In its radical form, it gives rise to a virtually insatiable craving for the warmth and the shelter that have been lost—or that, still more damaging, have never been experienced and, therefore, endlessly tease the imagination. It also involves rage at the parents who are felt to have withdrawn their sheltering attention and love. Dickens's orphans feel that their parents have abandoned them both to the brutality of the world outside and to the violence of the conflicts that fill their souls.

These conflicts, with fantasies to which they give rise, help to explain the toll that orphanhood and abandonment take in the stunting of human possibilities, as Dickens explores them. At one extreme, fantasies overwhelm his heroes, and most notably Oliver Twist, with a craving for a return to a state of protectedness and secure maternal nurture. At the other extreme, they mobilize the rage stirred by the sense of abandonment and impel them to crave just retribution against those who are responsible for the abandonment.

Ultimately, Dickens's protagonists are trapped within a vicious circle of desires and fantasies that numb and neutralize them and that culminate in paralysis or even, in fantasy, extinction. Both the wish to merge with the lost mother and the desire to kill her threaten a loss of self. Fusing with the mother, the abandoned child loses its identity; killing her, it is subject, in its imagination, to retributive violence. This double fantasy of merger and also of murder subverts the possibility of evolving a stable identity. Having eliminated its mother from the field of its inner life, the abandoned child loses the basis for grounding its identity in its real experience.

Hence, the pallor and the paralysis—ultimately, the relentlessly self-consuming depressiveness—of Dickens's adult protagonists, who cannot effectively come to grips either with passive wishes or with murderous rages. In the great works of his maturity, Dickens gives us stunning, stylized portrayals of people who are subverted by these difficulties. In Esther Summerson, he renders the dire conseqences for personality of the struggle to contain the desires and the rages that fill the imagination of a child who started out in life as a discard on a dustheap and was raised under the tyranny of punitive hatred for her as the incarnation of her mother's transgression. In Arthur Clennam, he portrays an essentially failed struggle to overcome the repressive depression of an orphanhood that turns out to be literal but that is undergone under the conditions of punitive rejection by a surrogate mother he believes is his own. In Pip, Dickens renders both the quintessential sense of brutalization that is the core of the orphan's sense of the world, and of a hampered struggle to overcome the subjective consequences of that battering as well as of the guilt that springs from it.

Dickens's insight into the psychology of orphanhood is profound, and the depiction of individuals such as Esther and Clennam that springs from it has no counterpart in English letters. Yet to linger with the psychology of orphanhood or of individual characters, even with the astuteness of critics such as Alex Zwerdling in his treatment of Esther, is to lose sight of the larger horizons of Dickens's achievement. Dickens's insight into the orphan condition not only gives him a grip on the phenomena of orphanhood, but it also generates an extraordinary gift of world-making and the capacity to use the worlds he generates in his novels to create perspectives for judging the world outside.

For though Dickens identifies with the orphan condition, he is, after all, not a Clennam or an Esther, and certainly not a Nell. His unique ability imaginatively to engage and then to transmute the orphan state permits him to furl out a galvanizing vision of life, a vision that refracts the dreams and desires of the orphaned and the abandoned and embeds them in works of astounding coherence and overhelming moral and imaginative force. Indeed, it is our thesis that both the substance of the novels and their decisive formal and stylistic features spring from Dickens's unremitting concern with abandonment and from a titanic struggle with the propensities it gives rise to.

Substantively, the greatest of Dickens's novels dramatize polarized possibilities. They concretize utopian impulses implicit in the Edenic craving of the orphan imagination, as it reaches for images of restoration to the comfort of the lost mother. At the same time, they mobilize the abandoned child's vindictive rage both to create and to excoriate a fiercely threatening world which is also, as Dickens comes to see it, apocalyptically dead and deadening, and which makes it impossible to achieve a more satisfactory mode of existence.

The brilliant literary formalization of the materials out of which the novels are shaped does not mute or muffle the cravings of the orphan sensibility but rather focuses them sharply. Indeed, that formalization serves, among other things, to reflect the impossibility, for the orphan imagination, of envisioning a normatively embodied novelistic "world," or of imagining more complexly integrated personalities than its internally rifted sensibilities can allow.

The radical sense of disinheritance, placelessness, and declassing that marks the orphan condition gives rise in the novels to an intense search for ways of reembodying the exposed and naked self. Each of the novels relentlessly probes reality to envision some mode of being that will both provide the stability that comes from belonging to the world and yet confer upon the self the realization of unmet childhood needs. It is the absolute nature of those needs and their irreducibility that, in our understanding, dooms to failure the struggle to embody the self in viable forms. At the same time, however, it is this unresolvable tension that accounts for the radically humane quality of Dickens's work and for the depth and power of his persistent indictment of social falsehood.

The very development of Dickens's art pivots on this tension—on Dickens's fierce need to temper his own orphan sensibility and to qualify the imaginative patterns it instinctively gives rise to. By the middle of his career, we find Dickens engaged in a mortal struggle between the tendency to abandon himself to the impulses and fantasies of the orphan condition and the effort to contain and even countermand them. Indeed, the present study argues that Dickens's deepest engagement with the orphan condition stems from his effort to wean himself and his reader from the temptations of that condition and to master the passivity and paralysis it entails. A major turning point in Dickens's career is the effort, in *David Copperfield,* both to vanquish the passive needs of the orphan imagination and to contain its aggressive thrust.

Before we proceed to trace the logic of Dickens's development, it is important to characterize the features of the work that are most visibly shaped by the logic of his own version of the orphan imagination. Both the passivity and the aggressive luridity of the orphan state are schematically evident in the early novels—most notably, in *Oliver Twist.* Within it, we see virtually all the basic elements of the orphan condition as they manifest themselves in Dickens's writing.

Oliver Twist embodies an abandoned child's wishful fantasy of gratuitous warmth, love, and identity-conferral. This is achieved for Oliver through the benign operation of a providential plot that saves him both from corruption and the gallows. Within the prototypical fantasy that *Twist* embodies, the inheritance of property and of a ready-made place in the world symbolizes the safety of a mother's unconditional love, permitting a passive enjoyment of that love and of everything it stands for. It should not surprise us that his mother's spirit is said to hover over the family tableau that at the end surrounds Oliver in contemplation of the tablet that has been erected in her memory outside the country church.

It is, moreover, not only the positive wish-fulfillment elements that refract Dickens's most forthright version of an archetypal orphan fantasy. The dark, enraged hemisphere of the orphan imagination finds its expression in the concerted hostility of the world with which Oliver must contend, and more specifically in Monks's plotting to ensnare Oliver in the coils of Fagin's malevolence and hence, of the law.

This polarization of the novel's world into extremes of good and evil finds expression in the splitting of its action between what we find convenient to call "paranoid" and "providential" plots. Paranoid plots entangle the protagonists and threaten to destroy them. They are usually organized by malevolent characters who literally plot and scheme against the protagonist. Fagin's collusion with Monks to entrap Oliver in crime is such a plot. Providential plots work independently of the characters' volition to counteract the paranoid plots. They provide their victims with release and, in the simplest instances, redemption. In *Oliver Twist,* as we have already noted, the inheritance plot serves this function by freeing Oliver from the fate Monks would generate for him and restoring him to a substitute family that is a simulacrum of the one he has never known.

In *Oliver Twist,* as in the other novels, the melodramatic plot is the correlative of the absence in Oliver himself of a complex inwardness, an inwardness that might grapple with both passive desires and aggressive needs. Altogether, the plotting of the novel reinforces our sense of Oliver's passivity by its intricate ordering of coincidences that determine his fate. It seems to us that what is vital and energized in the novel springs from Dickens's immersion in Oliver's passivity; it is Dickens's failure to imagine a psychically and imaginatively active Oliver that dictates the displacement out of him of the impulses and energies that would otherwise be in him. The rampant evil of Monks must be seen, in this perspective, as the projection outward of the rage inherent in Oliver's orphan condition. This displacement foreshadows the splitting that in later novels displaces aggression out of Pip into Orlick, and surrounds David Copperfield with figures that embody impulses and emotions he cannot come to grips with. Displacements of this sort are responsible for the simplicity and the transparency of Oliver, but also for the attentuation of the heroes of the later novels. The process of displacement is also responsible for some of the stunning formal innovations of the later novels—most dramatically, for the splitting from Esther of the third person narrative voice in *Bleak House.*

The decisive turning point in Dickens's development as a novelist comes when he tries actively to bring under control the passivity that dictated the form and substance of *Oliver Twist.* Already in the novels that immediately follow, we see him groping toward envisioning more active modes of being than are possible in the world of *Oliver Twist.* Little by little he begins to try to imagine ways of making it possible for his protagonist to forge an identity that can actively meet the challenge of adaptation to the world—more specifically, to the Victorian middle-class world that he and his readers inhabit. In *David Copperfield,* he finally portrays a character who must, in form at least, renounce his orphan desires and strive actively to survive.

This challenge, of renunciation for the sake of adaptation to a repressive world, is in fact the trigger and pivot of his richest and most challenging work. As we have already noted, the ongoing dynamism of Dickens's writing springs from the conflict between his susceptibility to the yearnings of the orphan condition and his growing conviction that he must move his characters out of the debilitating circuit of orphan imaginings. His achievement as he moves from novel to novel reflects his changing relation to the psychic and historical pressures that determine the shape of his novels and the way they express the conflict.

The historical dimension is indispensable. In speaking of the tension between the need to hold on to primordial orphan desire and the imperative of embodying the self in adult modes of socially viable being, we are not invoking what is often taken to be a universal psychic reality, of conflict between a pleasure principle and a reality principle. Rather, we are talking about a culturally determined, historically specific set of terms that are at play. Dickens's treatment of the orphan condition refracts, not only an idiosyncratic personal vision, but a prevailing middle-class preoccupation with children and childhood. This preoccupation, which had already emerged by the middle of the eighteenth century, is one term of what in Victorian England becomes a nighmarish contradiction within the middle-class ethos. The concern with childhood in the prevailing middle-class culture of Dickens's time opens the way to a powerful identification with the passive desires of infancy even as it calls for their strict control. Dickens's emphasis on adaptation catches up the latter impulse. It expresses the wish to control passive needs and desires to impose a stringent ethic of work and vocation—in effect, the Protestant ethic as it figures in the Victorian world. That ethic promises self-advancement which is to be attained through upward social mobility in a market economy. Only powerful control of childhood desire and regressive imaginings can achieve the structure of self required for such advancement.

The way he lives out the tension between adaptive and regressive impulses gives Dickens a unique insight into the realities of childhood. Dickens is the first novelist to render on a considerable scale the subjective experience of childhood; he is also the first deliberately to realize on any scale in his fiction Wordsworth's dictum that "the child is father of the man." However, because the fathering of Dickens's adult heroes is carried out by abandoned children, his characters can never successfully complete their project of self-integration or negotiate a satisfactory accommodation to the world.

If we stay within the terms of this paradox, the abandoned child is sterile; as we have already noted, though in very different terms, he cannot father himself or engender a process of development that results in a fully realized adult. The abandoned child continues to occupy his ostensibly adult self, haunting that self with archaic memories and desires, and forcing it into a position of estrangement. Even in *David Copperfield,* where Dickens strives to represent a positive process of becoming a productive middle-class adult, the abandoned child in David will not allow itself to be incorporated and trapped in the adult form. Rather, his blocked energies spill out into the energized doubles of the novel. The evacuation from David of the abandoned child that he was leaves him in a state of empty maturity.

Dickens's relation to both childhood need and to the work ethic is not static; it changes as he boldly explores the relation between them. So does his response to the outer historical reality with which his characters must deal. He moves from angry rejection, in *Oliver Twist*, of the external reality of scarcity and of the struggle that springs from it, to a qualified acceptance in *David Copperfield* of that reality and its dictates, and then to a horrified contemplation of its negativity in *Bleak House* and *Little Dorrit.* The horror stirs up ever-greater depths of rage and yearning that make for an exploration in both of these novels of dimensions of the orphan imagination unimaginable in the earlier, more obviously orphan-centered work. Indeed, it is in these novels that we find Dickens's truly magisterial depiction both of the psychological ravages of the orphan condition, as in the portrayal of Esther and Clennam, and of an inhuman world created by the projection of their orphan subjectivity. It is as though the struggle to renounce passive desire stirs up a more vigorous imagining of its nature and consequences than was possible in the earlier and less self-conscious fiction.

There is a deep irony here. By the time he writes *David Copperfield,* Dickens shows all the signs of having mobilized himself to relinquish a fantasy of inheritance that is central to the early work, and with it, the orphan fantasy of renewed access to the mother's lost body and breast, and all the forms of passive yearning that inform it. In fact, *Copperfield* celebrates that renunciation. Yet the representation of David's development reflects a deep conflict; despite its earnest commitment to an active work ethic, *David Copperfield* is rifted from within by fantasy elements that undercut David's affirmation of work and purposive identity. It is these elements that contribute to the creation in *Copperfield* of one of the richest meditations on individual identity in nineteenth-century fiction—and to the emptying out of David's vitality.

Dickens's conflict with regard to the ideal of personality implicit in the work ethic erupts still more vigorously in *Bleak House*, where it produces a sharp polarization of values between Esther Summerson and the third-person narrative voice and generates one of Dickens's most striking stylistic and imaginative achievements. In Esther, *Bleak House* represents a strenuous struggle to achieve a normative middle-class identity. Through her, it directly explores the terrible price of a *Bildung* which is governed by the imperative not only of renouncing regressive needs but also active, sustaining desire. So high is the price that Esther pays for achieving functional adaptivity that she undergoes a splitting more dramatic than David Copperfield's.

Esther's dramatically significant other is the novel's third-person narrative voice. Through the third person, Dickens projects a protean, narcissistic response to life that, not only breaches the boundaries of personality that Esther sets for herself, but also defies the normative forms of personality itself and violates the ground rules of normative discourse. The third person abrogates the most fundamental narrative conventions, like telling stories in the past tense, and gives itself the freedom indiscriminately to project its fantasies into the world.

More than anything else in his work, the third-person narrative voice epitomizes aspects of the creativity that Dickens managed to elicit by simultaneously containing and expressing the extraordinary tension between unmet, unevolved childhood needs and the will to become a productive, socially embodied adult. Through the third-person voice and the world it evokes, he in fact distills the essential qualities that characterize his art at its best. We mean the freedom of his novels from false conventional values, the depth of their tragic vision of life, their gift of macabre and often cynical comedy, and the capacity, visible everywhere, for identification with the afflicted and the oppressed.

The presence of the third-person voice, with its psychological and imaginative underpinnings, in fact casts light on the sustained intensity of the novels' imagined worlds. Even when a novel renders the deadness of its world—as in *Bleak House* and *Little Dorrit*—there is very little that is neutral or dead in Dickens's representation of that world. Indeed, Dickens has the capacity to irradiate every moment in the world he creates with an energy of meaning perhaps unparalleled in nineteenth-century fiction. The source of this capacity is, finally, a mystery, but we believe that our focus in this study on the never-absent figure of the abandoned child sheds some light upon it. As in the whirling discourse of the third-person voice, we come to feel that every moment of represented experience is informed by the life and death issues posed by the horror of abandonment. Everyone and everything in the novel, from Tulkinghorn's ominously rusty presence to the complex injustice perpetrated by Chancery, is given vital meaning by the rage and the need for nourishment of the abandoned child. Everything represented by the third-person voice has the quality of always being on the edge, as all of Dickens is on the edge, simultaneously resonating with terrible danger and promising rescue and reparation. That energy of representations emanates from the bruised consciousness of the abandoned child.

In *Little Dorrit,* the critique of the personality ideal implicit in the work ethic is still more dire than in *Bleak House*. *Little Dorrit* dramatizes through Clennam how the vitality of the self is drained by the repressiveness of the Protestant Ethic in its most radical form, as pressed to a grotesque extreme in his mother's distorted version of Calvinism. If Esther invests her energy in generating the self she needs to survive, Clennam, shown in his debilitated maturity, has withdrawn his energies from that struggle, and seeks release from the terrible depression that afflicts him. It should come as no surprise that around him, *Little Dorrit* projects a world still more desolate than the world of *Bleak House*.

Nor should it surprise us that the desolation of *Little Dorrit*'s represented world contains an extraordinary range of utopian images. Throughout Dickens's work, the restitution wished by and for the abandoned child is the source of an uncommon range of utopian themes, images, and motifs. Typical of these are Miss Flite's apocalyptic vision of a world in which estates are conferred at the end of time, the communitarian ideals that play themselves out in Micawber's discourse, and the pastoral rentier heaven at the end of *Oliver Twist*. These earlier images have their analogues in *Little Dorrit* in an astonishing range of pastoral and golden age references and in the text's insistent reversion to images of Christian redemption. Both sets of images, however, evoke the inaccessibility of any form of transcendence and the pathos (but also the pointlessness) of longing for transcendence.

Little Dorrit, moreover, pushes to the extreme another aspect of the hopelessness of utopian fulfillment. Partly because of their origin in the abandoned child's passive need for nurture and merger, the visions of transcendence in Dickens never achieve historical and political specificity. This is so because these visions hover on the boundary line between fantasy and vision. In *Little Dorrit,* where the deadness of the world is an overwhelming reality, these images seem more than usually ghostlike—dim, wavering echoes of nearly extinguished desire. At the same time, the fitful light they emit, like the distant, inaccessible stars to which the text of *Little Dorrit* refers, serves to highlight in a poignant, intermittently tragic way, the darkness of the scarcity-ridden world that has exacted from Clennam and Amy so exorbitant a price in renunciation and repression. It also serves to intensify our awareness of the pain of the hopelessness and meaninglessness that informs the world of Society as represented in the novel, and of the heart-rending consequences of living within the falsified values not only of the Merdles, but of all the pathetically yearning souls in the arid places that surround the Merdles' garishly lighted realm.

In *Bleak House* and *Little Dorrit,* Dickens, for the moment at least, seems to have exhausted the possibility for imagining any kind of vital selfhood that can be generated through striving within the work ethic. *Great Expectations,* for its part, renounces the possibility of an actively striving selfhood, at least in the world as Dickens knows it. In *Expectations,* Dickens again confronts the workings of the orphan imagination, and he does so on an unprecedented scale and with unprecedented felicity. Pip is shown to emerge from the mists of his illusions into a life that is not very vital, but that is also not wholly vitiated by his orphan needs. By renouncing the despair-fraught challenge of portraying an energetically striving protagonist, Dickens realizes in Pip an extraordinarily rich portrayal both of orphan desire and of the difficult process of trying to achieve liberation from it. He also realizes the vision, implicit everywhere in his work, of the orphan condition as the human condition—a vision that implies that the grief, the sense of loss, and the longings that fill the imagination of the Pips of the world are paradigmatic for all of us.

The development we have been describing leads Dickens toward a growing sense of the world as blocking every possibility of finding the fulfillment that David Copperfield ostensibly achieves. In *Bleak House,* we have a near-apocalyptic critique of Victorian society and then in *Little Dorrit* a still more generalized negation of the possibility of life itself. *Great Expectations* takes a more temperate view of life, but its sober representation of Pip's maturation conveys a sense that the possibilities of the self are drastically limited, as is the possibility of conferring meaning on the world.

There is, of course, no correlation between the novels' sense of life's severely depleted potentialities and the energizing richness of the novels themselves in representing that depletion. Quite the contrary. The more deeply Dickens engages the challenge of mediating between his identification with the orphan condition and his sense of the need to accommodate to the world, the more desperate his vision becomes—and the more brilliant his orchestration of the elements that convey it. This is especially true in the novels that depict the draining from the world of possibilities for vision and desire.

That draining is, to be sure, not solely an expression of Dickens's considered judgment of the world he knew. It is also a manifestation of the double bind of the orphan imagination, which cannot escape the vicious circle of its impulses. Dickens's vision of the empty world and the correspondingly empty self is rooted in one of the limiting conditions of the orphan imagination—in its inability to liberate itself from the cravings that consume it. Dickens's great novelistic success lies in his ability not to break out of the orphan impasse, but rather to derive from it images that project its substance and also provide a vantage point for envisioning and judging the world.

Read in this way, the sequence of novels suggests that the moment Dickens even provisionally affirms the normative Victorian way, he embarks on a thoroughgoing critique of its consequences for his characters—and for the world in which his characters must take shape. The affirmations of *David Cop-*

perfield engender the darkness of *Bleak House,* as Dickens more deeply engages the psychic and historical implications of David's values. That darkness deepens still further in *Little Dorrit,* and is not wholly dispelled in the last novels. *Great Expectations* represents a moment of great lucidity and balance that casts dazzling light on the orphan condition but offers no point of positive emergence from its dilemmas.

The pain as well as the splendor of the development we are describing lies in Dickens's inability (or unwillingness) to affirm the values linked to striving—that is, ultimately, to affirm the ethos of the Victorian middle class. As he explores its implications, he moves toward an evermore trenchant critique of it. The narratives in which this critique is cast are overwhelmingly drawn from the reservoir of fantasies implicit in the orphan condition.

* * *

In one sense, our reading affirms a very traditional view of Dickens. We think that the plight of the insulted and the injured stands close to the moral and imaginative center of his work, and we feel that the power of his work derives from his passionate identification with the outcast, the downtrodden, the abandoned. We believe that this identification is rooted in an imagination of abandonment possibly unmatched in literature. In this we align ourselves with many readers, ranging from Dostoevsky to Dorothy Van Ghent. Indeed, we affirm with Van Ghent that for Dickens the two unforgivable sins were abuse of children by parents and abuse of social power for any purpose whatever. We hold, moreover, that in dealing with these "sins," Dickens achieves a level of articulate indignation probably surpassed in nineteenth-century fiction only by Dostoevsky himself.

Although we agree with a variety of traditional readings, we also differ from some of the readers who have weighed heavily in the critical tradition over the past sixty or so years. It seems worth trying to place ourselves in relation to that tradition—doubly so, because in laying out our argument we will rarely engage directly with other readers.

In his essay on Dickens, George Orwell complains that Dickens shared the Victorian middle bourgeoisie's dream of passive leisure. What he does not grasp in his discussion of *Oliver Twist* is the depth and the imaginative value of the regressive needs that are satisfied by the Brownlows and the Maylies. We will show that these needs are rooted in Oliver's pathetic orphanhood and that it is precisely Dickens's identification with these needs that provides him with grounds for a fierce and informed critique of the marketplace from which the Victorian bourgeoisie derived its power. This critique is made by identifying Fagin, as entrepreneur, with the philosophy of "number one." Indeed, the demonization of Fagin is part of a judgment of the economic marketplace which is informed by Dickens's participation in the orphan experience, a participation that uses the lurid unexpressed fantasy life of the orphan to subvert the very middle-class values that Orwell sees Dickens as affirming. Steven Marcus's reading of *Oliver Twist* as a critique of utilitarianism as the apotheosis of "number one" seems to us dead right; we differ from him chiefly in that we derive its rich imaginative resonance from the stressfulness of the orphan condition, as it is brought to bear on a world increasingly dominated by the market and the ideology that supports it.

Unlike Orwell, Northrop Frye has a strong sense of Dickens's critical stance toward the world, and, like Frye, we take that stance as one of the great strengths of his work. We differ, however, with Frye's notion that behind the devitalized mechanization of the Dickensian characters and the creaking mechanism of the Dickens plot, both of which for Frye reflect the life-denying realities of the world Dickens knew, we can hear the rustling of an excluded sexuality that vitalizes the work. We believe that the vitalizing element is not a marginalized sexuality, but rather the rage of abandonment and its craving for restitution. We argue that this rage, in all its myriad refractions, fuels the imaginative enterprise that is Dickens's work and vividly colors the substance of the vision it embodies.

We would also qualify Edmund Wilson's sense that Dickens's great work after *Copperfield* springs primarily from his engagement with the issues of declassing that are figured in the Murdstone and Grinby episode. Although we think that the blacking factory experience was seminal for Dickens's sense of self and of life, we feel that earlier, chiefly preoedipal experiences are probably what feed the intensity of his response to the blacking episode. Both experiences—the inaccessible early experience and the all-too-accessible blacking factory experience—trigger what we call an orphan response in him, and open the way to his prodigious involvement with the orphan condition. Dickens himself was, self-evidently, not an orphan, yet earlier experience, of neglect or rejection, as activated by the trauma of the blacking factory, would seem to have given him broad access to the radical imagination of orphanhood. Positive evidence for such early experience is hard to find, yet, as we argue in our Bibliographic Essay (201–217), the body of his work bears witness to it. It is the concern of this book to excavate and interpret that evidence.

With Wilson we do hold—as Wilson writes in "The Two Scrooges"—that Dickens's greatest work is the work of the 1850s. But we differ seriously with the New Critics who valued the great "social" novels of that decade for the power of their unified moral judgments and for their splendid formal articulation. What rivets our attention in these texts is, rather, the conflicts that animate them, and the expression of these conflicts in their rifted formal structures, as exemplified in the two voices of *Bleak House*. It is these conflicts that not only generate visions of staggering power but also are the grounds for Dickens's straining to find a vantage point for envisioning a transcendence which, ultimately, the novels can neither achieve nor represent.

We further differ from the New Critical tradition in our conviction that it is Dickens's relentless struggle with the values he futilely tried to affirm which is the source of his value for us. We differ no less with those postmodernist readers who would deny the stabilizing value of his commitments. We hold that it is from within a preoccupation with crystallized identity that Dickens generates his powerful representations of a world that precludes the realization of identity or the fulfillment of the potentialities of the self.

Hence we feel that it is not, as David Musselwhite and other neo-Marxists will have it, Dickens's early, free-wheeling representation of the world, including the world of England's proletariat, that constitutes his towering achievement, or the dominant statement of value within it. It is, rather, his relatively claustrophobic representation of the struggle for being of middle-class characters such as David, Esther, Richard, and Clennam that generates his most vivid imaginative work, and informs his most telling critique of the world. Dickens operates within the imaginative arena of the bourgeois individualist imagination. His culture, essentially, is the culture of bourgeois humanism, his values are essentially the values of that culture.

In taking this view, we align ourselves with Georg Lukacs's sense that the strengths of the nineteenth-century novel stem from its simultaneous identification with dominant ideologies and its creation of a world which contradicts those ideologies. In this perspective, we would suggest that what are often taken to be Dickens's novelistic failures—that is, his failure to work within the conventions of nineteenth-century novelistic realism as established in the work of writers such as Stendhal, George Eliot, and Tolstoy—do not stem from mere idiosyncracy or sheer incapacity. Rather, they are the result of identification with humanist values that lead to a revulsion from the world in which it is impossible to realize those values.

Dickens's failure to embody character in the realist manner is not, as many have suggested, a given limitation of his talent as a writer. Nor is it only a result of his entanglement in the imaginative orphan condition, which precludes both the envisionment of integrated others and the achievement of a viably integrated selfhood within the victim of the orphan condition. It is also a refusal of an aesthetic mode and of its substantive implications. For him to have represented character in the realistic manner would have been to affirm the possiblity of self-realization within the world he knew, and hence, implicitly, to have affirmed the world itself. Dickens's refusal to portray character as other great nineteenth-century novelists did is grounded in the judgment that the world does not permit such self-realization.

In this perspective, we see a radical error in the tendency of the more traditional of the recent critics to read Dickens simply as a positive exponent of embodied identity. In very different ways and for very different reasons, John Kucich, Karen Chase, Lawrence Frank, and others have tried to retrieve something resembling a vision of embodied individuality from the texts we are dealing with. To read Dickens thus, even with the sensitivity to nuance that Karen Chase brings to the analysis of his work, is to miss one of the main thrusts of the oeuvre, whose final refusal of such direct representation is one of its salient qualities.

At the same time, we distance ourselves from postmodernist and neohistorical readers who deconstruct Dickens with a view to showing that character has (and can have) no coherence and that the nineteenth-century bourgeois sense of the unity or the givenness of character is no more than an ideological illusion. We affirm, with them, that Dickens's representations of people are rifted and grotesque and that his struggling heroes never come to autonomous "life" as convincingly "real" or coherent entities. But we insist that this is not because he did not believe in the desirability of such reality and such coherence, but because he felt that it was not achievable in the actual world.

Dickens, of course, is not alone among novelists, even among nineteenth-century novelists, in his pessimism with regard to the possibility of achieving an integrated and life-affirming identity, or a vitalizing relation to the world. In his *Theory of the Novel,* Lukacs proposes that the novel tradition itself arises from the effort to envision coherent worlds and identities in a state of universal alienation within which such coherence and meaning are unachievable. Lukacs's view develops the Hegelian notion that modern—that is, nineteenth century—culture is dominated by the unhappy consciousness, and there is a strong critical tradition that understands the history of the novel as an unfolding of that consciousness.

Although the nineteenth-century British novel is not, on the whole, informed by articulate worldviews such as those that shaped the beginnings of German prose fiction, it does in fact develop in the shadow of writers who were haunted by a sense that the world was losing its vitality. The first generation of British Romantics were preoccupied with a sense of the world as being drained of vividness and of mankind as losing touch with its life-affirming power. Blake, for one, articulated a full-blown nightmare vision of the fallenness of the post-Lockean universe, with its entrapment within its modes of scientific ratiocination. And Wordsworth's sense that the shades of the prison house close around the growing boy was not a mere figure of speech, or a universalizing sense of the dimming of the primordial light as the child matures. It was, rather, a concrete sense of the impact of urbanization, and of alienation from the underlying realities and rhythms of life.

Indeed, Wordsworth's vision of life pivoted on the dire necessity for mediation, between the soul of the child that is intruded into a potential state of alienation and the vitality of nature. For Wordsworth—significantly, in our context—it is the maternal presence that mediates between the child and the world. Wordsworth himself was, in fact, no stranger to the orphan condition. Unlike Dickens, who suffered with his parents till he was well along in life, Wordsworth lost his mother very early, and his father not so many years later; we think not enough has been made, in studying his work, of the link between his personal sense of orphan desolation and the poems, from those of *Lyrical Ballads* through *The Recluse,* which deal with loss. Hence the special poignancy of the germinal passage, in which he enunciates the centrality of mothering in the child's relation to the circumambient scene—to the world:

> Blest the Infant Babe
> (For with my best conjecture I would trace
> Our Being's earthly progress) blest the Babe,
> Nursed in his Mother's arms, who sinks to sleep
> Rocked on his Mother's breast; who, when his soul
> Claims manifest kindred with a human soul,
> Drinks in the feelings of his Mother's eye!
> For him, in one dear Presence, there exists
> A virtue which irradiates and exalts
> Objects through widest intercourse of sense.
> (*The Prelude,* Book II, ll. 232–41)

In the absence of such mediation, we have a dead world.

With Wordsworth, but with Blake as well, and certainly with Dickens, what matters, however, is not the particular biographical source of the sense of the world's desolation but rather its pervasiveness—and the power to infuse it with culturally negotiable imaginative contents, many of which are rooted in the orphan condition.

This is also true for Emily Brontë. Brontë is haunted, from within her own overwhelming sensibility of the orphan condition, by the possibility of such deadness, which she formulates with unparalleled intensity in one of the climactic scenes in *Wuthering Heights.* In the course of her "catechism" by Nelly, Catherine, weighing the life-affirming and life-denying implications of her relation to Edgar and Heathcliff, says:

> What were the use of my creation, if I were entirely contained here? My great miseries in the world have been Heathcliff's miseries, and I watched and felt each from the beginning; my great thought in living is himself. If all else perished and *he* remained, I should still continue to be; and if all else remained and he were annihilated, the Universe would turn to a mighty stranger. (122)

The final reach of Catherine's outburst is theological: "My love for Heathcliff," Catherine says, "resembles the eternal rocks beneath," but the language of her formulations, and especially her insistence that "I am Heathcliff," again and again echoes the issues of separation and fusion that inform the orphan state. Critics have often noted this; J. Hillis Miller's treatment of this motif in *The Disappearance of God* foregrounds the theological orphanhood implicit in Catherine's eloquent outburst—and typifies the sense of experience we are foregrounding here.

What is important in Dickens is not the abstract statement of alienation, but the concrete contents of the feeling. Dickens's emphasis in *Little Dorrit* on the remoteness of the transcendent Christian world—on the impossibility of transforming "the crown of thorns into a glory" (862)—renders the theological and existential implications of such unmediated and unmediateable distance. His achievement, however, lies in the richness of the contents that he can give to the abstract formulation. In *Little Dorrit,* as in the entire range of Dickens's best work, we have the interreverberation of the psychic and the substantive, of the orphan sensibility and the firmly grounded historical judgment, so that the issues of deadness and of loss, of social corruption and institutional lethality take on concrete and meaningful shape in our imagination.

It is the concrete articulation of Dickens vision, as it takes shape within his imagination of orphanhood and his simultaneous confrontation of his world, that we shall lay out in the rest of this book. Although it seems useful to us to point out the congruity between Dickens's core vision and that of his fellow nineteenth-century novelists, his importance for us rests on the particularity of his vision and its power. That power is what we wish to explore.

As for the structure of our book, it is radically simple. In the chapters that follow, we engage what we take to be an essential dialectic of Dickens's work, as it figures in a series of texts that, to our minds, provide the best material for tracking it. We engage the issues of the orphan condition where they first emerge with clarity, in *Oliver Twist,* and then as they develop through confrontation with the work ethic and the demands for crystallization of identity in *David Copperfield.* From there we follow it into the major novels that follow, that is, *Bleak House,* where the plight of an embattled subjectivity erupts in the split narrative of the novel, and *Little Dorrit,* where the apocalyptic implications of the impasse expressed and explored in *Bleak House* are pressed to radical conclusions. We conclude with a consideration of *Great Expectations,* which we see as a renewed confrontation with issues of identity and meaning, from within the hopelessness of the perspective achieved in *Dorrit.* The individual chapters are meant both to lay out the governing dialectic, as it emerges in and among particular texts, and to offer more or less global readings of each text.

The bibliographic essay with which we conclude explores biographical and historical material and surveys recent work on Dickens that bears on our interests.

2
Oliver Twist

OLIVER TWIST BOLDLY EPITOMIZES THE ISSUES WE ADDRESS. NO other Dickens novel centers so directly on the terrors and threats of the orphan condition, and none represents so vividly the working of the paranoid and the providential axes of his plot-making. None, moreover, provides so schematic a representation of Dickens's vision of the abandoned child; none illustrates so vividly the implications of total submission to the fantasies it implies; and none can be shown to derive so directly from what we take to be the repressed elements of its protagonist's elided subjectivity.

Oliver is utterly passive and helpless. He is not able to experience very much besides fear, loneliness, gratitude, and an aching need for love. No other Dickens hero so effortlessly gains, not only love, but a providential inheritance that provides him with a name, a preordained identity, and a ready-made world that enfolds him in the warmth and security he has never known. And no other Dickens novel carries its protagonist to so safe a haven with no hint of inner development or independent effort.

Nor can any other Dickens novel suggest so vividly the root terms of the conflict that informs the entire oeuvre. None can illustrate so schematically how the governing conflict, and the fantasies it gives rise to, generate both the world of the novel and the nature of the protagonist. *Oliver Twist* provides a paradigm for the ways in which the radical experience of being abandoned and the need to master that experience generate the action of the novel, the "world" within which the action unfolds, and the situations shaped within the action to achieve the ends of mastery.

Oliver Twist centers on an action of rescue and recovery that undoes its protagonist's initial exposure to brutal institutions. It does so by means of an inheritance plot that necessitates a protagonist who must be so passive and so good that he is denied anything approaching a credible inner life. The terms of his father's will demand that there be no stain on Oliver's character. It not only is criminality that must be avoided, but also any action or feeling that might deny him his lawful place in the world, and in doing so strand him in Fagin's world of violence and betrayal. In effect, the fantasy of redemption inscribed in the inheritance plot mandates an emotional self-mutilation that empties Oliver of such experience as he might have undergone and of such identity as he might have forged in the course of an active engagement with the world. Compared with Little Dick, Oliver is vivid, vital, and energized. He "asks for more" and lams into Noah Claypole for disparaging his mother. But his moments of spunky striking-out are as nothing to the wanness and the vulnerability that endear him to Mr. Brownlow and the Maylies.

It is obvious that the evacuation from Oliver of active aspiration, rage, and desire cannot be motivated by the need to meet the external demands of the inheritance plot. It is, rather, rooted in the conflict implicit in Dickens's version of the orphan condition—the conflict stirred by the orphan's anxiety about survival, and its fear of the rage to which its plight gives rise. It is from within this conflict that Oliver, Oliver's world, and the plot of the novel arise. Dickens writes, in the Preface to the second edition, that in Oliver he set out to show the possibility of natural goodness in the world. The novel, as we read it, suggests that the source of Oliver's "goodness," as of his wan lovableness, is terror in the face of his own repressed rage, and the depths of his craving for a reparative fusion with the mother he never knew. The text at whose center Oliver stands suggests that his pallor and his passivity spring from fears and cravings inherent in the version of the orphan condition—the condition of abandonment and brutalization—which he so vividly exemplifies.

Formally, to be sure, Oliver's cravings cannot be represented through Oliver himself. Oliver's life history precludes the rendering of his experience of abandonment. Oliver is born motherless, into a condition of loss. Absence is the prime condition of his existence; consciousness of what he has lost would seem to be beyond the pale of possibility.

Yet the craving for the tenderness his own mother could never give him can be glimpsed through the novel's plot and the wish-fulfillments it represents. This is especially evident in the nursing Oliver gets in the Brownlow and Maylie households and in the driftings into passivity associated with their ministrations. Here an archetypal narrative of orphanhood fills in, as it were, the necessary gaps in Oliver's concretely represented experience. Dickens's construction of the Oliver narrative provides intimations of experiences implicit in his situation—experiences that confer meaning and value on what Oliver underwent as an infant. These intimations figure most tellingly in the moments when Oliver is poised between sleep and wake, and when his experience is rendered in language that suggests fantasies of paradisal oblivion and graveyard felicity. That language, with the images it generates, bears witness to Dickens's imaginings of what Oliver, who never quite dares actively to crave very much, nonetheless must be understood to have envisioned in the course of his development, albeit in an inchoate way.

Oliver's reveries are empty of concrete biographical content, however. In principle, both the need for love and the rage at its absence might be expected to overwhelm a person with Oliver's life history. Oliver's need for parental presences as shelter from the vicissitudes of infant exposure can never have been assuaged and therefore must presumably be total. Indeed, the rage at the absence of such sheltering presences should be so great that, were Oliver to experience it, he would turn out to be a Heathcliff in the violence of his inner life—or, alternatively, an Esther Summerson in the grip of her struggle to contain that violence. The rage is, in fact, potentially so great that it cannot be acknowledged or engaged. The failure to engage it, of course, determines the character of both Oliver and the novel that bears his name.

The result of the failure to engage that inner violence is the Oliver we have. He is so sweet, so full of craving for approval, so responsive to affection, and so invested in his struggle against being absorbed into the criminal world, that he hardly exists as a locus of energy, imagination, or active desire. It is as though Dickens, in imagining Oliver, must exclude everything that we might expect to inhere in his essential structure of feeling. The result is an emotional evisceration that not only produces the Oliver we have, but also a novel that abandons itself to affirming Oliver's failure to experience strong feeling, active desire, or vigorous activity, and that projects outward all the aggression that Dickens cannot allow his protagonist to engage or even to experience. One consequence of this splitting is, as we have already noted, the novel's melodramatic polarization of good and evil.

For we must suppose that it is out of the inner violence which Oliver, like Dickens, cannot accommodate that the novel generates the energized presence of Fagin, Monk, Sikes, and the frenzied crowds that rage and rampage in pursuit of Sikes. These presences must be thought of as animated by Oliver's unassimilable rage, and drawn from the arsenal of fantasies implicit in his existential situation. They derive their energy from the depth of Oliver's *un*experienced adhesion to the fantasies and feelings involved.

What is remarkable about these projections and splittings, in *Twist* as elsewhere in Dickens, is that they not only generate fantasies and wish fulfillments, but also serve to animate Dickens's searing indictment of the given, the historical world—the contemporary world of the British marketplace, as the novelistic imagination intuited it. For in *Twist,* as elsewhere in Dickens, the fantasies that generate both the plot and the world of the novel mesh with and are vitalized by his perception of socioeconomic and political realities. Alongside its fiction of a happy ending, *Oliver Twist* projects a vision of threat and oppression that expresses Dickens's judgment of historical realities. The reality in question not only is the Poor Law, which is the immediate target of the novel's satire, but also, as Humphrey House and Steven Marcus have shown, the ideology of Number One—of the predatory market economy that relied on the workings of raw self-interest, such as Fagin is shown to enact.

It is to this reality, as it configures for his imagination, that Dickens responds with dread. His anxiety leads him to provide his hero with a safe haven in the suburban retreats and country homes of the novel's *rentiers.* Here Oliver, whose early experience has, in any case, not charged him with vivid desire, survives in a state of idyllic but deathlike passivity consonant with the suspended vitality of his saviors. This passivity is the imaginative counterpart of the aggression Dickens perceives in the market-dominated world.

The world of the Poor Law and the marketplace is nightmarishly envisioned in terms of Dickens's representation of assaults on Oliver. The world into which Oliver is born is relentlessly monstrous, brutal, sadistic. The physical threats to Oliver are stunning. Apart from the ubiquitous starvation to which he is subject and the beatings that he suffers, he is exposed to endless dangers: of falling into the fire, being smothered, scalded, eaten alive by boys wild with hunger, suffocated by smoke, fattened up for the slaughter, flogged to death, having his brains knocked out with an iron bar, stabbed by a knife, beaten with a club, hunted like an animal by a crowd, having his windpipe torn out by a dog. Fagin himself is represented as a child-eating ogre who relishes Oliver's pale face and trembling limbs; at one point, he is represented as emerging from his lair like a "loathsome reptile ... crawling forth by night in search of some rich offal for a meal" (186).

Abutting on the direct threats to Oliver is a constellation of images and situations that reinforce the sense of a nightmare world intent on consuming its young. The novel attacks utilitarianism and classical economics by the use of ghoulish metaphors that involve loss of body substance, equating one man's profit with the diminution of someone else's physical being. The new Poor Law system, with its calculation of expenditure, is "rather expensive at first, in consequence of the increase in the undertaker's bill, and the necessity of taking in the clothes of all the paupers, which fluttered loosely on their wasted, shrunken forms" (55). In burying the poor, Sowerberry tells Bumble, "We must have some profit," but this profit is jeopardized by the fact that "all the stout people go off the quickest ... [and that] three or four inches over one's calculation makes a great hole in one's profits" (69). At least three or four such inches of stinted body substance also figure in the profit to be made out of Oliver by Gamfield, the master chimney sweep, who finds in Oliver "a nice small pattern, just the very thing for register stoves" (61); by Sowerberry, whose ingenious speculation it is to employ Oliver as a mute-in-proportion at children's funerals; and by Fagin and Sikes, for whom Oliver's small size is indispensable for robbing the Maylie household.

The idea of profit as consuming body substance is further energized by its linking to active and passive images of cannibalism. Not only do we hear of a starving boy in the workhouse who is afraid he might some night happen to eat the boy who sleeps next to him, but we hear of how Oliver, given a little more food than usual, is overtaken by the fear that the board must "have determined to kill him for some useful purpose, or they never would have begun to fatten him up in this way" (63). In its more specifically oral form, the cannibal motif recurs in Oliver's nightmare journey with Sikes, in which Oliver ("the lamb" as Nancy refers to him—he being the son of *Agnes*) is led through the slaughterhouse which is Smithfield Market in a state of bewildered terror. The same image lurks in the meal of sheeps' heads previously made by Sikes (201), soon after Nancy refers to him as a lamb, and after Sikes speaks of his "carcase" (200). It is also inscribed in Mr. Grimwig's repeated threats to eat his own head; in the crowd surrounding the bleeding Sikes, "snarling with their teeth and making at him" (445) like wild beasts, and pressing "forward with the ecstacy of madmen" (449), while the women swear "they'd tear his heart out" (445); in Fagin's death-cell fantasy of sawing Morris Bolter's head off (472); and finally in Fagin's desperate cry, "What right have they to *butcher* me?" (472; our emphasis).

The imagination from which the novel springs is haunted by images of cannibalism, which ramify in several directions. Juxtaposed with the more obvious images, there is a set of associations that suggest that the functionaries of the workhouse batten on the bodies of their helpless victims. Mrs. Corney and Mr. Bumble drink the port wine intended for the hospital infirmary, and their corpulence suggests that they have incorporated the wasted flesh missing from the pauper bodies. Mrs. Corney comments succinctly on the connection between the death of paupers and her experience of eating when she complains, "They always die when I am at meals" (217). This connection possibly explains why Dickens must tell us that the corpulent but virtuous Mr. Losborne "had grown fat, more from good humour than from good living" (266). It would also seem to be no accident that the members of the Workhouse Board are fat, and that its chairman is "a particularly fat gentleman with a very round, red face" (53).

Oliver's moral life involves threats less infantile but no less lethal than the threats posed to his corporeal being; indeed, they threaten to land him in the same place as the physical threats to his existence—namely, on the gibbet and in the grave. Oliver's way to the hanging place is vividly mapped. He is trapped in Fagin's den, where the only option is criminality, and all roads seem to lead to the gallows, especially because Fagin's zeal for keeping him is fueled by Monks's frenzied commitment to doing away with him. At the end of the broad road to perdition over which Fagin presides there stands not only vice, but the gallows, to which Fagin's operatives, like Fagin himself, are consigned. The magnitude of the terror that informs this eventuality is evoked by the luridly accusing eyes that glare at Fagin, first in the courthouse and then in his prison cell, and that haunt Sikes after he has murdered Nancy, precipitating his lethal leap from the rooftop on Jacob's Island when he hallucinates them at the end. If we wish to conflate these eyes with the "all the better to eat you with" of the classical fairy tale, we have a no less vivid cannibalistic projection than in the more manifestly man-eating motifs. All these images are rooted in the luridity of the child's imagination.

This is also the case with the crowd images that cluster around Fagin and the hounding that corners Sikes. Dickens's preoccupation with the orgiastic gloating of the crowds that surround Sikes and Fagin reinforces the leering cannibal impulses that epitomize Oliver's condition. Taken together, these images invert what we take to be Oliver's deepest wish, namely, to sustain himself at the same time as he avenges himself on his abandoning parents, and this by eating them alive. They also implicitly reflect his fear, that it will be done unto him as he would have done to others—that he will be eaten even as he would eat.

Eating and being eaten do not exhaust the nightmare dimension of Oliver's suppressed inner life, and of the circumstances—including the aggressive side of the novel's plotting—that surround him. The world that conspires to annihilate him may be taken to be a projection of a wide range of wishes and anxieties that implicitly fill Oliver's imagination with threatening images. The point of the convergence on Oliver of people and circumstances inimical to his being is that he himself cannot imagine positive possibilities beyond passive nurture. Instead, he projects outward the frustration that comes of not getting the nurture he craves, and out of that frustration the novel's plot of pursuit and persecution is projected. As for the underlying wish for fusion with the phantom presence of the mother who never held him in her arms, that wish involves another sort of negation of his being. In this case, we have the negation of every possibility for experiencing active desire, desire that would motivate him to claim his own in any way, shape, manner, or form.

Indeed, Oliver's passivity is not only a manifestation of his desire for fusion, but is also determined by all the aggression that is displaced out of him into the represented world and into the language of the novel. Far from being the actively hungry urchin that his impulses might lead him to be, he is represented as lovable in his harmlessness. Much of the novel is given over to rendering Oliver's diminutiveness, his vulnerability, and his feebleness. It not only is that he lacks at least three or four inches of a full-bodied being, but that he is often sickly, and is actively sick or wounded. Little Dick's pathetic sickliness may serve to underscore Oliver's relative heartiness, but in the end it only echoes and amplifies his attenuation.

Oliver's illnesses are not represented as undesirable. They tend, rather, to be the condition for his lapsing into the still delight of nursing and nurture. Indeed, the moments of his entry into the world of the good and nurturing people—that is, of the Brownlows and the Maylies—are moments when Oliver is desperately in need of nursing. Mrs. Bedwin tends him at Mr. Brownlow's when he is sick and feverish in the crisis of his collapse after being rescued from charges of theft at Newgate, and Rose Maylie ministers to him when he is wounded during Sikes's effort to break into Mrs. Maylie's house.

In these situations, his weakness is heavily underscored, and with it, his innocence. We are told that the Maylie servants, expecting to see a violent criminal, "beheld no more formidable [an] object than poor little Oliver Twist, speechless and exhausted, who raised his heavy eyes and mutely solicited their compassion" (261). Soon after, Mr. Losborne jokes about how Oliver "has not been shaved very recently" (267), thus foregrounding his childlike, prepubescent, unsexual condition. In this, Oliver is sharply contrasted with Sikes, who, we hear, wakes up with a three-day growth of beard after a fierce bout with a fever, during which time Nancy was "nursing and caring for [him] as if [he] had been a child" (346).

Oliver's lovableness, it would seem, is in good part a concomitant of his feebleness. This holds for others as well. The condition for being loved in the "positive" parts of the *Twist* world—that is, in its Brownlow-Maylie part—is that one be poor, sick, and helpless. This not only applies to Oliver and to Harry Maylie, who must cut himself off from the world of action and politics to achieve his heart's desire, but also to Rose herself. Rose must pay the price of sickness almost unto death to become a woman and to marry. Conversely, in the *Twist* world, to be robust, to have energy, to be sexual, like Sikes, is to become a brutal, murdering monster. Better be sickly and renunciatory; at the very least to renounce, like Harry Maylie, the world of active social and political striving for the sake of harmonious existence in the bosom of nature—and of Rose.

It is congruous with this system of values that Oliver's intrusion upon the world where he finds his salvation is passive, involving no action or assertion on his part. He enters that world, not to ask for something, or demand his own—as Richard Carstone will later, in *Bleak House,* attempt to demand his own. Rather, he is taken into that world, as a victim of the forces that beleaguer him in that other world, the world of thieves and villains. There he is lulled into a state of somnolence. Injury, illness, unconsciousness, sleep are the hallmarks of his lapsing into the paradisal world which finally accommodates him; weakness, helplessness, dependency are the grounds on which he is welcomed. It is on these grounds that he is granted "a kindness and solicitude which [know] no bounds," in the realm where he will accede to the inheritance, the name, and the identity that have been providentially awaiting him.

Indeed, the world into which Oliver fades at the end of the novel—the world into which he is absorbed—is as static as Oliver himself has been throughout the novel. Socioeconomically, it is a world of *rentiers,* far removed from the turbulent marketplace where, as we shall show later in this chapter, people come to be rubbed out like long-circulated coins, and where Fagin pursues the voracious self-interest of the free-market entrepreneur. Humanly, it is a world of mild-mannered, feebly energized people who are not only surrogates for the loving family Oliver never had, but are also direct stand-ins for his own parents—that is, a fulfillment of a fantasy of restoration to the bosom of his own particular family of origin. Rose is his mother's sister, and Mr. Brownlow was his father's closest friend. The paradise into which Oliver's life is assimilated is a paradise of unstinting familial bounty.

It is, in short, a regressive world, which may be taken to represent one term of Oliver's fervent heart's desire, namely, the desire to return to the mother he never knew. Its pastoral tranquillity is a manifestation of the desire for nurture and finally for fusion, and as such it represents as great a threat to Oliver's potential life as does the violence of Fagin's hellish den, or the gallows to which it leads. It is Oliver's fate utterly to lack active, accessible desire, to be subject to a set of conflicts that obstruct his way to vital life. Behind both the happy ending of the novel and Oliver's harassment through most of its action lies a dead end of lifelessness.

Signs of the regressive tug of Oliver's conflicting wishes are strewn throughout the novel. There are moments when we glimpse, fleetingly, the deflected content of his governing conflict. Those moments give us access to Oliver's otherwise elided subjectivity. On the whole, these moments represent the experience of twilight states, between sleep and wake. During those moments, the text throws up images and ideas associated with absorption into the world of nature and finally of death, but also associations that link nature and death to the mother that Oliver craves.

The first of these episodes takes place as Oliver gets ready for bed in Mr. Sowerberry's shop. His spine-tingling images of death, induced by the appurtenances of the undertaker's trade, and the "recess beneath the counter in which his flock mattress was thrust [which] looked like a grave[,]" (75) make him wish, "as he crept into his narrow bed, that that were his coffin, and *that he could be lain in a calm and lasting sleep in the churchyard ground, with the tall grass waving gently above his head: and the sound of the old deep bell to soothe* him in his sleep" (75; our emphasis). This wish follows a definition of his uncared for state. "The boy had no friends to care for, or to care for him. The regret of no recent separation was fresh in his mind; the *absence of no loved and well-remembered face sank heavily into his heart*" (75; our emphasis). To have experienced "no recent separation . . . no loved and well-remembered face" is, of course, to *imagine* having had a face to remember, or to stand on the threshhold of such memory—for a moment to glimpse, however obliquely, the abandoned child's experience of the total absence of its mother. Indeed, in a later episode he sits in a graveyard, "thinking of the wretched grave in which his mother lay" (291).

Another episode in fact provides a more direct encounter with what we take to be the object of such imagining. Dozing at Mr. Brownlow's after his rescue from the vengeful crowd that pursued him and from the instruments of ostensible justice that were poised to imprison him, he lapses into "that deep tranquil sleep which ease from recent suffering alone imparts; that calm and peaceful rest which it is pain to wake from" (127–28). On waking from that sleep, we find him sitting with Mrs. Bedwin in Mr. Brownlow's house. He is partaking of a basin full of broth "strong enough to furnish an ample dinner . . . for three hundred and fifty paupers at the lowest computation" (128). At that point, his gaze fixes on a portrait of a woman with a "beautiful, mild face. . . . [which] makes my heart beat . . . as if it was alive and wanted to speak to me, but couldn't" (128–29). The woman in the portrait, whom Oliver very closely resembles, is, of course, his dead mother, whom he has never seen, but whose spirit is shown to pervade the world into which he is absorbed at the end of the novel. Weak as he is, he is moved so deeply by the sight of this never-before-seen mother, that he faints away.

This scene is seminal. It is the one place in the novel that directly elucidates, in direct relation to the image of his mother, all the moments when Oliver communes with the tranquillity of waking from healing sleep or with nature in the countryside. Thus, when we are told of Oliver's entry into the orderliness of the Brownlow household, we hear that "They were happy days, those of Oliver's recovery. Everything was so quiet, and neat, and orderly; everybody was so kind and gentle; that after the noise and turbulence in the midst of which he had always lived, *it seemed like Heaven itself*" (143; our emphasis).

Heaven is the ultimate place of safety, of shelter, implicitly of merger; and Heaven keeps cropping up in the text. It is vividly evoked at the Maylies'. "The boy stirred and smiled in his sleep, as though these marks of pity and compassion had awakened some pleasant *dream* of a love and affection he had never known" (268; our emphasis) even "as a strain of gentle music or the rippling of water in a silent place, or the odour of a flower, or the mention of a familiar word, will sometimes call up sudden dim *remembrances* of scenes that never were in this life; which vanish like a breath; which some brief memory of a happier existence, long gone by, would seem to have awakened" (268; our emphasis).

During his recovery, Oliver is shown to have an experience of nature that appears to be a further development both of the sleep states and the muted memory of a happier existence—of "a vague and half-formed consciousness of having held such feelings long before, in some remote and distant time" (290). In the Maylies' country house, Oliver experiences "peace of mind and soft tranquillity," and a sense of continuing, uninterrupted pleasure: "The days were peaceful and serene. . . . Nothing but pleasant and happy thoughts . . . the same quiet life . . . the same cheerful serenity."

In the elaborate, elegaic evocations of Oliver's lulled communion with nature and memory, the text suggests the extent to which Oliver's experience of the Maylies' world is based upon fantasy, wish fulfillment, and regressive memory, of absorption into a nirvanalike state of being, in mother earth—in the womb. We are told that at the Maylie retreat, "three months glided away; three months which, in the life of the most blessed and favored of mortals, might have been unmingled happiness, and which in Oliver's, were true felicity" (292). Within this timeless, stressless, ostensibly friction-free world, there is neither meaningful change nor development for Oliver. "Oliver had long since grown stout and healthy; but health or sickness made no difference in his warm feelings to those about him. . . . *He was still the same gentle, attached, affectionate creature that he had been when pain and suffering had wasted his strength*" (293; our emphasis).

Oliver's situation here elides whatever active desire Oliver might have for the nurturer, and the fantasy of fusion it implies, that he has never, in fact, enjoyed. It also sidesteps direct imagination of the mother who should be the source of that nurturing. We "see" Oliver's mother only as a spirit hovering around her memorial plaque in the never-never-land of the novel's end. Neither does the novel relate to the conflicts Oliver surely must have had with regard to nurturing. We hear nothing of the voracity and the rage and that, in our understanding, are in fact projected out of him and into the ramified cannibal imagery of the text. The lulling so marked here, with its abstraction from time, as well as from the conflicts that spring from desire, is therefore not only an escape from the violence of the Fagin world. It is also a circumvention of conflicts that Oliver must be imagined to have had: conflicts that would have stirred a bit of the Magwitch or of the Heathcliff in him or that might have exposed him to the self-consuming activity that destroys Richard Carstone in *Bleak House*. Richard will be consumed by his desire; Oliver can remain lulled within the bleached-out echo of the objects of his repressed desire. The end of the novel, with its never-never-land evocation of the rustic retreat and idyllic relationships for which Oliver is the occasion, represents the lulling (and the lifelessness) involved.

Oliver Twist does not, of course, stay within the strict confines of the repressions and polarizations we have been tracking. Many things complicate it, including the displacement of a good deal of rage from Oliver into the writing of the novel itself. As happens throughout Dickens's career, the suppression of the protagonist's rage leaves Dickens's narrative voice free to play, to rove, to engage in magical manipulation of narrative, utilizing the absent elements of his characters' subjectivity to create the grotesques for which he is famous, and to construct vivid, if highly tendentious, visions of social and historical reality. Here, the outrage at abandonment that is left out of Oliver himself finds uninhibited expression when directed at political economists, utilitarian philosophers, and their institutional agents. The novel's fierce assault on the marketplace, with its brilliant conflation of infantile fantasy and social parody, constitutes a remarkable consolidation of the aggression implicit in Oliver's existential situation. Other features of the novel bear witness to this process. Among them are the self-containment of the voice that assaults the world of the marketplace, the compactness of the story that the narrative voice recounts, and its use of images from the orphan imagination for the purpose of social satire.

In substance, the representation of Oliver's world conflates judgments and interpretations of the real-world marketplace with the fantasies of the cruel, sadistic, cannibalistic behavior that haunt the orphan condition. Significantly, the predators of Oliver's world—from Bumble and Corney and the magistrate Fang through Gamfield and Sowerberry to Fagin and the Artful Dodger—are at once incarnations of cannibalistic sadism and devout adherents of the principles of the political economy and utilitarian morality with which England, in the rhetoric of the novel, is identified. They simultaneously function as interpretations of doctrines that were coming to govern the moral, political, and economic life of the England Dickens knew, and materializations of the fantasies that haunt Oliver's orphaned consciousness.

Thus, the child-eating monster Fagin, who is a reptile in search of some rich offal for a meal, and who relishes Oliver's pale face and trembling limbs, is at the same time an exponent of the utilitarian doctrine of enlightened self-interest. Indeed, part of the comedy of the novel stems from the felicity with which Fagin parrots and parodies the rhetoric of utilitarianism. "To keep my little business snug, I depend on you. The first is your number one, the second my number one. The more you value your number one, the more careful you must be of mine; so we come at last to what I told you at first—that a regard for number one holds us all together, and must do so, unless we would all go to pieces in company" (388). The portrait of the avid, ideologically committed entrepreneur is filled out by his espousal of the doctrine of self-interest, by his almost aesthetic appreciation for the inherent beauty and fitness of contracts, and by his addiction to the formal rhetoric of contractual arrangements when he is setting up some criminal venture.

It is no less striking, how richly the criminal world is infused with the transactions, the rhetoric, and the self-consciousness of the Victorian bourgeois world. The life of criminals is referred to always as a trade (248) or business (244). Field Lane is "a commercial colony of itself: the emporium of petty larceny: visited ... by silent merchants" (235). Fagin declaims with great vehemence on the misery of idle or lazy habits. In trying to persuade Oliver to join the gang, the Dodger articulates a familiar Victorian dream when he suggests that Oliver will be able to "make [his] fortune out of hand," and thereby "be able to retire on [his] property, and do the genteel" (182). When Oliver is reluctant to join, the Dodger disparages the very wish fulfillment the novel is in the process of providing for Oliver: "Why, where's your spirit? Don't you take any pride of yourself? Would you go and be dependent on your friends?" (182).

A link is established, moreover, between the world of the criminals, with their ideology, and the Poor Law administrators. It is forged, among other things, by means of Oliver's small size, which, as we have seen, serves so many functions in the novel's imaginative economy. He is ideally sized to serve as chimneysweep for Gamfield, as miniature mute for Sowerberry, and as instrument for penetrating the small aperture by which the criminals plan to gain entry to the Maylie house. Clearly, as we noted earlier, Dickens links the loss of human substance engendered by starvation with the cannibal activity of economic exploitation in general. This motif not only is stressed in the effect on the mortician's profit of "three or four inches" too many in a pauper's corpse, but also in Fagin's conviction, as he contemplates the hanging of his cohorts, that "capital punishment is a fine thing for the trade."

The repulsiveness of this conflation of profit with the wasting away of body substance in the context of rampant cannibalism is elaborated in some of the representations of sexuality in the novel. The grossness of Mr. Bumble and Mrs. Corney's courting suggests something obscene, as does Noah and Charlotte's lovemaking. Part of the obscenity lies in the reduction of Noah and Charlotte's sexuality to gloatingly self-indulgent eating and drinking, as they gorge on oysters, or in the self-congratulatory investment of the Bumbles' energies in a teapot and its little daffy. The obscene aspect of the Bumbles' sexuality is further heightened by our knowledge of the gradual process of starvation to which the paupers under their tutelage are being subjected.

The horror of economic activity and its linking to nightmare images out of the orphan imagination reaches another kind of climax in the Smithfield episode. There is a sense in which the moment when Oliver is helplessly dragged through Smithfield Market comes to stand for experience of the marketplace in general, or at least the marketplace as perceived by Oliver.

> It was market morning. The ground was covered, nearly ankle-deep, with filth and mire; and a thick steam, perpetually rising from

> the reeking bodies of the cattle, and mingling with the fog, which seemed to rest upon the chimney-tops, hung heavily above.... Countrymen, butchers, drovers, hawkers, boys, thieves, idlers and vagabonds of every low grade, were mingled together in a mass.... [T]he shouts, oaths and quarreling on all sides; ... the roars of voices that issued from every public house ... the crowding, pushing, driving, beating, whooping and yelling, the hideous and discordant din that resounded from every corner of the market ... rendered it a stunning and bewildering scene which quite confounded the senses. (203)

The intermingling of men buying and selling animals about to be slaughtered; the nearly undifferentiated character of the individual and the "mass"; the merging of language and physical action into a nearly indistinguishable gesture; and the way buying and selling are reduced to a hideous and dicordant din instead of constituting meaningful human exchange—all these typify Dickens's sense of the public world in general and of the market in particular. The combination of moral and imaginative horror aroused by the market, and with it the anxieties that haunt the world of ordinary desire and striving, makes any activity dangerous, linking it ultimately to the child-consuming nightmare from which the novel shows us that Oliver must find refuge.

Given the firm link between the criminal world and the marketplace, it is striking that inheritance and coinage, posed as antithetical spheres, provide the novel's strongest metaphors for the moral life. These metaphors reenact and reinforce the "moral" of the action, as we have extrapolated it: that to act, or even to expose oneself to experience, is to be consumed; that only the sequestration of the treasure of one's being (and the pecuniary treasure that sustains one's being) can preserve it.

The coinage metaphor is most directly applied to women, but it is equally relevant to Oliver, and through him, to everyone. The best way Brownlow has of understanding the shape of Nancy's life is to suggest to her that "the past has been a dreary waste with you, of youthful energies misspent, and such priceless treasures lavished as the Creator bestows but once and never grants again" (414). The moral content of her identity seems to be a kind of inheritance, analogous to Milton's "one talent which is God's to give." Here that inheritance constitutes a moral stock of finite quantity, unengendered, not learned in the course of experience, and incapable of being renewed, replenished, or replaced through any human action. It must, therefore, be protected and conserved at any cost.

An analogous metaphor organizes the picture we get of the prostitutes gathered at The Three Cripples. They are rendered as follows: "Some with the last lingering tinge of their early freshness almost fading as you looked: others with every *mark* and *stamp* of their sex utterly beaten out, and presenting but one loathesome *blank* of profligacy and crime" (158; our emphasis). The loss of innocence, feminine identity, and virginity is interpreted here as a process of coin circulation—that is, as a series of spendings that lead to the wearing out of the coin, and hence to the loss of original identity and value. The process of erosion as Dickens renders it entails an expenditure and therefore a loss of what is seen as some original nature. "The girl's life had been *squandered* in the streets . . . but *there was something of the woman's original nature left in her still*" (360; our emphasis). Similarly, we hear of "the womanly feeling . . . which alone connected her with that humanity, of which her *wasting* life had obliterated so many, many traces when a very child" (361; our emphasis).

The metaphors are rampantly economic: circulation, spending, misspending, wasting, squandering of some given moral sum or inheritance. And they insist that such moral and spiritual capital as one has should be protected from the world rather than invested or transacted within it.

This insistence confirms the "moral" of the Oliver action and validates its relevance to the human condition. It reinforces what the novel insists is the desirability of the lulled, static world into which Oliver is absorbed by the end. And it sanctions the feeling that permeates the novel: that the only safe haven in a world of demonic predatoriness, economic and otherwise, is a pool of quietude grounded in inherited wealth, like the Maylies', or in accumulated wealth, like Brownlow's—wealth which, as the Artful Dodger puts it in his advice to Oliver, allows you to "retire on your property, and do the genteel" (182). It also mandates a desexualized world, sex leading to rubbing out of the coin that one is, as well as to the cataclysmic violence that follows from Nancy's sexual love for Sikes.

For inheritance, regarded from an economic viewpoint, and not as a metaphor, is conceived by Dickens in *Twist* as a kind of property that is not generated in the world, that is not social, that does not have its origin in any mediated exchange process, and that does not come into being through deprivation or exploitation of others. It is, moreover, something that comes to one without economic effort; it is given without asking. As such, it is also a convenient stand-in for the imagined bounty of the mother's body—her unsullied, desexualized body—which, if it yields sustenance without being asked, absolves the potential asker of the guilt of asking, as well as of the anger that may attend upon refusal. The trouble with inheritance is that life in the island of peace that Oliver finds is more like death than life, and it exacts a toll in debility—of character, of feeling, of experience—far greater than that exacted by the passing of coins from hand to hand in the world of The Three Cripples. The ambivalence that readers have felt about the novel's facile solutions has sprung, we think, from discomfort with the lulling lifelessness of the ending, and an underlying affinity with the vividness of the alternative world—the world of the thieves, however threatening.

Oliver Twist's identification of the marketplace with coin and of active life with the rubbing out of the images stamped on coins has the ring of gratuitously denigratory invective. It is a reduction of economic doctrine and economic practice to the terms of infantile fantasies about how living consumes life itself, fantasies that conflate eating with sex in ways we have talked about before. But it also provides a mordant reading of the "real" world, using the terms of what we take to be Dickens's primordial sense of experience, to make an imaginatively meaningful interpretation of that world.

The closeness of *Twist*'s lurid vision of the world to Dickens's inner life is confirmed by a striking detail in the text. We refer to a pair of curious references in the text to his experience in the blacking warehouse. We twice hear that the medicine sent for the dead woman in the Sowerberry episode was sent in a blacking bottle. Bumble, explaining to Sowerberry how and why they had never heard of the woman who needs to be buried, says,

> We only heard of the family the night before last, ... and we shouldn't have known anything about them, then, only a woman who lodges in the same house made an application to the porochial committee for them to send the porochial surgeon to see a woman who was very bad. He had gone out to dinner; but his 'prentice (which is a very clever lad) sent 'em some medicine *in a blacking-bottle,* off-hand. (80; emphasis ours)

That medicine, which Bumble tells Sowerberry "was given with great success to two Irish labourers, and a coalheaver, only a week before—[was] sent 'em for nothing, *with a blacking-bottle in*" (80; our emphasis).

It is curious, that *blacking* should intrude itself on this episode, which constitutes the novel's most harrowing direct representation of the life of the poor under the New Poor Law. The episode involves the death of a mother, the demented, self-involved grief of that mother's mother, and the orphaning of a brood of chidren; and it projects a nightmare vision, unparalleled even in this novel, of people who "seemed so like the rats he had seen outside, . . . which here and there lay putrefying in [the kennel's] rottenness, . . . hideous with famine" (82). Even the evocation in *Bleak House* of the putrefying cemetery where Hawdon is buried is anticipated here.

The sequence of the dead woman who could not be helped by the blacking bottle is, to be sure, strident and melodramatic. But it is also saturated with affect, expressing the narrative voice's—we would say *Dickens's*—horror of neglect, and his deep identification with the plight of the outcasts involved: of the dead wife, the raging mother, the desperate husband—though least of all, curiously, of the children, who figure only as "some ragged children in another corner" (82). With regard to this last point, it is as though Dickens, displacing Oliver's rage into this narrative, cannot enter into empathic relation to children who are in fact the chief objects of his own identification. Here Dickens does not or cannot empathize with the most luridly represented victims of the situation of neglect, amounting to abandonment, that engages his imagination through out the novel.

This is not altogether suprising. The blacking episode constituted Dickens's own clearly attested experience of abandonment and loss of identity. If we are to take seriously the centrality Dickens gives to this episode, we must assume that the blacking experience grafts back onto some other, earlier, still more traumatic, thoroughly infantile experience, or fantasy, of abandonment.

Just what this experience may have been we have no way of knowing—no way, that is, outside the eloquent evidence of the novels. We have some evidence that Dickens held his mother responsible for his misery in the blacking warehouse—that he resented the fact that she arranged for his sister Fanny to study in the Royal Academy of Music when "she was warm for sending me back" to the blacking factory after he had been sent home from there. We may speculate that this favoritism on her part echoed much earlier, and probably more radical, difficulties he had had in relation to her—difficulties that, presumably, Dickens himself had no significant conscious access to, but that could well have determined his passionate identification with the orphaned and the abandoned. The abandonments he portrays in his novels are those of characters whose abandonment is still more radical and still more decisive than his experience of the blacking factory, though there is no doubt that Dickens was overwhelmed by the fact that when he was relegated to it, he lost his place in his family and in the middle-class world, as well as the sense of his identity as a member of that class, whose gifts entitled him to an honored place within it. Certainly the evidence of the novels—their persistent concern with abandonment and its threats—suggests that Dickens, more than most writers, was deeply implicated in issues of abandonment and the feelings and fantasies that spring from it and that these fantasies are so vivid and touching because of the depth of the infantile experience they draw upon.

Still, abandonment and the melodramatic polarizations it mandates do not define the full range of issues and imaginings. There are moments—and they are among the more dramatic moments in *Twist*—that complicate the structure of issues we have been exploring. Such moments point to richer possibilities for exploring subjectivity and engaging the objective world, even though they do not, in the end, significantly qualify the novel's vision of the world.

First of all, there is the pair of half-sleep episodes involving Fagin—the one, when Oliver, adrift between sleep and wake, sees Fagin gloating over his treasure chest of watches and jewels, and is seen by Fagin as he watches; the other, in the country, when Oliver has his terrifying vision of Monks and Fagin peering at him through the window. In both, neither Oliver nor the narrative voice drifts off into the vagueness of nature worship or the doctrine of preexistence, as in other, seemingly similar episodes we have discussed already. Rather, in both we have a representation of incipient terror and violence, not outside Oliver, but within him. In these episodes, the twilight state does not provide the satisfaction of a passive wish for fusion, but rather it serves as the ground of a nightmare that would seem to spring from Oliver's otherwise vague and passive inwardness.

No less striking is the fact that in both scenes there is a blurring of reality and fantasy; the second is even introduced by a long digression on uncanny states in which the sleeping mind sees realities. The suggestion is that what Oliver sees in these states is a dream—that is, a manifestation of his own inwardness, and of the violence his inwardness might give rise to. These scenes in fact suggest a link between what is outside Oliver and what is inside him, so that the outside world is also inside, like a dream. For a moment, Oliver's subjectivity reveals elements of a violence and a violation of boundaries that the novel as a whole works so hard to exclude.

Hence our special interest in Oliver's response to the book on criminals that Fagin gives him, when he is terrified by stories of people who dream of crimes and find themselves enacting them. It is as though Oliver unwittingly recognizes in himself the possibility of a criminal violence, a destructiveness, and a criminality that his entire portrayal is designed to exclude.

To note this vivid intimation of the excluded dimensions of Oliver's character is momentarily to break down the novel's radical polarity of guilt and innocence, criminality and domesticity, absolute suffering and most perfect happiness—ultimately, hell, presided over by Fagin and his toasting fork and heaven, lapped in Rose's tenderness. It in effect undoes, for a moment, the polarized nature of the reality that the novel renders when it gives us an Oliver who is born into a totally rejecting, actively malevolent social state, and then, at the end is given a familial reality that is purely benevolent.

For the novel, even as it insists upon its airtight polarizations, continues to violate them in subtle but insistent ways. Not only does it recurrently blur the ostensibly clear line between dream and reality, but it breaks down its seemingly inviolable polarity of good and evil. Thus, the very characters who preside over the "good" world of the novel—at different times, Mr. Brownlow, Mr. Losborne, Harry Maylie, and, of course, Mr. Grimwig—erupt with anger and violence that are otherwise absent in their characterization. Mr. Grimwig's threat that he will eat his head is only one of the links between Mr. Brownlow's world of ostensible harmony and wholeness and Fagin's devilish den.

In this perspective, *Oliver Twist* jeopardizes the polarity between its worlds to such an extent that we are not sure which is the dream, which the reality: the criminal world or the Brownlow/Maylie world. The text at one point even suggests that possibly neither is real. It tells us that Oliver, who is carried unconscious from the prison to Mr. Brownlow's, "awoke at last from what seemed to have been a long and troubled dream" (125). This confusion is compounded by Oliver's asking, when he wakes, "What room is this? Where have I been brought to? . . . This is not the place I went to sleep in" (125).

More blatant confusion, with more dramatic crossing of the novel's highly polarized lines, takes place in the representation of the criminal world. The humor, the energy, and the camaraderie of the Artful Dodger, even of Charley Bates, tempts us to favor Fagin's den over the enervation of the Brownlow household. The motherliness of Fagin, despite all the irony of its self-interested effort to seduce "my dear" Oliver, or "my dear Noah," is certainly linked to the nightmare cannibal images associated with him. But it also points to surprising (and threatening) possibilities for tenderness and nurture. These possibilities are sometimes felt to be more powerful than any that are evoked by Mrs. Bedwin or the Maylie women. The same is in a different way true of the homoerotic and autoerotic undercurrents linked to the field of experience suggested by the camaraderie of Fagin's minions and by the suggestiveness of Master Bates's naming. The implicit intimacies of the community of boy thieves are meant, we think, to be admonitory, but they have an imaginative immediacy that the Maylie mollycoddling lacks.

Still more dramatically, the characterization of Nancy blurs the patness of the novel's organizing polarizations. Nancy's deviation from the novel's simplistic norm of characterization is dramatic. Her tenderness for Oliver and the sacrifices she makes on his behalf violate not only the ostensible moral negativity of the criminal world, but also the novel's vigorous avoidance of complexity in motivation. Nancy is the closest thing in the novel to an adult self—or at least to a self perceived from other than a child's perspective. She is shown to exist in a state of sustained conflict, as in the scene where we see her at once able to act on the impulse to protect Oliver and to yield to the wish to kiss Sikes on the lips.

Indeed, Nancy is shown to be trapped in an impossible bind. She is caught between her love for Sikes and her tenderness for Oliver. The bathos of the risks she takes on Oliver's behalf and the price she pays for saving him may be aesthetically problematic. But within the novel's overall circumvention of every possibility of complex experience, the drama of her commitment to the life she has lived, as expressed in her refusal of Rose's offer to "save" her from it, comes at us with unusual force. We not only perceive it as the consequence of her pathetic enslavement to her past, as Rose perceives it, but also as an affirmation of her experience as her own. Nancy is not only "good" in that she aligns herself with the ineffably "good" Oliver, and in effect saves him from sinking into the morass of criminality. She is also a more effective novelistic figure than most others in the text, in the sense that she embodies, from the reader's point of view, a possibility for conflict, process, and development that is otherwise kept out of the novel.

Yet the novel does everything it can to avert any direct or deliberate affirmation of her mode of being. The moral of the Nancy story, as of the novel as a whole, is that reality—life itself, complexity, conflict—is dangerous, and the Nancy action is shaped to drive this point home. It is Nancy's capacity to hold on to two loyalties at once that evokes the most radical violence in this powerfully violent novel. That violence involves not only Sikes's brutal bludgeoning of her, but the whole of its aftermath, from Sikes's paranoid haunting by endless accusing eyes to his pursuit by the raging mob and his gruesome death by hanging: a death that lines up with all the other images of hanging to drive home Oliver's potential fate, if he were to reach the end of the criminal line. At another level, the eruption of Sikes's violence toward Nancy may be related to the fact of their sexuality—a sexuality perceived by the text, and certainly by Oliver, as dangerous. The representation of sexuality in *Twist* suggests why Dickens tended to avoid later engagement with such material, and why he failed when he tried to deal with it.

Nancy's death—like Sikes's death and even Fagin's death—is in a way cautionary. Oliver's absorption into the hushed half-life of the country retreat the Maylies and Brownlow create for him is finally a response to the dangers, not only of belonging to the criminal world, but also to the dangers of being active, grown-up, subject to conflict, and involved in the world of desire. The representation of Nancy, which is probably the novel's most vivid foray into the adult world of conflict and ambiguity that the child's-eye view of the world does not completely control, only serves to affirm the desirability of the child's clinging to the safety of its vision of salvation in the passivity of the Maylie/Brownlow world and in its nullification of active desire.

For better or worse, *Oliver Twist* remains essentially true to its identification with the terms of the vision rooted in the orphan condition. The novels that follow it struggle, with varying success, to break free from the absoluteness of that vision. On the whole, they no longer admit the patness of the providential plot that governs *Twist*'s ending, though they preserve the paranoid plot and its sense of a world polarized between wicked, often grotesque figures who pursue and persecute the protagonist, and the innocent protagonist who undergoes extreme suffering. The bathos of *The Old Curiosity Shop*, for example, is more extreme than anything in *Twist*, but it may be derived from the effort to get clear of the simplism of *Twist*'s providential plot that snatches the protagonist from the jaws of death itself. The story of Little Nell tries, we think, to engage with the brutality of the world in the absence of an effective deus ex machina in the form of inheritance. Yet the novel is dominated by fantasies and displacements that fill *Oliver Twist*. The process of Nell's dying and then her actual death elaborate the fantasies of fusion that are submerged in the scenes where Oliver hovers on the threshhold between the waking world and the world of nightmare, and they are, by our lights, the result of Dickens's involvement with the archetypal orphan fantasies that fill *Twist*. The novel, moreover, betrays no consciousness of the fact that the sense of brutality conveyed is itself a projection, derived from of a tormented subjectivity that identifies with Nell and her state of abandonment, even as the brutalities of *Twist* spring from Oliver's repressive innocence.

The novels of the 1840s continue to struggle with the challenge of breaking free of the *Twist* paradigm, but they succeed in this only to a very limited extent. It is only in *David Copperfield* that Dickens succeeds in freeing himself from both the providential and the paranoid plots, and in projecting a protagonist who claims to be able to suggest a moral and psychological position from which to achieve a viable identity. It is this apparent liberation that provides the stimulus for the more creative recrudescence, in the novels that follow, of the conflicts embedded in the orphan condition, and for their utilization as a ground for judgment of the world on the one hand—and on the other hand for the shaping of novels whose imaginative power is unrivaled in English.

3
David Copperfield

David Copperfield REVERSES THE ORGANIZING ASSUMPTIONS OF *Oliver Twist,* and it does so in the service of the values of striving and renunciation that generate the conflict that informs Dickens's greatest work. *Twist* lodges its hero in the shelter of inherited wealth and identity; *Copperfield* renounces inheritance as a buffer against the world and affirms striving as the way to make one's way in the world. *Twist* conceives of the world as a child-eating monstrosity, and generates it out of Oliver's repressed terror and rage; *Copperfield* conceives of the world, if not as receptive, at least as accommodating. *Twist* empties Oliver of feeling; *Copperfield* gives us a copious sense of David's experience and uses it as a basis for affirming both the world he grows into and its values.

The shift is dramatic. It is as though Dickens has emerged from within the structure of imaginings that dominate the novels from *Twist* through *Dombey,* and has for the moment relinquished his identification with the passive, victimized orphan and with that orphan's sense of the malevolence of the world. Even *Dombey* is still in the grip of the need to dramatize the wickedness of Dombey Sr.'s blind passion for Paul as an extension of himself and the destructiveness of his rejection of Florence. *Dombey and Son* is also closely identified with Florence's craving for the love that Dombey cannot give. We may, of course, take Florence's eventual flight, and her struggle to cut herself off from her need for Dombey's love, as a move toward liberation from the passive yearning and utter victimization that marks the early novels; we may also take Walter's resilience as a move toward the automony David is said to achieve. Yet there is nothing in *Dombey* or in any of the novels that intervene between it and *Twist* to anticipate the extent of Dickens's effort, in *Copperfield,* to represent the process whereby a fairy-tale Walter becomes at least a simulacrum of a real-world individual, actually making his way in the world. Nor is there any sign in *Dombey* of the ideological consciousness that shapes *Copperfield*'s treatment of the process.

In this perspective, what we have in David Copperfield, the character, and *David Copperfield,* the novel, is a tour de force of tranformative imagination, which strives, not only to project a character who undergoes what is presented as an effective *Bildung,* but also to depict the processes and the values that facilitate his coming into being as an individual. The processes of that coming into being are inextricably bound up with those values. *Copperfield,* in fact, is a radically ideological text, whose conception of character reflects a cultural norm.

The present chapter sets out to describe the value-system established in the novel, and to pinpoint the successes and failures of its representation of David's development. Our intention is to show a series of things: how deeply committed the novel is to affirming a particular set of values; how the pressures of its affirmations make for hollowness in David's characterization because it filters out elements of rage and desire that are implicit in David himself and are native to the orphan condition; and how the handling of David not only gives rise to displacements, like those in *Twist,* but also makes for a critique of the value-system with which Dickens is working. Later, we will show how the stress of David's (and Dickens's) renunciations gives rise to the desperate vision that emerges in the novels that follow.

The ideological scheme is crucial to understanding both the novel's affirmations and the difficulties they create. *Copperfield* affirms an ethos that embraces hard work, vocation, goal direction, and a renunciatory husbanding of psychic resources to facilitate the emergence of a balanced, stable, and coherent self. The values embraced within that ethos are those of the mid-nineteenth-century secularized British version of the Protestant ethic. The values in question are laid out with great clarity in a seminal passage, where David formulates his ethos together with the psychological disposition that is needed to sustain it.

David's creed speaks for itself. He writes:

> I feel as if it were not for me to record . . . how hard I worked. . . . I will only add, to what I have already written of my perseverance . . . and of a patient and continuous energy which then began to be matured within me. . . [T]here, on looking back, I find the source of my success. I have been very fortunate in worldly matters; many

men have worked much harder and not succeeded half so well; but
I should never could have done what I have done, without the habits
of punctuality, order and diligence, without the determination to
concentrate myself on one object at a time ... which I then formed.
Heaven knows I write this, in no spirit of self-laudation. The man
who reviews his own life ... had need to have been a good man
indeed, if he would be spared the sharp consciousness of many talents neglected, many opportunities wasted, many erratic and perverted feelings constantly at war within his breast and defeating
him.... My meaning simply is that whatever I have tried to do in
life, I have tried with all my heart to do well; that whatever I have
devoted myself to, I have devoted myself to completely; that in great
aims and in small, I have always been thoroughly in earnest. I have
never believed it possible that any ... ability can claim immunity
from the companionship of the steady, plain, hard-working qualities.... Some happy talent, and some fortunate opportunity, may
form the two sides of the ladder on which some men mount, but
the rounds of that ladder must be made of stuff to stand wear and
tear; and there is no substitute for thoroughgoing, ardent, and sincere earnestness. (671–72)

Without the *perseverance,* the *diligence,* and the *earnestness* on which the activity he celebrates is built, the striving that David affirms is inconceivable. Indeed, one of the striking things about David's credo is the way it does not separate the psychic or moral disposition from the outer trait or the objective activity. David must not only *persevere* and be *patient,* cultivating the *habits of punctuality, order, and diligence,* but he must also purge the *perverse, wayward,* and *erratic* feelings within his breast.

This declaration of faith occupies only a minuscule part of this sprawling narrative; for the casual reader, it is easily swallowed up in the novel's ramified action. Yet it defines the pith of *Copperfield*'s manifest affirmations; the entire novel may, on the face of it at least, be read as an effort to demonstrate their validity. There is a massive alignment of material within the novel, reinforcing its programmatic assertion of the value of earnest and sustained endeavor, and not only stressing the value of work, but the danger of avoiding it; not only the need to be goal directed, but also the traits of character that sustain the purposiveness required. This material supports the commitment that Dickens affirms, but is inextricably bound up with the problematics of David's characterization and of the novel itself.

The text provides numerous examples of defeat through self-indulgence and frivolity. We need think only of the cautionary figures of Micawber and Steerforth, as well as, in a lesser way, Maldon and Mr. Wickfield. They differ in the particular traits that lead them astray, being variously subject to extravagance, fecklessness, and obsessiveness. All of them, however, err in their failure to calculate the consequences of their actions for themselves and for others, and in their inability effectively to devote themselves to their self-posited aims. In this, they are contrasted with David's mounting capacity to husband his energies, muster his resources, profit from his experience, and direct his will toward sanctioned ends. As against David's emergent sense of his self-consolidation, these figures variously dissipate themselves in self-subversive activities.

There is also an abundance of figures to point the positive value of work. Those who accept the burden of work willingly and with integrity are consistently affirmed. Mr. Dick is finally saved from insanity by learning to work as a copyist; like Goethe's Harper, his madness disappears when he takes on useful labor. Traddles expresses his value as a character by his admirable industry and self-denial. Once he accepts the reality of work, saving, and accumulation, he stops drawing skeletons. Ham, after he has been betrayed by Emily and Steerforth, shows his high moral nature by working "as well as a man can." He seems able to tolerate the burden of his pain and anger only by virtue of his commitment to work.

Mr. Peggotty is exemplary in this respect. He works nobly, both at creating a coherent family out of the shattered fragments of other families and in the single-minded labor of his journey to redeem Emily. Mrs. Gummidge overcomes her self-indulgent querulousness and becomes an uncomplaining worker in the Peggotty household. Peggotty herself is an industrious servant. Even as a child cast into Murdstone and Grinby, David insists on doing his work at least as well as others.

The emphasis on work as a moral value has its correlative in the ideal of character whose achievement is represented in the novel. Chief among the character-related elements dealt with is the importance of evolving a discrete, coherent, and purposive identity from within the disruptive flux of experience. Indeed, the formation of a firm character has the function, among other things, of serving as a buffer against such flux and as a basis for effective functioning in the world. Unlike *Twist,* with its almost undeviating consistency of Oliver's "character," *Copperfield* dramatizes the volatility of the self, the tenuousness of its boundaries, and the fragility of its coherences. But it does so to underscore the need for stability in the self and for firmly marked boundaries.

Much of the kaleidoscopic, often dreamlike, sequencing of David's childhood is devoted to the representation of moments of emergence from the flux of his real and imagined world and his reimmersion within it. Such moments of submergence and return appear later at some of the most vividly rendered junctures of his life. This process is first epitomized by the moment in his early childhood, when, drifting off to sleep, he feels engulfed by a billowing Peggotty. Later, at Salem House, he is threatened by his tendency to "dreamy" and "romantic" mooning. Finally, David's most vigorous self-mobilization for a purposive life follows the episode of self-surrender to the storm in the course of which Steerforth and Ham are killed. Indeed, the later stages of David's development unfold under the imperatives of the need for cumulative, controlling consciousness. What is stressed is the need for thrift in garnering what is profitable in experience and for consolidating and sustaining it within an identity that can thrive in the world. No less urgent is the need to accept the world as it is, and for the sake of doing so, to curtail the incursion of fantasies that might put one in conflict with it.

As with the issues of work, the themes of clarity, identity, and coherence are richly dispersed through the text. Probably their most dramatic manifestation is in the character of Betsy, who may be seen to have been generated to provide David with a surrogate mother whose self-containedness allows him to become what he must be. The logic—even the teleology—of her representation can be derived from her function in providing shape and boundaries for David, boundaries his own mother never provided.

In effect, Betsy is the fairy godmother who presides over David's rehabilitation in the wake of the Murdstones and then through his later development. If David is to be reborn after arriving at Dover almost naked, he must be tightly swaddled, and must not, under any circumstance, be of woman born. Betsy must be constructed of sturdier stuff. She must, to begin with, at the very beginning, cow the murderous Murdstone and beard a lioness—Jane Murdstone—in her den. Hence, Betsy must be ritualized, defeminized, and masculinized to produce the strength that will protect David and guide him in his development. An effective humanity toward the child can be engendered, moreover, only through a series of powerful defenses erected to give order and structure to her own feeling life—to set limits for her rage, her terror, her aggression, and her desire. If she were directly to express her own subjectivity, the consequences for David would be devastating. On the side of resentment, she stands in danger of becoming another Rosa Dartle, whose throbbing scar is a direct expression of her rage at being violated as well as abandoned. On the tender side—and the novel shows us the depth of tenderness and vulnerability of which she is capable, when her defenses are down—Betsy might configure as David's threateningly seduceable mother, who is not only taken from him by Murdstone, but also by the "second David" he sees at her breast.

It is in the context of such threats to the integrity of David's being that we must understand Betsy's outlandish appurtenances and traits: the pruning knife with which she welcomes David; her fear of being burned alive and poisoned by food; the incessant war she wages with boys to keep the donkeys off the green; her masculine dress; the absolute order and cleanliness she obsessively pursues; the castrated man she benevolently keeps with her; her inflexibility; the arbitrary way she insists on naming David after his unborn sister. All these may be understood as expressions of her terror of and rage toward a brutal, aggressive masculine universe. They also serve, however, to provide boundaries for a self within whose strict modes of defense and containment a moral and coherent life is possible. It is within such boundaries that she can effectively assume responsibility for David. At this level, Betsy is the antithesis of David's mother, whose childlike qualities and trusting femininity have, as David sees it, led to the preempting of her personality by Murdstone and therefore to her betrayal of David. Even more, she is counterposed against the seductiveness of the mother who shook out her curls at him in early childhood, and who presumably still threatens him with his own desire for merger with her.

Thus Betsy functions, not as an exemplary figure in the sphere of work and productivity, but rather as a concomitant locus of value—as an instrument for the production of the David Dickens wants, a David whose balance, stability, and coherence sustain the values he affirms. Betsy will ultimately be replaced by Agnes who is said, significantly, not only to be the center but also the circumference of his life; it is her presence that, by

David's repeated testimony, keeps him within the bounds he sets for himself.

Clearly, the harshness of Betsy's bizarrely bristling surface and the firmness of Agnes's character and commitment are necessary to David because of what he conceives to be his own "erratic and perverted" propensities. His self-conception reflects his anxiety about his psychic and moral disposition. Indeed, one of the more heavily worked themes of the novel is the danger of submission to the impulses of "an undisciplined heart" (730). Annie Strong defines this danger in her impassioned declaration of loyalty to her husband, formulating it in the course of castigating herself for indulging her affection for Maldon. Maldon himself is, of course, a cautionary instance of the dangers of an undisciplined heart, and Steerforth is obviously the prime example of it in the novel. David elaborates these warnings with a view to presenting himself as another potential victim of an undisciplined emotional life; he stresses the place of his undisciplined heart both in his marriage to Dora and in his irrepressible love for Steerforth. He does so, clearly, to stress the importance of cultivating the virtues celebrated in the credo and to warn readers that they too must beware of the impulses of the undisciplined heart. And he makes much of his courage and assiduity in subduing his dreamy and romantic nature, even as he affirms the place of his disciplined character, as finally formed, in doing so.

The novel, however, does not sustain a consistent and consecutive sense of the emergence of this firm and rigorous David. It certainly does not dramatize him as the drivingly energized figure he claims to have become by the end of the novel. Indeed, David does not quite convince us that he has hewn out an identity consistent with his credo; he does not configure in the imagination of the reader as a person who has evolved a character that effectively contains his energies and imaginings. Nor can the novel itself finally confirm the conception of itself, as a text, which it promulgates. Even as it struggles toward representation and affirmation of David's values, *David Copperfield* dramatizes the ways in which it is not the edifying novel it claims to be, even as David, who cannot be thoroughly contained within the boundaries he sets for himself, proves not to be what he says he has become.

The problematics of the novel in this respect have often been noted. They materialize with special clarity after David's emergence from the relatively enchanted world of his childhood, when much of the charm, the emotional power, and the comedy of the earlier episodes leaches out of him. Once he leaves the initial condition of benign tutelage with his mother and Peggotty, and then of brutal battering by the Murdstones, David is increasingly emptied of the vivifying inwardness of his childhood. Once he begins to assert a relatively autonomous sense of his identity outside the childhood world, we lose contact with the stresses and tensions of his subjectivity, and especially with the reality of the suffering and the bliss that mark his early life. To the extent that he preserves an immediate sense of his own subjectivity, he dramatizes the survival in himself of the qualities of bemusedness, hauntedness, and boundary-blurring which in effect contradict the image of himself that he affirms in the credo—the self that seems meant to be achieved in the elaborately rendered process of his *Bildung.*

Altogether, David is riddled with absences. This is the case at all stages of his development. In his account of his childhood, he muffles the acuteness of his miseries; this becomes especially evident if we compare them to the highly amplified sufferings of Oliver and Nell. In the later stages of his development, we are by and large hard put to believe the survival in him of important traits that figured in the representation of his earlier life. Moreover, there is virtually nothing in the adult "David," as he presents himself, to sustain his claim to being a rigorously disciplined, hard-driving, single-minded person. Nor do we find in David's self-presentation meaningful manifestations of the friction, not to speak of the potential abrasiveness, implicit in the self-mobilization on which his adult identity and achievement are said to be founded. It is difficult to give credence, for example, to the possibility that the aggressive side of the self he claims to have become actually incorporates the fierce self-assertion that finds expression when David bites Mr. Murdstone—the self-assertion that is foregrounded in the cruelty of his labeling, at Salem House, with the sign "take care of him. He bites" (130). Even in the representation of the biting episodes, which are frightening in themselves, we do not fully experience the grinding wretchedness, as well as the insufferable rage and humiliation, which his persecution by the Murdstones must have stirred in him. Nor are we given a clue to how his mordant canine rage may have been transformed within David's striving self, or integrated within it, as he develops.

The conception of writing that David espouses is as problematic as his representation of himself, and as constraining. Indeed, the treatment of writing in the novel underscores all the other issues that cluster around David's self-presentation. David does not define the memoir he is writing—the memoir that is the novel he inhabits and we read—as an imaginative enterprise, as a literary undertaking, or as a rhetorical project. It is presented, rather, as a record of his life, a copy of his memory: as a positive, even positivistic transcription of what is *there,* untouched by the complex processes of conceptualizing, verbalizing, and organizing the story of his life from within the perplexing perspective of a vital, dynamic, conflict-ridden present. It is as though the final stabilization of his life has rendered it static—as though it provides a platform from which to see what has transpired in his life, without continuing involvement with either the shaping subjectivities of his *then* or the coercive needs of his *now.*

There are, to be sure, moments when David lays out the place of literature and of imaginative identification with literary figures in his development as a person. At such moments, he depicts the process of self-projection onto characters in novels and of making over his own world and self on the pattern of what he has brought back from his forays into them. Moreover, the manner of the novel's telling—most notably, the teasing playfulness of the first pages, with their question, as to who is the hero of David's life, and its comic account of the caul, and of the aversion to meandering of the old woman who came into possession of it—runs athwart of the speaker's later commitment to earnestness and sobriety.

The main thrust of the novel, however, is to stress, not the literary, imaginative, and linguistic nature of David's autobiographical enterprise, but rather the fidelity to the fact of the record it purports to constitute, and his earnestness, diligence, and perseverance in producing it. Only in climactic moments—especially in David's experience of the storm where Steerforth is drowned—is there any direct extended dramatization of counterfactual subjectivity, and even this subjectivity is represented as having largely been overcome before the end of the narrative.

Yet such subjectivity does pervade *Copperfield,* even as it pervades *Twist,* though it takes a very different form. It is displaced out of David, as it is out of Oliver, but here it does not control the world of the novel, and is not concentrated in the villainy and violence of characters such as Monks and Fagin, or by institutions such as the marketplace, which fill the world of *Twist*. The displaced subjectivity in *Copperfield* is not consolidated within a coercively paranoid plot. It is, rather, dispersed throughout the text, and finds its most vivid embodiment in the series of flanking figures—of the figures generally recognized as David's doubles. These figures dramatize the magnitude of the dangers, seductions, subversions, and satisfactions that the novel, in its ideological dimension, strives to distance from David. At the same time, the subjectivity that these figures represent generates a powerful countertext which not only subverts the conception of character and art that the novel promotes, but also points back to the conflicts that fill the orphan condition—the conflicts that *Copperfield*'s system of values tries to send underground. Indeed, it is the force of what is displaced into *Copperfield*'s countertext that triggers much of the violence that emerges in the third-person voice in *Bleak House* and finally leads to the impasse of *Little Dorrit*.

The countertext of *David Copperfield* tells us that David's conception of art, like his representation of his character, is part of a cultural system that systematically seeks to deny the operation of "perverted" imaginative and emotional materials in David's emergent self, and that banishes them from the sphere of his direct experience, as represented in his memoir. It is only by grasping what has been displaced into the doubles that we can understand more fully what it is that David's final vision of himself is designed to exclude, and how the excluded material bears on the novel's value system, as well as on the novels that follow.

The nature of the displaced material, and its modes of transposition, can be exemplified in the representation of Mr. Dick. Dick serves as a stand-in for David in the specific matter of writing, as well as in other crucial areas of conflict and motivation. Striking facets of Dick's life illuminate analogous dimensions of David's experience.

Dick's symbolic dimension is roundly confirmed by Betsy. She explains to David that King Charles's head is "his allegorical way of expressing [his plight].... He connects his illness with great disturbances and agitation," she says, "and that's the figure or the simile or whatever it's called, which he chooses to use" (261). King Charles's head is a metaphor, but so, of course, is Dick.

The question of course is, what is Dick himself a metaphor for? Our suggestion is that he represents one of David's ways of

3: *DAVID COPPERFIELD* 65

dealing with his own "disturbances and agitation" (261), which, as we shall see, are analogous to Dick's. Agitation is banished from David's writing for the same reason, and by the same strategy, that it is banished from Dick's, namely, by a commitment to copying. Although expunged, it can be seen to figure in David through what is displaced out of David and into Dick.

Like all David's doubles, Dick is, to begin with, dramatically contrasted with David. His age, his thumb sucking, his blandly benign temperament, and his hallucinatory propensities all distinguish him sharply. Yet there are also striking parallels. He is, like David, a ward of Betsy's; indeed, Betsy took him in just after David betrayed her by failing to be the girl child she wanted him to be. Like David, moreover, he is brought into the pale of respectability by Betsy's unrelenting rigor in setting limits.

The similarities are striking. Dick, whose real name is Babley ("babbly"?), is writing a memoir, as the grown-up David is doing when he produces the text we read. Dick's memoir differs from David's both in its purpose and in his chronic inability to finish it. If David's memoir purports to be a gratuitous record of his memory, ostensibly for himself alone, Dick's is purposefully designed to inculpate his brother before the authorities for mistreating him, and thus to exculpate himself. The suggestion is that Dick wants to prove that he is not a madman, or that, if he is, he is mad because he has been mistreated by his brother.

Although committed to completing the memoir, he cannot get it written, and he cannot do so because the head of King Charles the First keeps "getting into it." What is involved in the matter of King Charles's head is the intrusion of a wholly irrational obsessive element into the flow of his discourse. If we strip away the hilarity of the representation—like the surrealist effect of the intrusion itself, and the fact that instead of finishing the memoir and submitting it, Dick goes and flies its pages as a kite—it becomes clear that the decapitated king's head intrudes on a complaint that Dick intends making to one authority—the *king*'s Bench—about another, who is Dick's brother and guardian. That is, a usurped and murdered royal authority intercepts an appeal intended for submission to a royal authority, condemning still another authority.

The suggestion is that the intention of bringing down an authority summons the image of an already brought-down authority and that this image inhibits the carrying out of the intention. For Dick, to indite his memoir is to indict his brother. Presumably, the self-assertion involved in finishing and submitting the memoir prevents Dick from writing it. It is as though Dick cannot write because he would like to kill—to behead—the king. In this way, Dick's own wish to affirm himself—to exist—to live, by writing his memoir, is aborted by King Charles's head. Hence, it is not only King Charles who is decapitated, but Richard (another murdered king!?) Babley as well. Whether we press interpretation further, and read decapitation as castration, is a matter of choice: it is a question, in part, of whether we need or want to find further grounds for the de-effectualization of Dick and, indirectly, of David.

The only cure, for Dick, as for the devotee of the Protestant ethic, is work; for him, copying, as we have already noted, is the antidote to madness. Once Dick gives up the project of aggressively memorializing, and takes to copying—copying for the pragmatic purpose of providing security for Betsy—King Charles's head, which is a token of his madness, stops invading him.

David, of course, finishes his memoir, but copying is what he claims to be doing when he puts down the story that is ostensibly the record of his life, a transcription of things remembered. His emphasis on copying is suggestive. It implies that his work involves no imagination, no obsession, certainly no aggressive self-justification, no incrimination of those who have wronged him! At the same time, although he does write his memoir, he does not imbue it with the energy and the outrage that we might have expected to "get into" the life of an orphaned and abused Dickensian hero—a hero whose very initials echo, by inversion, Dickens's own, and point directly back to Dickens himself, even as do Mr. Dick's name and his haunting by King *Charles*'s head.

Like Dick, who gave up writing a memoir that incriminates—but also like Oliver, who never, except during his altercation with Noah, strikes out or accuses anyone directly—David forgoes direct incrimination of those who might have been held accountable for his plight. His dead father is criticized by Betsy for his testamentary arrangement, and David mentions that his mother's annuity died with her. David himself expresses only pity for his loneliness in the grave. Instead, he deflects onto others the anger he must have had against an absent father and an incompetent mother. He does so by viciously caricaturing the Murdstones who, in effect, are the closest thing to a *set* of parents that he ever had. The ferocity of his caricature flies in the face of his own copyistic insistence on verisimilitude. It is as though, like the livid, lightning-slash of Rosa Dartle's scar, which shows itself only in the white heat of her rage, David's hostility can only manifest itself against his will, through the involuntary bias of his writing, so that it shows up (as he says of Rosa's scar) like invisible ink—like the handwriting on the wall, to which Rosa's scar is also compared.

Anger also seeps out in David's muted but devastating portrayal of the fathers (or father-surrogates) who abound in the novel. We have his own father, whose annuity lasts only until his mother's death, and leaves nothing to him; the intestate and impecunious Spenlow, who has nothing to leave Dora; the obsessionally self-involved and ultimately irresponsible Wickfield; the absconded (through death) progenitors of both Steerforth and Annie Strong; and the uncle-guardian of Traddles, who arbitrarily disinherits him. Through all the living fathers and father surrogates in the novel, and with no overt sign of malicious intent, Dickens/David indicts paternity as absent, inadequate, and irresponsible. Even Daniel Peggotty, who is so thoroughly idealized, cannot begin to cope with the challenges posed by his foster children, Emily and Ham. David insists, moreover, that, like everything else in the novel, the parents and stand-in parents that he renders—even the Murdstones!—are a copy of "reality," rather than projections that derive from his inner world, projections that surely defy rather than reflect the orderliness and containment of the copyist and his well-ruled page.

In this perspective, we might suggest that Dickens's choice of *Copp*erfield over other names considered for David may well have been determined, in part at least, by its phonic overlap with *Copy*field. In this context—that is, the context of the need to suppress the decapitating, even the dementing, rage implied by the story of his life, and by the wish to tell it as an indictment—we may also find a key to the pervasive charm of David's memoir, as well as to his evasion through his charm of the resentment and frictive aggressiveness that we might have expected to find in him. *Copperfield* beguiles with David's charm, but it does not engage us with what may underlie or motivate it. David is not ineffectual, on the face of it; he is not emasculated, like Dick. His narrative, however, is curiously lacking in the thrust we might have expected it to have. As we have already noted, there is no sign, in the flow of David's narrative, of the mordant energy of retaliation that David expresses when he bites Murdstone's hand. Nor do we have the displacement of aggression into the outside world, as we have in *Twist,* or the fabrication of a plot (a paranoid plot) in which David is pursued from the outset. The Uriah conspiracy provides a miniature version of such plotting, but it is insignificant as compared with the kind of plot that organizes *Oliver Twist* or that will figure in *Great Expectations.*

If we ask where the resentment and aggressiveness have gone, one answer is that they have largely migrated into Uriah. Uriah is a highly energized monster of resentment, the incarnation of a vindictive aggressiveness toward much that David comes to value. His scheme against Mr. Wickfield and Agnes is a scheme against the novel's richest emblems of bourgeois order and of Christian rectitude.

Like all David's doubles, Uriah is sharply distinguished from David. He has no redeeming charm, and little manifest relation to the issues of creativity and artistic expression that figure in Dick, Steerforth, and Micawber. He is, moreover, the only character toward whom David sustains continuing animosity, and one of the very few toward whom he directs physical violence. The only other figure besides Murdstone whom David assaults physically is the butcher's boy in Canterbury, whom he fights because of an imagined slight to the light-of-his-adolescent life, and even there his contentiousness is elicited by his sense of having been affronted. With Uriah, David's violence is compulsive, expressing his sense of invasion by Uriah and Uriah's moral and physical stench. Uriah's intrusiveness is ubiquitous, but it is materialized most dramatically when he billets himself on David in London. In doing so, he appropriates David's living space and pervades it with his physical presence and moral violence.

David's fascination with Uriah would seem to be the fascination of the abomination. Uriah is one of Dickens's more repulsive but also more energized grotesques, and a whole catalog of off-putting traits is fused in him. Those traits are not the arbitrary fruit of Dickens's imagination, nor are they merely part of a caricaturistic playfulness that slyly subverts David's claims to copyistic verisimilitude. They are, rather, highly overdetermined social and cultural qualities, which provide a skeptical commentary on the modes of instinctual adaptation that are appropriate to David's credo. Indeed, they are displacements of everything in David that should have been there had he been wholly what he claims to be in the way of burgher enterprise.

3: DAVID COPPERFIELD

We do not have to probe deeply to perceive the scatological, phallic, and assaultive elements of Uriah's representation. What is it here, we are impelled to think, that lies in a he*ap*? Does *Ur*iah suggest still another excremental function? Why is it that his writing suggests snail-slime? And how will he sully Agnes, as both David and the reader feel he will, if he touches her?

To this last question we have a clear enough answer: He will sully her by sexual possession. Yet it remains a question: Why will sexual possession sully? That Heep is a phallic as well as an anal creature is self-evident. Otherwise, what does it mean that he writhes, snakes, eels, and plays with his hands as he does? And the emphasis on hands, together with his uneasy adolescent squirming—in which propensity he parallels Micawber Jr. in the throes of adolescence—suggests that he is not only phallic, but onanistic, and that his onanism, like the entire thrust of his lurid imagination, is more than ordinarily filthy. A cultural revulsion from masturbatory self-indulgence is compounded here by a set of scatological associations with masturbation itself.

Indeed, the text systematically links the phallic aspect of his presence to scatological aspects of his being. It is as though the anality of his money grubbing and ledger keeping besmirches his erotic impulses—as though the social and cultural activity, of amassing wealth and of scrambling up the social ladder, contaminates his sexuality—as though touching Agnes transfers to her the filthiness of his relation to money. The implication is that the very desire for Agnes is not wholly or even largely erotic, but rather socioeconomic; what magnetizes her for Uriah is her place in the social and economic hierarchy. It is as though the "lower" instincts that fuel Uriah's business and legal activity are heightened in their ugliness, rather than sublimated and refined, by his scramble upward on the social scale.

What is startling about the psychosexual drama of Uriah's plot against the Wickfields and especially against Agnes is the way his character is linked in this way to the ideological grid on which the novel is built. Heep, the consummate hypocrite, who masks pride with humility and resentment with servility, is a caricature of David's work ethic and of the ideal of personality he affirms. If we see David's credo as a mid-nineteenth-century distillation of character elements integral to the Protestant ethic, we should have no difficulty in seeing Uriah as a grotesque embodiment of that creed. He is a monster of self-interest, self-advancement, and self-aggrandizement, who covets power to compensate for humiliation. Uriah's own bitter representation of the ideology on which he was reared foregrounds a fundamental contradiction in its values. At bay after his unmasking, he snarls:

> They used to teach at school ... from nine to eleven, that labor was a curse; and from eleven to one, that it was a blessing and a cheerfulness and a dignity and I don't know what all. (829)

Uriah has lived according to the creed whose inconsistencies he savages at the end, whose imperatives he cringingly submits to—imperatives to which David capitulates as well. His sense of self-degradation is heightened by the blatant incoherence of the ideology in which he has been bred. That ideology not only contradicts itself on the issue of work. It also betrays its own disingenuousness in celebrating individual striving at the same time that it subordinates the individual to the imperatives of grueling work and a repressive moral code.

Within that code, Uriah, like the compliant creature he is, assiduously pursues his own self-interest. He works grindingly to this end, with a diligence and a single-mindedness that parallel and parody David's self-dedication in pursuit of his career. He conceives of his life atomistically, cut off as he is from all human affinities apart from his symbiotic relation with his mother. Uriah does dirt on the accoutrements of culture with which, as he sees it, his betters prettify their own pursuit of wealth and standing, even as he covets those accoutrements. And he insists, despite the help he received from his parents and his schools, that he is as self-made as he can be.

Uriah does not, to be sure, go as far in this direction as Bounderby of *Hard Times*. But he emphatically rejects every bit of extraneous help that he can, refusing David's offer to help him with the Latin in *Tidd's Practice,* through which he hopes to master the Law. What he is refusing not only is help, but also the patina of learning that goes with gentility and the professions—the kind of learning that so hilariously fills the novel in Micawber's buoyant discourse. So brutally aggressive is Uriah in his inner perception of his process of upward mobility that it is not suprising that David, in one of his worst nightmares, envisions Uriah as a buccaneer. In David's dream, Uriah the buccaneer is an outright predator, who sails on a pirate ship that flies a flag inscribed *Tidd's Practice* on its mast—a ship that carries Emily off to the Spanish Main—the very Emily whose wish to be a lady when she was a child foreshadows her susceptibility to the worldliness of the gentleman who is Steerforth. There is a curiously chiastic symmetry in the fact that the sexual threats to Emily and Agnes, both of whom are the objects of David's ostensibly unsullied love, are linked to issues of social mobility. Emily's seduction by Steerforth is facilitated by her childhood sense of wanting to be a lady, while Uriah's passion for Agnes is motivated by her place above him in the social scale.

David does not recognize the affinity between his ideology and Uriah's, between the inner imperatives of his ambition to rise in the world and Uriah's. Indeed, Uriah is designed to stand in stark contrast to David, even as his traits of greed and cunning are posed in contrast to David's ostensible generosity and grace. It is as though he is there to make clear that David is not what Uriah is. The whole drift of the narrative is designed to make us feel the appropriateness of the match between David and Agnes, and the repulsiveness of even the possibility that she might couple with Uriah.

And yet a powerful countercurrent is set up both by a considerable range of details in the text. David is horrified that Uriah wants to marry his boss's daughter, but David himself, in pursuing Dora, is pursuing his own boss's daughter. David reviews his life in his memoir, and Uriah, in his way, does the same in his impassioned explanation of his life during his unmasking.

In addition to all this, we must note the peculiar force of the pathos given Uriah at his unmasking; the energy of his presentation; and most of all, the ramified implications of Dickens's naming of David, Agnes, and Uriah. Indeed, through the cunning of naming, Dickens performs a subtle but dramatic reversal of the novel's manifest judgments. Pointing to a legitimate affinity between Uriah and Agnes, and to a licit bond between them, it undercuts the sharp demarcation between Uriah and David, and provides a cutting commentary on David and all he wants to stand for.

The drama of naming, with its reversals, is played out against the background of the biblical story of King David and Bathsheba. In chapter 11 of 2 Sam. King David ruthlessly takes Bathsheba from Uriah, whose lawful wife she is. That this associative link is not gratuitous is driven home, not only by the naming of David and Uriah, but also by the naming of Agnes, the woman who replaces Bathsheba in the triangle. Agnes is linked by her name with Christ, the "Lamb of God." But she would also seem to be linked with the "poor man's ewe-lamb" of the Prophet Nathan's "Thou art the man" parable (2 Sam., 12), where Nathan gets King David to inculpate himself by condemning the rich man who appropriated the "poor man's single ewe-lamb"—the poor man standing for Uriah and the ewe-lamb for Bathsheba.

The implication of this allusion is that Agnes is rightfully Uriah's, and that Dickens, at some level, feels she is. If we track the ideological sight lines of the novel, it makes sense that she should be. It is she who presides over the spiritual life of the ostensibly hard-driving, goal-directed, achievement-oriented David, whose double Uriah is, and whose credo Uriah lives by. Agnes is the guardian angel of that David, who nonetheless claims that he is not aggressive, not covetous, not crassly self-interested; who in fact performs magically, like King David, the Sweet Singer of Israel; and whose siren song of a memoir bears witness to the amiable side of his character.

If we acknowledge the affinity between Uriah and Agnes, there is a sense in which Agnes's self-subordinating, self-abnegating firmness may be seen as the natural complement of (or antidote to) the self-aggrandizing compulsion to mastery of self and others that is historically integral to David's credo. Feminists have made us aware of how the Angel in the House (here, Agnes) serves, for the Victorian imagination, as an agency for redeeming the Devil in the Marketplace that her husband must have felt himself to be. In this sense, Agnes is felt to belong to Uriah, or to that part of David that Uriah caricatures—the part, in fact, that makes him so fascinating to David. This is so even though (and because) the fascination is represented as the fascination of the abomination: of the abomination David may be imagined to feel he harbors within.

The last thing David can do is acknowledge Uriah as an aspect of himself, nor does Dickens foreground their affinities. Yet the novel subtly insinuates that the repellent aspects of Uriah's being bear upon David, and in doing so, bear directly upon David's code of values.

More vividly than Uriah, Steerforth embodies elements which David must shut out—in this case, not because they are repulsive, but because they are too, too attractive. Indeed, together with Micawber, Steerforth points to positive possibilities in David. More than that. Together, Steerforth and Micawber suggest a constellation of human potentialities that intimate paradisal and utopian fulfillments that must be eschewed, not because they are not desirable in themselves, but because they threaten the structure of personality that David aspires toward. Steerforth undercuts David, not by parodying his qualities, but by embodying qualities that are integral to his life as a writer but are excluded from his representation of himself.

Far from seeming repulsive to David, as Uriah does, Steerforth is irresistible, full of the very "wayward and perverted" feelings that David must master in himself. David is fascinated by Steerforth's boundless self-indulgence, and by the working in him of active sexuality, overpowering charm, imperious presence, imaginative energy, and artistic gifts. He is almost fatally drawn to all of these, and it takes him the better part of the novel to master his attraction.

By his own avowal, even at the end he has not fully purged himself of the fascination; in good part, he needs Agnes to help him contain what Steerforth represents, to make sure he lives by the dictates of his "disciplined heart." David is fascinated by Steerforth's masculinity, by the monarchical masterfulness that accompanies it, and by the traits that Steerforth shares with David-as-artist—paradoxically, the traits that are part of what David disparages as "dreamy and romantic" in himself but are felt to be part of Steerforth's generative power. What engages the reader in Steerforth—and what especially engages us as readers with a particular view of Dickens and the logic of his development—is the desirability of what he represents: how he signifies, not only elements that David must suppress, but energies he must renounce.

On the face of it, of course, Steerforth is a cautionary figure. He despoils Emily and destroys the harmony of the home Mr. Peggotty has created for her, Ham, and Mrs. Gummidge. In his destructiveness, he is an avatar of the rakes of the eighteenth-century novel, and within the ideological framework of the text, he illustrates the dangers of cultivation without restraint. In this dimension, he has an important place. If Uriah represents the deforming side of what David deliberately affirms, Steerforth embodies a free-wheeling sexuality that David denies in himself—a sexuality of which David, but not the novel that bears his name, is in fact oblivious. Indeed, an active sexuality is just what is lacking in his account of his infatuation with Miss Larkin and Dora and of his love for Agnes.

In addition to illustrating the dangers of a licentious sexuality, Steerforth shows how the absence of restraining influences gives free play to erratic impulses, and how such freedom allows these impulses to vent themselves destructively. Along these lines, Steerforth himself laments his lack of a judicious father. Rosa

Dartle is eloquent on the subject of his mother's corrupting indulgence of his every wish, and David, reflecting on his grief at the loss of this most beloved of his friends, adverts to both points, stressing the importance of limits in child rearing.

Steerforth represents subtler threats, however—to the emergent David, to the ethic of accountability that David propounds, and to the structure of personality that he affirms. His most attractive qualities epitomize the kinds of freedom and playfulness that David cannot indulge. In their second Yarmouth episode (chapters 21–22), David sets up a series of polarities between himself and Steerforth that dramatize these contrasts. During their visit, Steerforth throws himself into the activity of sailing, and David notes that "his restless nature and bold spirits delight ... to find a vent in rough toil and hard weather, as in any other means of excitement" (377). David spends his time very differently. While Steerforth sails and schemes, David revisits the old familiar scenes of his childhood, scenes "associated with the figure I was to make in life and the distinguished things I was to do" (378). In effect, he spends his time at Yarmouth amassing further impressions of his past, virtually hoarding them, and making them both an object for consciousness and a means of eventually generating fame and wealth.

David challenges Steerforth on the "fitful uses of your powers" in view of "how ardent you are in any pursuit you follow" (382). He goes on to argue for concerted effort in one's calling and incremental cultivation of one's capacities. Steerforth, of course, resists the challenge of vocation; he says he has an aversion to being bound "to any of the wheels on which the Ixions of these days are turning round and round" (382). And David's rendering of Steerforth's performance at Yarmouth sharpens the issue, stressing the exuberance but also the dangers of his mode of being. David enjoys Steerforth's prodigality but criticizes its wastefulness. All the "delightful" qualities manifested in Steerforth's delicacy in entertaining the Peggottys come to seem "a brilliant game, played for the excitement of the moment, for the employment of high spirits ... in a mere *wasteful* careless course of winning what was worthless to him, and the next minute thrown away" (368; our emphasis).

The quibble here on game as play and gaming as gambling is central to understanding the complexity of what Steerforth means in relation to David, and to perceiving the tension between Steerforth's role as a cautionary figure and his standing as a locus of value. On the positive side, he represents pure play;

within the plentitude and spontaneity of that play, he stands for the gratuitous exercise of human faculties, for whatever is mobile, playful, spontaneous in humankind. The text, however, tilts play—games—into gaming, or gambling, with the desperateness, the hazardousness, and the waste that are associated with it. As such, it must be censured—and the passage just cited harshly censures it.

Play is also tipped in another direction. The Steerforth who offers to dish up for David a sentimental or comical version of himself, and who sings a sea shanty more convincingly than the sailors, telling a tale of shipwreck as though he were there, is a person who plays parts, an actor who produces multiple rather than unified states of self. His impersonations involve a protean propensity, by which he flows into and out of varied forms of selfhood. The shapes he flows into and out of are often, moreover, the shapes of others—as when he impersonates Mr. Peggotty and, in singing, does him one better than himself.

This is experienced by David as an astonishing talent, performed with magical ease and linked to a fineness and delicacy of perception that allows him to enter into the moods, feelings, and aspirations of others with healing grace. Of Steerforth, David says that at moments—moments when Steerforth is not "heavy with himself"—Steerforth operates with "no noise, no effort, no consciousness in anything he d[oes]" (368). That ease, amounting to grace, is shown to work wonders in the face of sickness, suffering, and death itself. Even in a sickroom, we are told, he seems "like light and air, brightening and refreshing it as if he were healthy weather" (368). When Steerforth is there, David can read Foxe's *Book of Martyrs,* remembering the terror it stirred in him as a child but not feeling it.

In this dimension, Steerforth stands in stark contrast to Uriah's miasmal presence, but also, in the end, to the David who tells us that in his pursuit of Dora, "I strained every nerve, exerted every energy," and who, in his credo affirms the earnest, diligent, single-minded pursuit of defined ends.

In the perspective of his artistic aptness and therapeutic magic, Steerforth, linked as he is to the wind and the sun, seems almost to be an Apollo figure, whose regal authority in the realm of story, play, and dream has great power over David. This is most vivid when David first meets him and is drawn by him into a curious piece of playacting. David, otherwise "Daisy," plays Scheherazade to Steerforth's imperial person at the beginning of their acquaintance, and beguiles Steerforth, as Scheherazade did her Sultan, with stories: stories that elicit whatever is "romantic and dreamy" in David himself. What is interesting here not only is the reversal of roles, so that David gains power over the masterful older boy, but also the sexual role reversal involved in that assumption of power. That reversal is the more vivid in view of David's celebration of the beauty and sensual repose of the sleeping Steerforth, who is contemplated as an erotic object by the seemingly passive and feminine Scheherazade-Daisy-David.

Altogether, Steerforth suggests protean possibilities, of personality, even of gender, possibilities that challenge the ideal of single identity and singleness of purpose inherent in the ideal of a calling. Steerforth suggests a kind generative power beyond the sexual. He is endowed with a metamorphic potency that allows him to proliferate selves so that, without losing himself, he can transgress the boundaries of self, and appropriate—even transform—the world for his own gratuitous purposes.

These possiblities are anathema to the David of the credo. Cleaving to the purposiveness of his work, and the unitary earnestness of his character, David must suppress the powers Steerforth stands for. Yet they would seem to be essential to the David who writes the memoir which is the novel whose protagonist he is, and who is also supposed to be a novelist. They certainly are essential to Dickens the novelist. Indeed, the Steerforth who enters with such abandon into the characters and the feelings of others seems closely akin to the roving voice *Dickens* employed in earlier novels, flowing in and out of objects and people, partly out of the impulse to please, mesmerize, enchant, seduce, and partly out of a monarchical impulse—and kingship is one of the recurrent, dominant images for Steerforth's masterful mode of operation.

David, unlike his creator in earlier works, and unlike the fluent, mobile Steerforth who so enchants him, must cultivate a careful, deliberate restraint by which he renders others, while maintaining his boundary lines, as his psychic needs and ideological posture dictate. He must, in short, keep his distance, and, as writer, *copy* reality, even the reality of his own inwardness, rather than give himself up to the play of fantasy and desire that animates a Steerforth. He must also sidestep the fierce sadistic lashings out that the imperious Steerforth—the oriental despot Steerforth, who in his Arabian Nights dimension beheads wives and in his Salem House incarnation casts out upstarts like Mell—indulges, and curtail the "feminine" charm of his Scheherazade/Daisy nature.

The urgency of banishing the Steerforth within David is climactically represented in the storm scene. That scene not only represents the intrusion of what is felt to be cosmic violence on the temperate world of the novel. It also represents the incursion into David of all the boundary-breaking violence and fantasy that he strives to contain. During the storm, David feels as if the storm is a dream. In the course of it, he invokes a set of images that, in fact, allude to dreams that he has had throughout the novel: dreams that have unsettled him, of falling from cliffs and masts; of being pecked at by threatening, long-necked fowl; of being himself abducted to the Spanish main by a David-and-Steerforth-double who may be Uriah, and so on. By the time the storm is over and Steerforth is dead, he experiences a sense of exhaustion and of emptying-out that foreshadows the depression which is the prelude to his final pulling himself together for his great leap forward as a writer, as well as for his union with Agnes. It is as though the storm scene expresses the climactic quality of the threat to David's shape and existence that is posed by all the elements of fantasy, dream, and desire that Steerforth symbolizes. It also serves symbolically as a way of definitively purging them—though not, curiously, of purging him of his love for Steerforth.

Micawber, so different from Steerforth, provides another subversive counterweight to David's self-containment and to the values he affirms. Like Steerforth, he is a cautionary figure—a compendium of elements cast out of the officially sober David of the novel's end. He provides a ramified commentary on what David is, being a figure who in fact undercuts much that David wants to stand for. Still more than the other doubles, Micawber acts on David's self-image in a great variety of ways. He is the vehicle for the expression of a range of infantile impulses and of a set of complex linguistic and imaginative operations that transform those impulses. The transformations function in visionary ways. They enunciate a virtually utopian vision of a better life, they undermine David's (and the novel's) ideological asperities, and they bear upon David's life as a writer.

The cautionary side of Micawber is obvious. Until he takes on the task of exposing Heep, he spurns the values of diligence, earnestness, and integrity, in the burgher sense of the word. Micawber evades financial accountability, he fails to make money, to pay debts, or to defer consumption. He is unstable and discontinuous in his responses, hilariously lurching from laughter to self-pity to despair and back again. He resists differentiation within his personality, refusing the containment or expulsion of qualities that prevent him from functioning as a responsible father. As a wielder of language, moreover, he defies the reality-bound strictures of David's copyism, using language to defy reality and to transform it. In the course of doing so, he desymbolizes and materializes language, cutting the grounds of his discourse out from under itself.

Yet still more than Steerforth, Micawber elicits our admiration. Few readers are indifferent to Micawber's gusto—to the exuberant orality of his pleasures, in food and in language; to the anti-Malthusian irrepressibility of his philoprogenitiveness; or to the ease with which he substitutes the wish for the deed— the word for the thing—and defies the demand that he be accountable, consecutive, or coherent in any terms but his own.

As with Steerforth, moreover, the very content of his discourse provides a telling counterpoint to David's. Micawber's sense of life is inimical to the Protestant ethic. It is not only pagan, but communitarian, not only Latinate, but specifically and meaningfully late eighteenth century. His rhetoric turns out not only to reflect cultural and ideological imperatives, but also points to psychic issues, such as abandonment and privation, that we have seen percolating within the analogy between David and Dick. That configuration of motifs, quite startlingly, is one of the elements that links Micawber directly to David, and to the psychic needs that David elides in his story, even as it links Micawber to other figures in the novel. Indeed, through it, it becomes possible to formulate more closely the structure of the conflict that animates the entire narrative and some of that conflict's historical antecedents.

But first the cultural and ideological elements. Micawber's self-created and linguistically charmed world is deeply antithetical to David's more commonplace world. Micawber's world is ruled by the god of day; within it, one is married at the hymeneal altar, lives out one's marital existence at the altar of domestic life, and outside the family, serves as a worthy minister at the sacred altar of friendship. If one procreates, one renews one's youth like the Phoenix. It is possible, moreover, to find oneself wielding the thunderbolt or directing the devouring and avenging flame and commanding the devouring element. The human form one inhabits is a Temple. There are, moreover, states of pollution and taboo one falls into; even to falter morally is to fall under such a taboo. To remit guilt, one makes reparation to one's fellow man. When one dies, one is immolated on a funeral pyre.

For Micawber, the breasts themselves are not particular and finite; they are nature's founts. People who share what seems to be a common experience are comrades in the battle of life. Others are his trusted friends. The trust that should obtain between individuals is between man and man, even when one of those individuals is, like David at the beginning of their acquaintanceship, a boy; and all men are (or should be) his fellow creatures. If one has a sense of self-respect, one stands erect before one's fellow man. To do something moral is to do honor to our common nature.

Clearly, embedded in his discourse are fragments of an alternative worldview. Micawber insists, from the depths of his social and economic destitution, that men are not and should not be divided between buyer and seller, but rather be "comrades in the battle of the world" (477), linking hands and singing "Here's a hand, my trusty frere" (321). This vision is consecrated in a self-made (though comically distanced) communal feast, mediated by the ritual of the punch ceremony. If Micawber drinks punch instead of making his "fortune for his family down to the latest posterity" (473), the unpostponed pleasure proposed—and instant gratification, gustatory, bibulous, or verbal is the name of his game—has a communal rather than an individual cast.

Micawber's discourse celebrates the universality of man, and removes it from the mediating and limiting categories of class and status. With Micawber, we leave the world of David, in which, finally, "trifles make up the sum of life" (838) and of Traddles, where one must be as "prosaic and literal as possible" (596). With him, we enter a world where one worships at the "sacred altar of friendship" (315), and is free of the isolating discipline of the self.

Micawber's world is full of magic and fantasy. It is presided over, not by the degenerate Calvinist deity who sanctifies earnest worldly striving, but by older deities, headed by the "god of day" (231), often confused by David with Micawber himself, whose face he sees "shining out of a thin cloud of these delightful fumes" (473). Those deities smile benignly at the pleasures of the world, though they "wield ... the thunderbolt" (770) in the presence of selfish greed. In Micawber's mouth, words do not serve to produce an exacting copy of "reality," and, as they are meant to do for David, an ordered experience of the self. Rather, "real in his mouth and delicious to the taste" (225), words generate sensuous and aesthetic gratification. In Micawber, language revises, transforms, transcends experience, even as it produces, within the novel's comic exuberance, the image of buoyant selfhood that is Micawber himself.

Given the sharp polarity between David's reality-bound, goal-directed, renunciatory credo and Micawber's exuberantly self-gratifying, fantastical vision of life, it is startling to realize that Micawber's sense of things has its roots in an ideological configuration cognate with David's. If we track Micawber's language, it becomes clear that Micawber is a wielder of the crumbs of a schoolboy's education in classical culture, serving as an echo chamber for a specific eighteenth-century appropriation of that culture. As an ideological construct, Micawber's vision of humanity joins the rags and tatters of his simulation of eighteenth-century gentility with the pith of an ideology that found its formulation in the Religion of Man and figured centrally in the French Revolution. That ideology, of course, was promulgated by the culture and the class that produced David's credo and that generated the contradictions with which his credo, like his memoir, is rifted.

These contradictions are no less radical than those which Uriah pillories in his account of his school, except that the issue is not the status of work but rather the status of the individual and the meaning of individual freedom. *David Copperfield,* like the genre of the *Bildungsroman* to which it belongs, celebrates the notion of individuality. This is, at the most rudimentary level, reflected in David's undertaking to write an autobiography—that is, to take his own life, with all its presumed singularity, and to "write it" in the form of an autobiographical memoir, on the assumption that there is communicable meaning and value in its representation of himself as an ostensibly unique being. At the same time, the memoir as written affirms the subordination of that being to vocation and accountability: values that negate so much of David's individuality, and that mandate the need to flatten, restrain, and control the needs and desires that contradict or subvert these traits.

Micawber himself reproduces the essential contradictions of David's situation. To begin with, he does not escape the constraints of the world that David's ideology reflects and sustains. Although he negates David's values, everything he is may be seen as a response to them. Feckless and un-Malthusian in his generativeness, he is nonetheless family bound; irresponsible and shirking, his life is nonetheless defined by issues of income and outlay, by the process of contracting debts and discharging (or not discharging) them. He exposes Uriah's machinations, but the very task of exposing him involves accounting and account keeping analogous to Uriah's life's work; it is as though Micawber, unlikely as it may seem, is Uriah's double, as well as his natural watchdog.

At the same time, Micawber enacts a comic version of the untrammeled individualism implied by insistence on the intrinsic value of his individual life. It is easy to see Micawber's entire impersonative, rhetoricizing stance as a way of preserving his sense of the pristine wholeness of his being. In practice, it serves to repel the demand that he accommodate and let himself be bound to (if we may borrow Steerforth's trenchant metaphor) the Ixion's wheel of vocation, of a life invested in work. Indeed, the very mobilization of the language of the law and of Latinate sententiousness may be taken as a defiance, through parody, of the whole system of Nays, of Thou-shalt-nots, implied by the work ethic and by David's conception of affirmative selfhood. At the same time, Micawber's triumphant self-presentation as intractably and ineradicably himself may be understood as an insistence on his own irreducibility as a person and as a locus of value—as his stubborn refusal to be born into a world where parts of himself can and must be separated from him and, like David's caul, be put up for sale. Micawber, we might say, will not part with his caul, even as he will not embrace a calling.

His refusal may be seen as springing from an unwillingness to renounce the wholeness that is implicit in as yet unrealized and untested potentialities. When he must adopt the standard language of the law, he feels a terrible constraint upon the mind's capacity to soar exaltedly. When he commits himself to the labor of exposing Uriah and of saving the fortunes of Betsy and the Wickfields, he feels that he has cut himself off from himself and his vital relation to his family, and becomes subject to unprecedented outbursts of violence.

We have here, of course, the enactment of one of the radical contradictions of the world Dickens imagines and reflects. We have, in Micawber's sense of the split between his subjectivity and his newfound work, an anticipation of the treatment, in *Great Expectations,* of the splits in Wemmick's world. The difference is that here we have a laying-out, in Micawber's vision, of satisfactions and potentialities largely excluded from Wemmick's dissociated consciousness. Micawber, to be sure, has no home to serve as his castle; the world cannot forcibly be shut out of his domain. In the unbuttressed reality of his life, his experience of the world works abrasively upon him, much as the market rubs out the figuration on the stamped coins that are the characters in *Twist*. The difference between Micawber and Wemmick—or between Micawber and Nancy or the Artful Dodger—is that Micawber's exuberant linguistic and imaginative gifts float him (or seem to float him) outside reality, at least for the space of time allotted to his charmed life in the novel.

At every level, Micawber's make-believe buoys him up. Even his impersonations serve to suggest possibilities shut out of a working life within a vocation—as, in the extreme, when he dresses up as an emigrant on his way to Australia. They serve, inwardly, to keep the finiteness inherent in the nature of work and vocation from becoming real. The erratic leaps of his imagination, moving as it does toward desired ends without considering the means to those ends, turn out to reflect a magically providential view of the world—a totalizing trust in the benign possibility of achieving consummations devoutly wished. Micawber, contemplating finite possibilities—of callings, for example—keeps invoking fulfillments that circumvent process, that isolate him from the frictive resistance of the outside world, and that spare him from the workings of time itself, as well as from the challenge of working in ordinary human time. Within Micawber's system, for Wilkins Jr. to become a choirboy in Canterbury means for him to be a clergyman; Wilkins Sr.'s very baldness becomes an attribute that qualifies him for being a judge, once he "goes into" the law by taking a job with Uriah.

None of his hocus-pocus works, of course—except in the charmed life he leads within the novel, where Dickens's whimsy and David's comically rendered sense of Micawber's resilient bouncings-back create a world of make-believe where he can survive and entertain. David finally rejects Micawber's magical sense of reality, which contradicts his need to bring his wish-thinking under control and to resist his tendency to read the world in terms of his desire. Yet there is a sense in which David's entire memoir, which is the novel we read, performs a Micawber-like transformation of what must have been the reality of his life.

For one of the salient features of *David Copperfield* is the programmatic containment of the horrors of the orphan condition in David's early life. The *données* of the novel elide such horrors. David starts out, not in a baby farm, like Oliver, but in a home where not one but two mothers coddle him, and a third—Betsy—already lurks in the wings at the outset, while Agnes waits for him further along his way. The terrors of his life with the Murdstones are harrowing enough, but the pathos of David's experience with them is mitigated by their stylization within the rueful comedy of David's interaction with the monsters Dickens makes of them, as well as by Peggotty's presence and by the conviction that his mother, if she weren't under Murdstone's thumb, would take his side. Even the account of the flight from Dover, following the restrained representation of David's experience at Murdstone and Grinby, constrains direct expression of the terror, self-pity, and rage that inform the depiction of analogous situations in other Dickens novels. The reader who recalls the representation of Oliver Twist or Little Nell becomes aware of how rigorously Dickens has in fact curtailed these elements to suit the relative amiability of David's narrative, to facilitate its affirmative resolution, to make plausible the susceptibility of the novel's world to David's qualities and values, and to affirm the viability of his ethic as a means of finding a place in the world.

David is not the only character whose experience of orphanhood is contained in a heretofore uncharacteristic way. Although *David Copperfield* does not proclaim itself to be a book concerned with orphaning, it abounds, like all Dickens's fiction, in orphans and orphanings. Vital to the novel's action are David's orphaned condition, and the greater and lesser orphaning of all the doubles, but especially of Micawber, who speaks of himself as "a waif and stray on the shores of life," and is a kind of orphan of the universe itself—of the universe that Mr. Jarndyce, in *Bleak House,* will characterize as an indifferent parent. No less vital to the texture of the novel's imaginative life is Agnes's plight as a motherless child whose father has in good part defaulted in his responsiblity toward her because of obsessional grief for the loss of his wife and an equally obsessional preoccupation with Agnes herself. These orphanings, moreover, are merely instances of a pervasive condition of loss, by death, betrayal, and arbitrary circumstance. Consider what Dickens might have done elsewhere, in representing the experience of Clara, the widowed child bride; of Ham and Emily, orphans of various storms; and similarly, in varying degrees, a further range of characters, including Peggotty; Steerforth; Rosa Dartle; Uriah; Traddles; Sophie and her sisters; Betsy herself and even her wastrel husband, Mr. Mell; and his mother; Annie Strong and *her* mother; and Jack Maldon. Essentially, in this regard, *David Copperfield,* for all the sunniness of its tone and its happy ending, contains as characteristically rich a Dickensian array of potentially needy children and analogues of such children as does virtually any other Dickens text.

Yet much of the misery implicit in these characters and their experience of suffering is elided. Part of the circumventions is facilitated by the ambiguous wish fulfillments of David's story as he tells it, culminating in his union with Agnes and in the stability and satisfaction it is said to provide. In fact, what we have in his marriage to Agnes is the realization of a fantasy of fusion with a protective figure—with a mother figure that compensates for all the potential misery of the very abandonment whose expression the novel effectively works to mute. Equally problematic is the novel's failure to articulate any sense of the process whereby the self transforms itself from the condition of pervasive rage and misery David is allowed to feel and express in dealing with the Murdstones into the shapely burgherhood he is said to achieve by the end of the novel. Both text and self emerge from the welter of early experience that generate them with something of the effortlessness that marks Micawber's recurrent appearances, "all complete". It emerges in a way that is congruous with David's magical sense that Agnes has stepped, integrally herself, out of a picture frame: that she is her mother's portrait, animate.

No wonder, then, that so many readers have chafed at *Copperfield*'s ending. So much of David's implicit experience, and much of the novel's potential complexity, has been displaced into the countertext, that David, in his union with Agnes, seems hollow. Not only has David not been endowed with the inwardness that has been projected into his doubles, but the doubles themselves have by the end been banished from his world. Furthermore, not only is David's adult condition not effectively portrayed, but his childhood has simply been replaced by his adulthood, with no concrete sense of how he has moved from the one state to the other. At the same time, it should not be a matter of surprise that, with the satisfactions provided by the story as written, Dickens can achieve, for himself and for his more trusting readers, his daylight saga of bourgeois virtue, secular reality, and personal achievement, with as much panache as he manages. Nor should it surprise us that, considering the Micawber-like charm he has given David, he should have written a novel that seems so balanced, so equable, and often so magical, a novel in which he celebrates a mode of being that tends to exclude everything we imagine his hero might desire or toward which he might aspire—everything that his doubles represent.

Hence, the force of the way the tensions that are pushed into the margins of *David Copperfield* return with a vengeance in *Bleak House*. *Bleak House* engages directly, in Esther, the constraining values that govern David's narrative. In doing so, it reflects back on both David and his credo, rigorously examining the strategies and the price of self-forging in David's mode. At the same time, it liberates in the third-person voice all the energy of rage and frustration that both Esther and David repress. It also places at the center of its vision the desperation of the insulted and the injured in their most radical form, namely, in their condition as children abandoned to the ravages of hunger and pain. In the course of doing so, *Bleak House* projects a global sense of the negativity of the world, such as is admitted neither in *Oliver Twist*, with its Manichean polarizations, nor in *David Copperfield*, with its equable insistence on possibilities. And it does so largely in the medium of a voice—the third-person-narrative-voice—that vents everything that neither Oliver nor David can express and that operates within Micawber's assumptions about the magical power of language and about the capacity of the imagination to remake reality in the image of its worst fears and its ultimate desires.

4
Bleak House

*D*AVID COPPERFIELD'S STRUGGLE WITH THE ISSUE OF VOCATION REflects Dickens's confrontation with the paralyzing passivity of the orphan condition. *Bleak House,* which follows it in the sequence of Dickens's work, explores with rigor the impact on a character of renunciations and repressions far more stringent than anything David attempts. Indeed, the novel is dominated by the tension between Esther Summerson's strenuous effort to control the incipient nightmare of her life and the unruly impulses she must repress.

It is no accident that the character who must undergo this struggle for control—namely Esther—was left for dead at birth and was then subjected to unprecedented moral abuse by her surrogate mother. It is as though Dickens is giving us as extreme an instance of abandonment as possible. He does so, it seems to us, to dramatize as vividly as he can what *David Copperfield* does not engage—namely, the magnitude of the struggle a victim of abandonment must wage to organize a self that finds a place in the world by exercising its own powers of control.

To give form to what Esther cannot integrate in consciousness, he creates an extraordinary medium through which to project the impulses and imaginings that must be contained in the course of her struggle. His medium is, of course, the third-person narrative voice, whose venting of everything that inhabits the orphan condition is one of the miracles of Dickens's art. It is a voice in which a stunning array of literary artifice is put in the service of unrestrained expressiveness.

Ultimately, the two voices are not discrete entities, but rather polarized facets of a single affective system. Dickens creates a form for the voice, but the voice itself is an inevitable concomitant of Esther's inner life. What unifies them is the shared experience of abandonment, as exacerbated by the struggle to accommodate to the world. In this sense, both voices are the outgrowth of a fierce contention, in Esther, between raging, infantile need and the need to subordinate such need to the imperatives of survival.

Seen in this perspective, the two voices play out a tension which, we have been arguing, animates Dickens's best work. We mean the tension between regressive needs, with the fantasies they generate, and the imperatives of life in the world—the imperatives of mobilizing oneself for the sake of enduring and helping one's children to endure in a world that is subversive of life itself. Esther, constrained by these imperatives, and the third-person narrative voice, which rejects all constraints, together articulate a single nighmare, the nightmare of contending with abandonment.

Because the two voices are so closely implicated in each other, it should come as no surprise that the stories they tell are essentially the same story—or rather, polarized facets of the same story. The story is, again, a narrative of the struggle with the primordial needs and the regressive impulses of the abandoned child, who is under pressure to accommodate to a world defined by scarcity and threat. It not only is Esther, among the characters in the novel, who enacts that struggle, but Richard as well. Richard is, in a sense, the novel's prime example of the struggle and its hazards because, still more than Esther, he is a normative *Bildung* figure. Poised between the two voices and embedded in both their discourses, Richard tries to accommodate and fails. He fails because he falls victim to a monster, in the guise of the Chancery Suit, which embodies all the regressive voracity that haunts and inhabits the orphan imagination.

Nor should it surprise us that the novel projects a vision of endless thwarting within a world inimical to desire. Esther survives in an enclave of amenity, providentially provided by John Jarndyce, but the condition for her survival is her successful struggle to define and contain desire; unlike Oliver, she actively earns the love that she gains. Moreover, the world surrounding the enclave that provides shelter for Esther is marked by a comprehensive negativity that exceeds even the destructiveness of the marketplace and the thieves' den in *Twist*. It is a world controlled by everything that is displaced out of Esther's imagination. Ultimately, the world of *Bleak House* is a world where desire consumes, contact contaminates, and the institutions of government and justice are monstrously voracious and destructive.

Bleak House is, as everyone has always known, "about" the condition of England, even as *Oliver Twist* is "about" the Poor Law. But the structure and the language of its representations are, this time too, rooted in the experience of a furious child, who craves reparative fusion with an imagined mother. That child is impelled by a vindictive rage that sadistically toys with both its world and with stand-ins for its mother, and it finally avenges itself on them; that child, who is impersonated by the third-person voice, is the opposite equivalent of the sedate and decorous Esther, who filters out of her experience every vivid impulse of cruelty and of energizing desire.

In Esther, Dickens retraces the dolorous path of instinctual and imaginative renunciation. Esther represents a far more extreme version than David of the processes of self-crystallization through accommodation to the social and psychic roles available in her world. She is an example of the process of mobilizing the will for the suppression of desire and with it of the memories and fantasies that fuel desire. That process leaves the will functional, but without the content that would give positive meaning to its activity.

Esther's self-suppression is foregrounded in the way she tells her story. Her narrative strategies are best seen in juxatposition with her counterpart voice. While the third-person narrative voice aggressively defies the normative conventions of narrative, Esther strives to preserve them all. Her predilection for the particularizingly personal pronoun, defining what belongs to whom—*my* Guardian, *her* baby; her preference, as has been noted by a variety of readers such as Karen Chase and Graham Hough, for the tidily historical past, as well as for events logically and causally laid out in temporal sequence; her prim grammaticality—all of these produce an ostensibly coherent narrative, with emphatically meaningful sequences and transparent motivation. Even the mysteries that impinge on her ordering consciousness, like the mystery of her birth, are in the end clarified, at least to her satisfaction.

Esther's stylistic preferences and her modes of understanding are, of course, the surface manifestation of the deeper modes of self-organization for self-suppression. Her insistent clarity in the use of pronouns bespeaks her need to define herself as separate, not only from others, but from the parts of herself that she must shut out, including her craving for a return to her lost mother. Her affinity for the historical past signifies her need to keep the past in its place—long ago and far away—so that it will not well up in her, and disrupt the identity and the life she has carefully constructed. She not only must learn that, as she tells us, she is no more responsible for her birth than a queen is for hers, but must also beat down the desire and anxiety that a less defensively deflective consciousness of her personal history might stir. Temporal order and tidy causality are all ways of containing whatever it is in her that might blur the boundaries she erects against a potentially unruly subjectivity.

In short, Esther's narrative mode is the product of the repressions that survival mandates. Esther seems to qualify the imperatives laid down by her "godmother" on her birthday, but in fact she doesn't. Miss Barbary tells Esther that "it would have been far better . . . you had never been born" (64), and recommends that Esther strive to live in "submission, self-denial, diligent work" as "preparation for a life begun with . . . a shadow on it" (65). Esther transposes this into the need to be "industrious, contented and kind-hearted" (65), and industriousness, contentment, and generosity are indeed the traits she stresses in her memoir. Yet Esther's story makes it clear that submission, self-denial, and diligence have in fact dominated her life. Esther is not so much contented and kind hearted as she is self-denying and submissive. Even at the crisis of her life, she cannot ask for Woodcourt or even acknowledge that she desires Woodcourt. Nor can she actively reject John Jarndyce for Woodcourt but must have Woodcourt given her by Jarndyce on the eve of her impending marriage to him. Not only can she not ask for the freedom to marry Woodcourt, but she must, for long stretches, deny the wish to be loved by him.

Underlying her renunciation of an active sexuality is a deeper denial—namely, suppression of the wish for a mother's love, the kind of unconditional love that children ordinarily expect from their mothers. As one of the multitude of orphaned or abandoned children in the novel, it is Esther's paradigmatic function within the text to renounce the wish for a mother. It is no less emphatically her function to suppress the anger that frustration of that wish gives rise to.

On the face of it, Esther renounces the possibility for unqualified love, freely given and freely taken, and replaces it with the notion that it is desirable "to do some good to someone, and *win* some love to myself if I could" (65). By renouncing the claims of her own narcissism, she hopes in effect nonetheless to gratify it by earning love for herself from others. The consequence for Esther's personality is evident in her self-effacement, in her excessive humility, and in the way she satisfies her own need for love by ministering endlessly to others.

The history of her doll is vital to her history of self-abnegation. Recounting how she was overwhelmed by grief and terror on leaving home after her aunt's death, Esther recalls the fact that on that occasion she had buried her doll in the garden. Her doll, she tells us, was the only being in whom she could confide in her unremittingly desolate childhood. To Esther, her doll was "what [she] was to no one on earth" (65). This means that no one responded to her as she needed to be responded to, that no one loved her, as she needed to be loved. The doll was or "contained" an imagined being onto whom she could project feelings she needed in response to her feelings and by doing so, get the support she needed. In burying the doll, moreover, she was, in effect, renouncing even the possibility of such response and such support.

This is why she tells us that she calls to mind her doll's burial when she leaves Greenleaf six years later. Leaving Greenleaf, she tells herself that she must control her grief because "I must not take tears where I was going" (75). What she is anticipating is the absence of anyone, "where [she] was going," who will respond to her tears and empathize with her grief. She anticipates that she will not even be able to allow herself the self-indulgence of imagining such a person and attributing to that person the responses she needs. The reason, presumably, is that she is afraid that by such an act of imagination she will stir herself up by feeling or remembering. She fears that if she is stirred up in this way she will not be able to function as she feels she must.

Indeed, what dominates her consciousness as she contemplates the love she leaves behind at Greenleaf is memory of the "resolution I had made on my birthday, ... to be industrious, contented, and true-hearted, and to do some good ... and win some love if I could" (73). Only much later, in the context of her encounter with Lady Dedlock, does the doll again crop up, in connection with her feeling that she is dressing herself as she used to dress her doll. Clearly, Esther's childhood admitted no harking back to the kind of yearning that she could indulge in relation to the doll. Her later life, even as early as her departure from Greenleaf, certainly has no place for recall of such yearning, or for the fantasies of love or retribution that might arise from such yearning.

There are many signs that these yearnings persist. They are present in the very opening of her diary. There she suggests that her memoir is not self-generated, but is rather instituted as part of a larger project—"I have a great deal of difficulty," she writes, "in beginning to write my part of these pages" (62). Yet the flow of ideas suggests that she undertakes it, at least in part, as still another way of winning love, or at least sympathy from the reader, even as she had earned it from the girls at Greenleaf, from the Jellyby children, and from Ada and Richard, among others. This is made clear by the fact that it is at that point that she tells us about her doll; the first thing she tells us about herself as she sets about telling her story is the specialness of her relationship with her doll, to whom, she says, she had confided all her feelings because she was "the only friend with whom I felt at ease" (63). Presumably her reader will be another such friend, and provide the responses of warmth and understanding she could attribute to her doll.

With her doll, Esther freely projected her inwardness onto the world. Burial of her doll signifies renunciation, not only of the possibility of imagining reciprocities of feeling, but also of the freedom to project her desires into the world, as a prelude to the struggle to fulfill them. It also signifies an interdiction on even imagining alternatives to her present situation, lest she make self-determined demands on the world.

Esther's prose style reflects this in a fascinating way. Her narrative consistently establishes a strict boundary line between the utilitarian functionality of her prose, with its tendency to cleave to known fact and reasonable conjecture, and any sort of metaphoric or projective usage that might blur the boundaries between herself and others. This finds expression in Esther's avoidance of metaphor and in the scrupulousness with which she notes every instance of projection on her part. Metaphors that crop up in her own discourse are attributed to others, explained away, or apologized for. Explanations and apologies also accompany Esther's treatment of her own self as an object, as when she addresses herself directly by name, adjuring "Esther" to do this or not to do that. On the rare occasions that she resorts to strikingly figurative language—and several brilliant images do crop up in her discourse—such language tends to be carefully controlled as simile rather than metaphor.

The need to control metaphor in this way reflects a need to draw a clear line between fantasy and reality. Esther's stylistic constraints bespeak a fear of breaching the boundaries of her self-definition. Esther, in effect, insists on avoiding any mode of discourse or relationship that openly confuses fantasy and reality and breaches the border between subject and object. Hence, she avoids the fusion of disparate elements that metaphor implies. She insists, not only on the discreteness and integrity of her own inner being, but also on the clarity and discreteness of the world outside her. Her "world" is a realm of discretely perceived objects, each of them carefully bounded. Ultimately, the curtailment of imaginative projection implicit in her curtailment of metaphor may be seen as part of a comprehensive refusal to hurl her inwardness into the world, to qualify or transform what is "out there" in the world on the basis of what is "in here" within the self. This curtailment must be understood as a manifestation of the need to prevent the surging up of unruly feelings, and to ward off the danger of regression, with the loss of control it involves.

The hide-boundedness of Esther's discourse becomes evident in a number of passages where she generates vivid images that bring to mind the opulently metaphoric workings of the third-person narrative or of Dickens himself. This is the case when she notes that Rachael, on her leaving for Greenleaf, "gave me one parting kiss upon my forehead, *like* a thaw-drop from the stone porch" (70; our emphasis), or when she says that Krook's "throat, chin, and eyebrows were so frosted with white hairs, and so gnarled with veins and puckered skin, that he looked from his breast upward *like* some old root in a fall of snow" (99–100; our emphasis). It is as though Dickens is signifying within Esther's own discourse that sharp distinctions must be drawn, for her, between her sense of hard-nosed, morally restrained "reality" and a realm of unruly subjectivity that might spawn autonomous images and threaten her system of iron control.

What may well be Esther's most striking image provides a parable of the threats to self that boundary-breaking entails. We refer to her perception of rope makers encountered on the shore at Deal:

> The sea was heaving under a thick white fog; and nothing else was moving but a few early ropemakers, who, with the yarn twisted around their bodies, looked as if . . . they were spinning themselves into cordage. (674)

This image—carefully qualified and circumscribed by Esther's "as if"—implies the existence of an inwardness to the self that is separate from the world outside. If we take the metaphor seriously, it seems to threaten the spinning subject with the emptying out of the passionate and conflict-ridden inwardness the self presumably contains, and with it a frightening loss of self. The sense that active involvement in the world uses one up is reminiscent of the coin metaphors in *Twist* and the treatment of writing in *Copperfield*. The idea that spinning empties out what is inside the spinner also brings to mind the insistent presence in *Copperfield* of a notion that writing is generated from internal body fluids—of the fact that the script of Peggotty's letters is dissolved in tears, that Daniel Peggotty's blood gushes when his grief at Emily's seduction is too great for words, and that Uriah Heep's script is like snail slime on the page. It is also of a piece with David's radical need to control the processes of writing, and what might erupt into it. What we have called David's copyism is a defense against a fuller expression of his inwardness in his memoir. Esther combats such anxiety in a more extreme way, dealing with it through the flat circumstantiality of her discourse, through the page-by-page conception of its unfolding, and through its stage-by-stage laying out of sequences in the story it tells.

Indeed, narrative mode and the personality organization that generates it coincide in the production of Esther's memoir—that is, they collude in the process of her scrupulously preventing herself from wholly spinning herself into her narrative. The tidiness of her narrative and its preoccupation with time, sequence, and order bear witness to the extent to which she obstructs by means of scrupulous organization any threatening reponses that lie hidden within her. We may in fact infer that for Esther the maintenance of a morally meaningful and practically effective sense of self is contingent upon maintaining a coherent, serial sense of temporal experience, a sense that prevents the spilling of Esther's turbulent guts. It is herself as well as her narrative that Esther is carefully composing when she writes the memoir we read.

How much turbulence is contained within her becomes clear in the course of her illness, which serves, much like the storm in *David Copperfield,* to dramatize the boundary issues we have been discussing. Possibly the most disruptive effect of the illness is a blurring of boundaries between herself and the world and between the disparate times of her life, so that the moments of her life become simultaneously present and momentarily indistinguishable from each other. This condition is not wholly unprecedented in her experience. Because the issues of boundary lines derive from her lack of a mother, it makes sense that she first experiences it when she first sees Lady Dedlock in church and much later when she finds her dead. In the first instance, she feels that Lady Dedlock's "face [was] like a broken glass . . . in which I saw scraps of old remembrances" (304), and is therefore overcome by a "strange emotion" (305). When she tells us of the movement toward the place where she and Bucket find Lady Dedlock, we hear that the "great water-gates" (867) of memory had opened up, so that she is overwhelmed by a surge of associations. Indeed, as she is about to identify her dead mother, she cascades into a mode of metaphoric discourse closely akin to that of the third-person voice.

During the progress of her illness, the bewilderment is both sustained and overwhelming. She writes that

> I lay ill through several weeks, and the usual tenor of my life became like an old remembrance. But this was not the effect of time, so much as of the change in all my habits, made by the helplessness and inaction of a sick-room. Before I had been confined to it many days, everything else seemed to have retired into a remote distance, where there was little or no separation between the various stages of my life. . . . In falling ill, I seemed to have crossed a dark lake, and to have left all my experience, mingled together by the great distance, on the healthy shore. (543)

The breaking of the dam—of the "water-gates"—of control is signaled, moreover, by "a curious sense of fullness, as if I were becoming too large altogether" (496) that marks her coming down with smallpox. The fullness intimates the welling up of things she cannot contain or control.

Also suggestive are the nightmare images that plague Esther in her delirium, when she cannot distinguish night from day, dream from reality. She remembers feeling that she is laboring up a colossal staircase, turning like a worm in a garden path as she goes, and then imagines a situation "when, strung together somewhere in great black space," there was "a flaming necklace, or ring, or starry circle of some kind, of which *I* was one of the beads!" (544). The necklace image would seem to refract the feeling that she has been forced into a state of being she cannot control, and is bound there by a power beyond imagining, with a coerciveness beyond bearing. The fact that what coerces her is on a necklace suggests that, among other things, she is being linked to something feminine, to something associated to the necklace of lights she sees at Chesney Wold at about the time she first meets Lady Dedlock—that is, to her mother, and to her feelings about her mother.

Esther's disease, in short, represents an overwhelming incursion of memory and desire. In the course of it, she becomes subject to several kinds of metamorphic process, which link her both to the world outside her and to her own repressed inwardness. Esther's illness is transformative in the sense that it breaks her forcibly out of the rigorously curtailed domestic scene on which she enacts herself—out of the sheltering walls of the bleak, bleak house of her ostensibly happy life—and connects her, not only to what wells up from within, but also to unaccustomed realities outside herself. Specifically, it reflects her connection to Jo, not in her ministering mode, but rather as an aspect of a larger social process: the process so resonantly dramatized by the fever Jo carries, which links all those who dwell in sheltered places to the hazards of life in society at large. It links her, in other words, to realities as coercive as those that determined her orphaning.

Another modulation within her illness connects her to elements of her subjectivity that have been suppressed by the need to achieve functional control. Indeed, one of the striking effects of her commitment to what we have termed the tidy historical past tense—to the recounting of the events of her life, not only in clear sequences, but also in the past tense—would seem to be the need, which we noted at the outset, to establish the definitive pastness of the past. Esther must put the past in its place, so that she can leave it and the feelings it generated completely behind her, out of sight and out of mind. Her disease disrupts this neat relegation; it undoes the elisions and repressions that make it possible for her to be herself as she wants herself to be. Undoing her habitual dissociation from her essential needs, it reconnects her, through dream and delirium, to elements of imagination that are ordinarily banished from her consciousness. For a moment, in her delirium, we experience her kinship to the third-person voice, whose unremitting commitment to the present tense suggests, as we shall see, an unwillingness (as well as an inability) to dissociate itself from the agony of its crippling past and from the fury it generates. This link to the voice also elucidates the depth of the dangers Esther wards off in containing her inwardness. Remarkable though the third-person voice may be in its capacity to express what it feels, this very capacity prevents, as we shall see, its existing, in the ordinary sense, at all. The ordeal of her sickness elucidates the coerciveness of the experience that Esther must, compulsively as it were, shut out of her conscious life.

Dream and delirium are, of course, quickly exorcized, and Esther, though disfigured after her recovery, quickly resumes her habitual structure of selfhood. Yet one striking thing about the presentation of Esther and her narrative is the way that, despite her asserted reconstitution of her identity when she recovers, the elements that erupt in her illness would seem to require repeated beating down. Her reconciliation to her image in the mirror and her return to her Dame Durdenesque routines, with their emphatic insistence on order, containment, and control, do not suffice. Although Esther would seem functionally to have mastered the need for unconditional love, the novel suggests the persistence of an abiding set of needs that gnaw away, not only at Esther, but at *Bleak House* itself.

These needs are most directly discernible in the representation of the figures that draw her harshest judgments. Skimpole is foremost among these. As Esther presents him, he is the epitome of the morally reprehensible manipulator whose selfishness and irresponsibility must be excoriated. The grounds of Esther's aversion to him are interesting, however, and especially in the perspective of Esther's repressions. As Esther's primary antagonist, Skimpole represents the claims of the narcissism— of the broader and more self-regarding emotional and imaginative life—that Esther buries together with her doll. That inner life survives in Esther as the subversive subjective content against which her formidable defenses are erected. Skimpole's claim that he has no sense of time; his denial that there is a meaningful distinction between intention and action; the primacy he gives to "poetry" and the projections it entails as a magic wand for transforming "reality"; and his repudiation of the normative world of work, of callings, and even of household objects—all these bear witness to the clash of values between them. In the end, his insistence that he is a child, and therefore not to be held accountable for his deeds, but rather to be indulged in all his wishes (no nectar, no ambrosia, not even mother's milk, but always, at any season and at any price, hothouse peaches, and nectarines!), signifies the unconditioned and unconditional narcissism that is, in fact, at issue between him and Esther, between Esther and herself, and between Esther and the third-person voice.

That narcissism, as we shall see, is not merely the selfishness excoriated by Esther in Skimpole. It is also the animating force of the third-person narrative, and in fact serves as the springboard for the moral and historical power of that voice, whose energized capacity to succumb to its impulses and vent its feelings stems from its direct access to the narcissism pilloried in Skimpole.

Esther repudiates Skimpole, the adult who plays the child while exercising the exploitative cunning of the corrupt hypocrite that he is. Not surprisingly, he is the character whom she judges most severely. It is not surprising, given the governing mood of *Bleak House,* that Dickens does not extend to Skimpole's vision of life the sympathy he lends Micawber's. Nothing in Skimpole's verbal flutterings approaches the buoyant utopian dimension of Micawber's discourse, and we are permitted little or no sympathetic participation in the pleasures of his existence or in his sense of life. Skimpole formulates thoughts that intrigue us and that are reminiscent of utopian speculations that were current in Dickens's time. We find evidence for this in his sense of the moral economy of the universe, in his conviction of the centrality of pleasure to our inner life, and in his need to stand clear of entrapment in narrow professional commitments. Indeed, the sense of the need to vary one's work, and to flit from activity to activity, specifically echoes Fourier's butterfly principle, even as his sense of pleasure and of play brings to mind Schiller's essay on the aesthetic education of man. Despite these associations, or possibly because of them, Skimpole himself is not allowed to become a Micawber-like locus of value, either as a person or as promulgator of a worldview. Quite the contrary. He is held up for criticism, not only by Esther, but—though ambivalently—by the novel itself.

It is characteristic of Esther that she applies the censoriousness she directs at Skimpole to all the childishly self-indulgent people in the novel. Skimpole epitomizes a set of traits that are dispersed with lesser intensity through a variety of other figures. Mr. Turveydrop has none of the energized articulateness and none of the self-consciousness of Skimpole, but like Skimpole he is castigated for his gross self-indulgence, for enjoying all his unearned prerogatives. His "children"—Caddy and Prince—enjoy Esther's sympathy because of their victimization by him, but at the outset Caddy herself is judged for her all-too-justified petulance at her mother. Esther's narrative is shot through with sympathetic accounts of the tribulations of children in families, like the Jellybys and Pardiggles, that neglect or abuse them. But her memoir is also peppered with censoriousness for those children who do not shape up, as she and Charley do, with good cheer, and pull themselves together, as Caddy eventually does, to renounce her anger and deal constructively with her afflictions.

Esther's censoriousness toward the self-involved and the self-indulgent, even when they are in distress, must be taken as a measure of her struggle to beat down her own resentments, and to suppress the narcissistic impulses that might surface within her. It is significant that the illness which opens the way for the incursion of Esther's repressed subjectivity also mars the beauty that links her to her mother. It is as though the narcissistic pleasures of her beauty, and the oneness with Lady Dedlock that her beauty symbolizes, must be marred in order that Esther be free to invest her all in the identity she forges and in the self-subordinating life of service and control to which she dedicates herself. Many of the equivocal elements of her self-presentation, like her sometimes comic denials of her perceptiveness, her beauty, and her charm—all these are part of the system of denial we have been describing. Esther cannot acknowledge to herself how lovely, clever, and charming she wants to be and in fact often is, even as she cannot accept her own anger, or those impulses in herself which might challenge the constraints she places on herself and on her activity in the world.

Esther's judgments, and especially her judgment of Skimpole, are harsh, and they seem on the whole to organize our judgment of what goes on in the novel. *Bleak House,* however, is not trapped in Esther's perspective, and her constraining judgments do not control its vision of the world. Because of her struggle for control of her own feelings, she cannot experience or express the horror and pain of abandonment that is central to the novel's vision of life. This is therefore projected through a variety of other means. There not only is the antithetical presence of the third-person voice, but also the play of thematic and imaginative materials that enlarge our field of vision beyond Esther's wildest imaginings. Within the novel as a whole, cutting across both voices, there is the resonance of an insistent, keenly orchestrated sympathy for all the victimized children in the novel. No Dickens text—not even Oliver Twist—pivots so largely on the image of the abused, abandoned, and doomed child. We have, of course, the newborn Esther, left for dead, but also the nearly feral but radically human Jo; Guster, with her fits; Ada and Richard, the orphans of the Suit; Charley and her prematurely self-reliant siblings; Jenny's dead baby and Liz's; the smudgy Jellyby brood and the uncharitably exploited Pardiggles; the opium-logged Hawdon, figured as his mother's babe; the maimed Squod and the wayward George Rouncewell; and, as a point of ultimate reference, the figure of the Christ child itself.

It not only is, or even chiefly, the number and range of doomed, abandoned, and abused children that expresses the depth of the novel's identification with the orphan condition. It is also the fact that so many of these children must literally die and that the pathos of their death is eloquently rendered. Much of the novel's narrative and figurative material addresses the reader's imagination of the horror of abandonment, loss, and death. That material is disposed so as to sluice into other contexts a great variety of universally available emotions rooted in the orphan condition. Even Lady Dedlock's flight and death at the end of the novel are represented in terms that link her, obliquely, to these emotions, and Hawdon, dead, is imagined as he was when he was a baby.

The novel's dead and dying babies are characteristically associated with the Christ child, and recurrently serve as a ground for indicting the neglectful God (or the absconded parents, or the indifferent secular authorities) who let the novel's suffering analogues of the Christ child die of deprivation or neglect. Jenny's dead baby is seen in the light of the newborn Jesus; on his deathbed, Jo uncomprehendingly addresses his Father, Who Is In Heaven; the outcast Hawdon's jaundiced corpse leads the third-person narrator to attack the powers that allow such deaths as his to occur. And there is, within the third-person narrative, a furious appeal on behalf of the multitude of outcasts, orphans, and foundlings who are epitomized by Jo. Reading across the split voices of the narrative, all these figures embody the intrinsic exposedness of the infant Esther, whose initial abandonment does not reverberate in her consciousness as we might expect it to but that resonates richly in the representation of others.

Indeed, we think that Esther's life project is repression of the pain, rage, and desperation that her infancy and childhood must have generated. The variety of mother roles she plays, including the way she, in effect, mothers her own mother, serve to deflect and transmute that pain and that rage. Her identification with the people she mothers may be seen to serve, moreover, as a satisfaction, but also as a deflection, of her underlying desire to merge with a mother. As for the novel as a whole, we take it that the most striking elements in its construction, namely, the splitting of its narrative voices, is determined by the need at once to suppress and to express her repressed desire, rage, and desperation.

Esther's elision of her own feelings, and her espousal of a code of conduct that precludes direct expression of either the need for love or rage at its absence puts in an interesting light the presence of all the suffering and abandoned infants of the novel. Located for the most part within the third-person narrative, these infants bespeak the radical need for redeeming love, but at the same time, like Esther, they cannot effectively express an active demand for anything at all. In this respect, their passive helplessness serves as an appropriate emblem of the essential passivity induced by Esther's renunciation of her right to demand anything at all, or even actively to wish for it. Their presence within the third-person narrative, however, suggests that they are also a touchstone to the antithetical sense of things that stems from the persistent rage Esther herself must have felt and that finds direct expression in the third-person voice.

For, if Esther, who is so carefully shaped and socialized, contains her suppressed anger and compulsively channels her potential energy into domestic and maternal pursuits, both anger and energy find expression in the third-person voice. Indeed, we take it that it is only by releasing the repressed contents of the Esther narrative—by allowing, in a manner of speaking, Mr. Jarndyce's beast to growl in the growlery and to emerge from it, howling—that the larger world of the novel can be articulated; it is only through the release in the third-person narrative of all that is implied by Esther's abandonment that the novel can link biography with history and subjective pain with the novel's vision of life. That is, it is only by making articulate the subjective realities of the orphan condition that Dickens can generate a coherent sense of a world that abandons its children and also give us tools for interpreting it. In this sense, the anger vented by the third person not only allows for an interpretation of the world, but also for the integrality of that world as an imaginative entity.

Although the voice that is the medium for the third-person world making is not characterized as a person, or as a character in the ordinary novelistic sense, it has many of the qualities of personhood. It vividly expresses a variety of responses and sustains a considerable number of attitudes that mark it, if not as a person in the everyday sense, then as a vital center of feeling. As such a center, it organizes itself in recognizable ways and expresses itself with a consistency and a coherence that signify what we ordinarily think of as "character" in both fiction and life. It is, in fact, probably the most vividly colored and urgently insistent presence in the novel.

One of its salient characteristics is, as we have already noted, the refusal (or inability) to define boundaries, either for itself or for its discourse. Hence it cannot, as Esther can, emerge from the text as an articulated being, with firm boundaries in space and time. Instead, it reverberates freely to elements that are excluded from the careful formalization of Esther's existence. These things include narcissism, magic, vision, vindictiveness, rage, and an imaginative reaching for some conception of a better world, side by side with aching consciousness of the intractability of the "real" world, a world that is epitomized by the way it abandons and even persecutes its Esthers, its Hawdons, its Gusters, its Jos—even, in the last analysis, and at the behest of the third person, its Lady Dedlocks. All these qualities, together with the discourse that the third-person voice produces—that is, the third-person narrative—are just what characterize it.

As with Esther, the stylistic traits and the narrative modes of the third-person voice provide convenient ways of apprehending both its form and its contents. Most striking is the fact that the third-person voice relinquishes the historical past in telling its story. That is, it forgoes the tense that is necessary to normative narrative. In doing so, it renounces one of the central aspects of Esther's sense of the world—namely, her insistence on the absolute pastness of the past. It refuses to put the past—the insufferable, unspeakable past—in its place. Instead, it insists on the presentness of the past—on the relevance, at every moment of present life, of what happened in the past, and on the power of the past to determine every word, thought, and action in the present.

Altogether, its relation to verbs is revealing. The opening paragraphs of the novel dramatize in the extreme a tendency to renounce verbs and what they signify—namely, manifest actions and positively declared states of being. Insofar as it utilizes verbs, it does so in ways that violate our sense of narrative ordering. It assaults us with the strangeness of being suspended, as we read, in an ongoing present, a present whose presentness is also undermined by the paradox that the narrative voice nonetheless organizes its materials in sequences that imply narrative and that concede the existence of temporal sequence. As we shall see, this voice, which does not use the past tense, nonetheless looks before and after, and seeks for what is, as well as for what is not; it not only represents narratives, but also conspires to generate them.

The opening of the novel speaks eloquently to the tendency to create the sense of suspension: "London. Michaelmas term lately over, and the Lord Chancellor sitting in Lincoln's Inn Hall. Implacable November weather" (49). The verblessness, the present participle (sitting), and the specific emphasis on a place (London) and a time (Michaelmas term), as in conventional stage directions, work together to give us a sense of suspended being, of suspended animation, of a space of time in which things hang, undirected and unresolved, and therefore cannot be pinned down or laid out as a temporal or spatial sequence, even while they teasingly retain the characteristics ("lately") of temporality.

Analogously, nominatives, both nouns and pronouns, are often elided, so that verb-related forms hang in suspension, subjectless, and therefore performing, as it were, their own actions. The stylistic ruptures, both verbal and nominative, are generalized to the point where they affect, sooner or later, most formal relations between subjects, actions, and objects, and therefore of agency in general. That is, the ruptures make it difficult for us to conceptualize, locally, the working or doing or being of whoever or whatever it is that performs actions. Ultimately, of course, everything comes clear, but the process of arriving at this clarity gives rise to a disorientation that puts us in a position somewhat analogous to that of the narrative voice.

For the disruption of agency, like the suspension of events in the narrative's continuing present, mirrors what we take to be the essential condition of the third-person voice. That voice is not a subject or agent. It is incapable of direct action, and it is unable to move objects or achieve objectives. It is, moreover, without self-consciousness or self-reflexiveness, and it is utterly lacking in the capacity for self-regulatory self-confrontation or moral accounting with regard to its own responses. As a corollary of this, it cannot, as Esther so compulsively must, look forward and backward in time; it remains, formally at least, suspended in a present akin to that of its narrative.

Yet the third-person voice is not absolutely trapped in that present, even as it is not trapped within its ostensible lack of inwardness—within its nonexistence as a character, or person, in the ordinary sense. With regard to the issue of time, it is a mistake to infer from its use of the present tense that the voice has no interpretive power and cannot organize a view of things.

Hillis Miller (1958) errs in this, as do other readers. From the voice's suspension in the narrative present, and from the correlative absence of the past tense and from the failure to anticipate the future in its recounting, Miller infers a state of interpretive paralysis. Our own reading is that the present tense of its discourse is, among other things, a sign of its entrapment in its earliest experience, and of its desperate clinging to it. The third-person voices clutches to itself the horror of abandonment, and will not relinquish either its experience of the helplessness abandonment gives rise to or of the fury it unleashes. Nor will it put a lid on the fantasies of fusion and vengeance of which it must have been subject in the course of its existence, from the moment of its initial abandonment to the present—the suspended present—in which it utters its text.

So far is it from being trapped in the present moment, the moment of narration, that the present in which and of which it speaks is the direct distillate of the fantasies generated out of the voice's ever-present experience of abandonment. Those fantasies are, in fact, profoundly future oriented. By this we mean that its narrative is both an expression of the pain of its abandonment and a vehicle for longed-for satisfactions that include the vengeance it must take on those it feels abandoned it and the merger it must achieve with them. Indeed, in this perspective, the very plot of the novel may be seen as the product of an omnipotence fantasy that appropriates the world, and transforms it into an instrument for its satisfactions.

Thus, while Esther contracts herself into the wee space of her humility, and does so by tidily placing herself in excruciatingly finite space and time, the third person refuses to confine itself at all. Its imperious appropriation of all time and all space is in fact a reflex of its relentless clinging to its sense of abandonment and of its desperate wish to undo that abandonment. It undoes it by projecting its fantasies and wishes into the world as a way of controlling the world. Indeed, this spewing of itself into the world serves still another fantasy. The third-person voice seems to feel that in doing so it can merge with the world by making the world a part of itself.

Perhaps the clearest sign of its appropriation of the world is its rampant use of metaphor. If Esther assiduously avoids metaphor, the third-person voice revels in it, at every point extruding its fantasy life into the world, to the extent of controlling the world by means of its metaphors. We have to go no further than the opening paragraph of the novel to perceive its strategies of projective appropriation for the transformation of reality. By the end of the paragraph, we not only have a megalosaurus at liberty on Holborn Hill, but a medley of disparate realities in the process of actively interpenetrating with each other, from snowflakes in mourning to pedestrians accumulating at compound interest. From within that insistent merging of separate entities, the voice evokes a vision of the beginning as well as the end of the universe itself. The megalosaurus and the mud suggest the emergence of the world from the primordial slime while the grime-blackened snowflakes and the snowflakes in mourning for the death of the sun bespeak an apocalypse.

The voice's use of metaphor not only tranforms what is outside it, but also controls it. Clenched as well as euphoric in its fury, it transforms all objects and people in its field of vision into grotesque entities that it controls through such transformations. Eighteen lawyers jumping to the bar in protest become eighteen hammers of a piano popping up; the entire legal profession is unnamed in the third-person voice's process of naming them. The use of Chizzle, Mizzle, Drizzle reduces them to a comic sequence of sounds, in a way that echoes their nullification of their clients as individual human beings.

The strategy of rhyming people out of existence is derived from children's rhymes and echoes the function for children of such rhymes in wishing away ghosts or other threatening presences. The particular rhyme series we have cited appropriately begins with a name that has a limited degree of meaning. Chizzle presumably constitutes a clean-cut play on chiseling—both cheating and chipping away with a chisel, but leaving some space for us to imagine a named being. By the time we get to the other terms, the clear trace of meaning diminishes, yielding only vague associations with mud, muzzle, and so on. An analogous obliteration is achieved in the naming of the politicians—Boodle, Coodle, Doodle, Noodle, and Buffy, Cuffy, Duffy, and so on.

Another kind of language magic and coercive will to control is at work in the voice's treatment of Chancery and the Chancery Suit. The novel suggests that the Suit is a representation of a complex social process; in the Preface, Dickens insists on the historicity of the Suit, even as he insists on the reality in nature of Spontaneous Combustion. The voice, however, deals with the Suit as anything but a historical reality, and Esther eventually follows it in this. Already in the first chapter the voice uses the power of words to transform the Suit into a horrendous monster that "stretche[s] forth its unwholesome hand to spoil and corrupt" (53), "shirking and sharking," "sow[ing] ... confusion broadcast" (53), and "drag[ging] its dreary length before the court" (52).

We understand its treatment of the Suit as a strategy for dealing with its bewildering incomprehensibility, as well as with the rage that bewilderment stirs. From within its angry child's-eye perspective the third-person voice transforms the Suit from a baffling and resistant historical reality into a living creature which, however, dangerous, offers the possibility of being confronted and even mastered. It as if only in creaturely form is there any hope of catching, defeating, and putting an end to the Suit. St George, after all, vanquishes the dragon.

The logic of the third-person voice's anthropomorphization and demonization of the Suit is congruous with Gridley's response to it. Gridley says that he should not blame the representatives of the system, but rather the system itself. Yet Gridley also insists that if he didn't personalize the system, so that he can blame it, he would go mad. "It is only by resenting [my wrongs], and by revenging them in my mind ... that I am able to keep my wits together" (266–67). The third person may be imagined to treat the Suit as it does, not only blaming it, but also transforming it, as a way of warding off the madness that might overtake it if it were to submit passively to the rage the Suit elicits in its failure to provide the sustenance it promises.

Through its use of language magic, the third-person voice not only externalizes its inwardness to control what is outside it, but in doing so it transforms its infant powerlessness into a sense of ominpotence. This reversal may be understood as part of a struggle, analogous to Esther's antithetical strategy of self-control, to master an intolerable sense of helplessness and to contain the chaos with which it is threatened. There are many traces of this struggle in the text, and the fantasy of omnipotence is only the most visible of them. For like the ubiquitous God of Creation, the powerless ostensible nonbeing that is the voice comes to fill all the time and all the space of its ostensibly time-free narrative and to tyrannize over it with the full force of its totalizing imagination. Not only does its language assail the world with the energized authority of a deity returned to deliver Doomsday judgment on its sinful Creation, but the sweep of its imagination is such that it invokes no less than the cosmos as the theater of its enactment.

The judgments it pronounces are, of course, made on behalf of the abandoned and the outcast. The fiercest eddies of outrage whip around the orphans, like Jo, and the victims, like Gridley, who have been persecuted by a world that hunts, teases, and destroys them—characters whose destruction by neglect, malice, harassment, and disease are the measure of the world's culpability. Reporting the death of Jo, for example, the voice makes a sardonic appeal to kings and Christian gentlemen: "Dead," it says, as Jo breathes his last:

> Dead, your Majesty. Dead, my lords and gentlemen. Dead, Right Reverends and Wrong Reverends of every order. Dead, men and women, born with Heavenly compassion in your hearts. And dying thus round us every day. (705)

Toward Chancery and the miseries it generates, it goes beyond this appeal and invokes the Heavens and the Earth. Seething with irony, it tells us, at the outset, that

> Never can there come fog too thick, never can there come mud and mire too deep, to assort with the groping and floundering condition which this High Court of Chancery, most pestilent of hoary sinners, holds, this day, in the sight of heaven and earth. (50)

The voice's rage and its gigantism show themselves, not only in the megalomanic conjuring of the theater of the universe itself for its doomsday drama, but also in a variety of rhetorical emphases in this passage: in its climactic iteration of the "nevers"; in its vituperative and redundant name calling of "hoary and pestilential sinner"; and, of course, in its grandiloquent reaching for "heaven and earth." All these bespeak the intensity of the rage being vented by the third-person voice, even as that rage is transformed into the coinage of traditional moral and religious discourse. The clearsighted heavens scowl at what may be obscured on earth by mud and fog, and God Himself judges what the voice sees and shows. It is the voice that utters His judgments. The effect is all the more powerful because of the exalted—and familiar—terms of that discourse.

As with Esther, again, every detail of the third-person narrative reflects the impulses that motivate it. Here we are in the presence of the voice's anger and its totalizing will to power, not over itself, as with Esther, but over the entire universe and first of all over the immediate objects of its animosity. The will to power has its most elaborate expression in the way the plot of the novel, as well as its thematic emphases, may be seen as derivatives of the third person's inner life. Both the insistent presence of orphans and the centrality of Lady Dedlock to the plot are integral to its sense of life and being. The proliferation of suffering children expresses the pain of the abandonment which is at the core of the third person's experience, as well as of Esther's; the hunting-down of Lady Dedlock reflects the need to allay that pain by avenging it on its perpetrator.

Hence, it is no surprise that the third person's fantasy of omnipotence is directed toward Lady Dedlock, on whose head it brings down a kind of kangaroo-court justice. It does so through the fantasy that is shared by Esther and the voice and that shapes the plot of the novel. In this respect, the third-person voice serves as Esther's surrogate in ferreting out her origins, providing the medium in which the unmasking of Lady Dedlock takes place. It also serves as the agent of Esther's repressed anger in avenging herself on the mother she so readily forgives in her own narrative, but toward whom it is inconceivable she does not harbor murderous rage.

The third-person voice, as surrogate for Esther and as her alter ego, may be said to be driven to expose and destroy what we take to be the original and ultimate source of "their" shared degradation, who is also the novel's pivotal agent of abandonment. The voice repeatedly takes on those who think they are inscrutable and, in Lady Dedlock's case, invulnerable ("quite out of the reach and ken of ordinary mortals" [59]) and exposes them in their vulnerability. With regard to Lady Dedlock, exposure is not enough; she must be hunted down and destroyed. Tulkinghorn's pursuit of her fatal secret not only leads to her exposure by the Smallweeds and to her unmasking by Bucket, but also to her destruction by exposure to the brutal elements.

In this perspective, the detective plot, with its doubling of investigators, may be read as an instrument of the third-person voice, realizing an unconscious fantasy of vengeance which is the pivot of the action. The voice not only cries out for judgment, but also may be taken to execute its judgment by generating a world in which it manipulates everything to avenge itself upon the source of its own ghostlike, disincarnate condition. In this perspective, Lady Dedlock's "sin," is not, as some readers have held, the sin of indulging in an unhallowed sexuality out of which her child is born. It is, rather, the sin of abandoning that child, a sin that she in fact committed, even though the plot of the novel exonerates her by having her believe her child was dead. Here, not the thought determines, but the deed. Esther has in fact been abandoned, whether or not Lady Dedlock meant to abandon her. Hence, Lady Dedlock is punished for that abandonment in retribution for Esther's absolute helplessness as the infant left for dead. The abandoned child does not split hairs; it does not distinguish between actions and intentions.

The third person, seen in this light, not only punishes Esther's delinquent mother, but plays sadistically with her along the way. The ultimate exposure of Lady Dedlock takes many, many hundreds of pages to accomplish. But all along the way there is a recurrent disposition to play with and revel in small moments of exposure and humiliation. The powerful, frozen Lady Dedlock is "hotly pursued by the fashionable intelligence," which is seen as a "mighty hunter before the Lord."

> She supposes herself to be an inscrutable Being, quite out of the reach and ken of ordinary mortals, but there are deferential people, in a dozen callings . . . who can tell you how to manage her as if she were a baby; who do nothing but nurse her all their lives . . . who lead her and her whole troop . . . and bear them off, as Lemuel Gulliver bore away the stately fleet of the majestic Lilliput. (59)

She is not, that is, the haughty figure that she is believed to be and that the third-person voice in fact collaborates in making her seem; she is in fact a helpless baby who must be "nursed," and who is toyed with and exploited by everyone around her. Seeing her in this way, the third person, in effect, subjects her to a helplessness analogous to that of the helpless infant Esther and of all of Esther's infant analogues, like the neglected Peepy—and, if we wish, of the never-born, eternally disembodied third person itself. The evocation of Gulliver and the Lilliputians has special resonance here, because it is a precipitate of a mechanism that is always present in the voice—the transformation through reversal by rage of an original state of shrinking helplessness into gargantuan power.

All the foreshadowing of Lady Dedlock's end and of the disintegration of the Dedlocks and their traditions—for example, the elaborate apparatus of the Ghost and the Ghost's walk, as well as the novel's banshees and other supernatural presences—are in the service of a gloating anticipation of what is to come. Traditionally (and rightly) viewed as proleptic devices, these details also serve to anticipate the pleasure of revenge. Indeed, everything is ruthlessly organized from the very beginning to whet the hunter's appetite for its prey. Nature itself is made to express the death that is to come (56), even the rain, the wetness, and the decay of Chesney Wold are in the service of the satisfaction of the voice's appetite for vengeance. In our first encounter with Chesney Wold, we hear that

> [a]n arch of the bridge has been sapped and sopped away . . . so wet that the trees seem wet through, and the soft loppings and prunings of the woodman's axe can make no crash and crackle as they fall. (56)

The dripping of the rain is already, or is about to become, the sound of the ghost's walk. Everything is in a state of preparation for the final blow, as the third person takes command of nature in the service of its vengeance.

The treatment of the Dedlock world and its decadence is intertwined with the disease motif which is central both to the playing out of Lady Dedlock's hunting down and to the thematic structure of the novel as a whole. In the end, Lady Dedlock is doomed to die on the threshhold of the plague-infested graveyard where Hawdon/Nemo is buried; the pullulating infestation of the graveyard becomes an emblem of the corruption that pervades the world as *Bleak House* presents it and of the world as the third person sees it. It is also an agent of the universal retribution the third person seeks—and of the Justice the third person invokes.

The Dedlock/disease theme emerges when the Dedlocks are first seen in the little church at Chesney Wold. At that point, the voice speaks of its smelling "as earthy as a grave," and of its "time and damp-worn monuments" (304)—elements that will be referred back to later, when it speaks of the house at Chesney Wold as pervaded by "a cold, blank smell, like the smell of a little church, though something dryer; suggesting that the dead and buried Dedlocks walk there . . . and leave the flavour of their graves behind them" (456). These evoke a relatively sanitized version of the novel's sense of the state of the corrupt body in death, of the oozing decay of Nemo's grave, and of the associations that link it to the deaths of both Lady Dedlock and Krook.

We recall that Nemo's burial elicits a vehement outburst, containing one of the third person's major invocations of disease as an instrument of apocalypse. Nemo is buried in "a hemmed-in churchyard, pestiferous and obscene, whence malignant diseases are communicated to the bodies of our dear brothers and sisters" (202). The heart of the vision is the unholy intimacy between life and death, in the form of disease:

> With every villainy of life in action close on death, and every poisonous element of death in action close on life—here, they lower our dear brother down a foot or two: here sow him in corruption, to be raised in corruption: an avenging ghost at many a sick bedside: a shameful testimony to future ages, how civilization and barbarism walked this boastful island together. (202)

We have here, among other things, an allusion to Paul's Epistle to the Corinthians, which tells us of the human body that "It is sown in corruption; it is raised in incorruption" (1 Cor. 4. 2). Here, however, corruption—decay—is incorrigible. It is not redeemed through love, as Paul implies, but rather is doomed to wander, grim and vindictive, like the avenging ghost of the Ghost's Walk. Here it "walks" like a miasma, to avenge the death of the outcast, the abandoned, and the orphaned, whose degradation and persecution are requited through disease, even as Lady Dedlock's death, at the entrance to this place of pestilential doom, will avenge her original sin of abandoning Esther.

When the voice invokes disease as the agent of retribution after Hawdon's interment, it anticipates the apocalyptic catastrophe it will unleash as it contemplates Tom-All-Alone's, with its heavy, "nauseous air" (682), its atmosphere as of a moonscape's "desert region unfit for life and blasted by volcanic fires," (682–83) and the devastation it harbors:

> But [Tom] has his revenge. Even the winds are his messengers. . . . There is not a drop of Tom's corrupted blood but propagates infection and contagion somewhere. It shall pollute, this very night, the choice stream . . . of a Norman house, and his Grace shall not be able to say Nay to the infamous alliance. There is not an atom of Tom's slime, not a cubic inch of any pestilential gas in which he lives . . . but shall work his retribution. (683)

This peroration obliquely anticipates the doom on the Dedlock house, as it shall be fulfilled through Lady Dedlock. In the plot of the novel, Jo, who is flesh of Tom's flesh, will infect Charley who will infect Esther who will, metaphorically and through the agency of the plot spun by the third person, destroy Lady Dedlock, who will die at the crossroads of corruption, at the very gate of Nemo's burial place, and Jo's, whose Banshee is linked to the plague-ridden atoms of Tom's infected blood and avenging slime.

This agonized appropriation of godlike power is the apogee of the third-person voice's prophetic response to its experience. The authority it arrogates to itself here to a considerable extent sets the moral tone of the novel as a whole. In effect, here the voice recruits the notion of an absolute moral economy in the universe—this, after all, is the meaning of the assertion that every cubic inch of pestilential slime will wreak justice—to rectify the nightmare of life within the horror of a world for which, again, abandonment is the perfect metonomy.

The horror, rather than the call for justice, is at the heart of the voice's vision. There is, to be sure, deep resonance in the voice's calling down of judgment on a corrupt world. Such resonance, however, cannot make anything happen or even alleviate the voice's desolation; finally, it remains only one more strategy by which the voice tries to bolster its sense of being. What characterizes the voice not only is its inability to be or to do anything, but also its inability even to envision anything substantive outside the narrow range of its drastically curtailed inner life. It careens exuberantly within its discourse, appropriating, in a manner of speaking, all of Dickens's comic and rhetorical powers for its own needs. In the end, however, it cannot escape the constraints of its unconditional orphan plight.

Even its mobilization of disease as apocalypse is in the final analysis the elaboration of a set of fantasies rooted, like everything else, in the orphan condition. Its susceptibility to the threat of contamination and pollution arises from its recoil from life in the world and specifically in the flesh. It expresses that horror when it perceives that the "flame of gas burn[s] so sullenly above the iron gate, on which the poisoned air deposits its witch-ointment slimy to the touch" (203); when it notes that the fluids that ooze out of Krook's spontaneously combusted body, are "a thick yellow liquor ... [,] a stagnant, sickening oil, with some natural repulsion in it" (509); and when it cries out that Tom's diseased blood and pestiferous slime dominate the world.

What the voice experiences is a horror of life itself—of life as lived in the body; of the ravages of sexuality as the voice perceives it; and of the deadly contamination that accompanies contact of any sort. Hawdon's room and the state of his body when Tulkinghorn comes upon them serve as a touchstone to the voice's ubiquitous sense of contamination. One sign of this is the poignant detail of how the air in his room, almost as nauseous as the atmosphere of Tom-All-Alone's, is so fetid that it extinguishes a burning candle (186). Jo serves a similar function. No character in the novel receives so profound a compassionate response as Jo, yet the figuration of his presence is to a considerable degree defined by the disease he carries from the pestilential plague spot which is Tom-All-Alone's. Jo, like Hawdon, is bound up with a corrupt world, where people are conceived in corruption, born in corruption, and die in corruption, with no hope of a better fate anywhere but in the Heaven that the third-person voice can barely evoke for the dead and dying victims of its world.

The nightmare of the voice's inner life can be epitomized by the magnitude of its conflicted response to Jo, Hawdon, and the series of babies, orphans, and outcasts in the novels. Together, they call forth the demand for cosmic justice, but they also elicit yearning for a better existence, soul-searing compassion, and revulsion from life itself. That revulsion is rooted in the pain, the corruption, and the horror that are inscribed within the voice's perception of a world in which life mercilessly spawns and then abandons its progeny.

For the voice's vision of life is informed by a sense that the very generation of life is both irresponsible and polluting. The irresponsible sexuality of parents is the primal source of the orphanhood, not only of Esther and the orphans associated with her, but also of life itself, as the voice perceives it. The primal begettors are also the primal abandoners. The humors of the body, in all their pestiferousness, are among other things signs of the sexuality that cannot be dissociated from disease and from the emotional nightmare of abandonment.

The voice, experiencing all this, and tracking it in the disrupted relationship between Hawdon and Lady Dedlock in her earlier life as Honoria Barbary, is in an almost paralytic bind. It is torn between its compassion, even for the begettors, whom in its pitying phase it sees as orphanlike beings, and its revulsion from the pain of abandonment. At the same time, it is repelled by what it perceived to be the taintedness of the act of procreation, which produces future victims of abandonment, and outraged by the irresponsiblity toward the beings they beget of those who indulge what is imagined to be an intrinsically corrupt sexuality.

The voice's complex response to the realities of life as it is imagined spills over into the "feel" of the novel as a whole and specifically into Esther's discourse. Seepage of this sort is evident at the climactic moment of the action, when Esther records the experience of finding Lady Dedlock dead on the threshhold of the pestiferous graveyard where both Hawdon and Jo are buried. Esther is at the end of the harrowing journey through day and night, town and country, storm and sleet, in quest of her mother. Her journey, as she recounts it, partakes of the nightmarish disorientations of the third-person voice. In the course of it, she loses the clarity of perception and firmness of orientation that marks her account of her experience. The journey, in fact, has a numbing but also a stimulating effect on her, similar to the effect of her feverish illness. "I have the most confused impression of that walk," she says of the last segment of the pursuit, in a passage we have already cited a part of:

> I recollect that it was neither night nor day; that morning was dawning, but the street-lamps were not yet put out; that the sleet was still falling, and that all the ways were deep with it . . . At the same time I remember. . . that the stained house fronts put on human shapes and looked at me; that great water gates seemed to be opening and closing in my head, or in the air; and that the unreal things were more substantial than the real. (867)

Here Esther clings to the circumstantiality and denotativeness of her own style, but the content, with its loss of the distinction between reality and unreality and of what is inside her and what is outside, brings her close to the third-person mode of perception and discourse.

The scene itself, with all its pathos and horror, is a kind of *Liebestod,* where Lady Dedlock rejoins her abandoned lover in the chill snow through which she has made her way, at the plague spot which is his final place of troubled rest—the place where we have seen rats, like the rats in the gutter where Oliver attended on the corpse of the dead woman, climbing in and out of the graves. As Esther horrifiedly contemplates this scene, her mind already inundated by the "watergates" of her momentarily liberated memory, it also seems like a primal scene, where love and death mingle with plague and pestilence. Toward this tableau, she remains numb, expressing little, and merely "recording" what she "sees" and holds her breath at what we take to be the pain, pathos, and horror.

Her inability to experience or give meaning to the horror of this scene, and the level of her abstraction from her ordinary orientation in time and space, bring her close to the third-person voice—so much so, that they seem to merge for a moment. What we have in the scene, in fact, is a conflation of so much that the voice, as surrogate for Esther, has imagined and suffered, that we can extrapolate the complexity and the anguish of the subjectivity from which it is projected—the subjectivity that identifies, not only with Esther, but with Hawdon, and with Jo, and with Lady Dedlock herself. Standing away from the scene, and treating it like a camera's eye, she nonetheless not only seems to merge with it, but also to be experiencing the merger of her mother, her father, Jo, and herself in an image of a merger of everthing into everything else within a single vignette of life-creating and life-destroying desire. The voice could not do better, in concretizing its essential sense of life.

This critical moment of melding, between the polarized sensibilities of Esther and the voice, should not blur the sustained tension between the two, nor obscure the impact of Esther's vision of life on our perception of the world of the novel. Much as *Bleak House* is not trapped in Esther's sense of things, so it is not entirely controlled by the voice. Although the voice's thundering outrage grips the imagination, and though the novel as a whole projects a vision of life that is closely attuned to the voice's underlying sense of things, *Bleak House* achieves, as it were, a stereoscopic effect by filtering its vision through its polarized voices. In this way, it complicates and qualifies the visions of both, though without significantly tempering the novel's global sense of the horror of life.

Ordinarily, Esther provides a telling commentary on the voice. She does this in her very existence as a person with a name, a role in society, and a consciousness that can reflect on herself and her experience. Esther does survive. Unlike Jo, she is not destroyed by her abandonment, and she is not disembodied by it, like the voice. In fact, she fills her fair share of the novel with her sober way of seeing things. She has come through, despite her initial abandonment; she is permitted to take the circumstances that make it possible for her to survive, including her fiercely repressive upbringing by Miss Barbary, and to use them to shape herself into the person she becomes. Despite her loss of control during her illness, her shape is all too clear and very sharply defined. The values she embodies, moreover, are shown to be indispensable for survival. The order, cleanliness, punctuality, clarity of perception, and the self-containedness that she achieves are what empower her to survive. So do the earnestness, the sincerity, and the single-mindedness that line up with David Copperfield's credo. It is suggested, moreover, that her governing values are what is universally needed for survival in the brutal world of the novel. Also indispensable are the tempering of desire and the self-doubt that leads her to suppress even her normative desires, like her wish for Woodcourt's love. Indeed, the very shaping of her desire, to make sure that it is directed at appropriate objects, is part of her formation as a candidate for survival. It is a cardinal aspect of her *Bildung*.

The price of her survival, however, is a profound cutting off both from her primary needs and her besetting fears. These are what emerge in the third-person voice, whose ability to project its fantasies and to shape its perception of the world in terms of them constitutes a stunning expression of what Esther herself must defend against. Yet it is part of the novel's radical confrontation with the issues of abandonment and accommodation that we can imagine no way of incorporating back into Esther, as we know her, any part of what is displaced out of her into the voice.

Esther's relation to her counterpart voice is very different from David Copperfield's relation to his doubles. If we stand away from David's representation of himself, we can imagine that he might incorporate some of the qualities that are displaced out of him into his doubles and still not lose his essential character. David need not be Steerforth, or be the predator Steerforth becomes, for him, in his own way and his own measure, to be charming, to impersonate other people, and to bring them good cheer. Indeed, his very narrative demonstrates the existence in him of these "steerforthian" qualities. For Esther, on the other hand, such a synthesis of what she accepts as part of herself and what she excludes seems impossible. By shaping Esther as an extreme incarnation of the values that David purports to live by, Dickens creates in her a character whose very ground of being is exclusion, not only of "wayward and perverted feelings," but also of the emotions and imaginings that are at the root of her being. But he also demonstrates the impossibility for anyone in the world of the novel to deal constructively with the elements excluded from the well-ordered sphere of her being, or to achieve greater flexibility and with it, a greater freedom to be. In fact, the novel dramatizes the difficulty, if not the impossibility, of shaping selves that can both experience and control desire.

Esther is not the only character who must erect powerful barriers against the dissolution threatened by the experience of a vivid subjectivity. Virtually everyone in the world of the novel must do that—the comically lovable Bagnets as well as the grotesquely repellant Smallweeds, the self-effacing Mr. Jarndyce as well as the self-important Sir Leicester. Indeed, as Martin Price has observed, one of the striking aspects of *Bleak House* is the presence within it of a constellation of characters preoccupied with form—Sir Leicester, Turveydrop, and Bagnet are his chief instances—and a scrupulous examination of the constraints that form imposes on them.

There is an impressive array of characters who are cut off from experience of their true subjectivity, or who shape themselves so as to avoid experience of it. There is Miss Flite, who contains her longing and her anger within the forms of the archaic courtliness that makes her so touching and so pathetic. There is George, who echoes Bagnet in a military formalization of his affective life. Very dramatically, there is John Jarndyce, who cannot be thanked because his experience of other peoples' gratitude is too threatening, and who must banish his anger to the Growlery, even as he must blame the East Wind for any upset he experiences. Reminiscent of Grimwig in *Twist,* there is Boythorn, whose booming voice externalizes an irritable eruptiveness in a comic formalization that contains and curtails its potential destructiveness. There is Tulkinghorn, whose rusty garb and tight professional mien reflect the suppression of whatever humane susceptibilities he retains. There is Lady Dedlock, whose gelid surface cannot survive the warmth of the feelings that well up in her when she is confronted with the consequences of her past life. And, of course, there are all the professionals, locked into the forms of the vocations they pursue.

The emotional aridity of the people who live within the world of the novel is linked to constraints that world puts on individual needs. The world of the novel is a world defined by an endless and irreparable miscarriage of justice, as in Chancery, and by the ossification of institutions within a soul-destroying system of greed, rapacity, malice, and folly, as in the Dedlocks' world of rotten boroughs. More than that. Within the reality represented in the novel, it becomes clear that the "system" that is the world undermines and obstructs every impulse toward striving beyond the stultifying "is." At all levels, abandonment lurks, disease festers. Even in the most sheltered places, it is virtually impossible to shape selves with meaningful feeling lives.

In the perspective of the polarization between Esther and the third-person voice, the Richard story holds special interest. Although it is embedded chiefly in the Esther narrative, it is the vehicle for psychic material that pervades both narratives and illuminates the underlying conflicts of the novel as a whole. The fact that Richard's story is embedded in a concrete and extended narrative, which records his experience from without, together with the figuration through which much of his inner experience is rendered, puts us more directly in touch with the issues that arise within the orphan condition than any of the novels, or any aspect of *Bleak House*, we have discussed so far. Esther and the third-person voice enact antithetical responses to the orphan condition; Richard further elucidates its underlying dynamic.

This dynamic hinges on crying need, variously expressed and suppressed by the Olivers, the Davids, and the Esthers of Dickens's fiction. The nature of that need is more than usually visible here in the imagery that accompanies Richard's struggle for identity and manhood. What emerges in the Richard action not only is the subversive nature of such need, but also the role of the world in stirring those needs and in destroying the characters who are subject to them. As one of the two most developed stories in *Bleak House*—the other is the story of Lady Dedlock's hunting down—the account of Richard's development underscores his importance in the economy of the whole. Through him Dickens picks up the theme of *Bildung* in its normative form, and in doing so, he foregrounds the inadequacy of Esther's mode of self-organization. He does so by portraying in him a character who cannot shut out the needs and feelings that Esther's self-fashioning represses. The Richard story illustrates the impossiblity for a person who remains susceptible to the needs enacted by the third-person voice, yet must embody himself in a role that requires containments akin to those that make possible Esther's survival. Indeed, what is revealed by the Richard action is the necessary failure of *Bildung* in the traditional sense. This is partly due to the stultifying deadness of the society and of the roles into which he must adapt himself. But it is also due to the power of his world to stir the regressive desire to which he is susceptible.

The Scylla and Charybdis of Richard's quest for identity are on the one hand the stony intractability of the vocations available to him and on the other the siren song of the wishfulness that the Suit, with its teasing lure of nurture, arouses in him. Worn out by the thankless effort to find meaning within a vocation, he lets himself be sucked into craving for the passivity that an inheritance would facilitate. Because that craving is insatiable, he becomes subject to the dissolution of being that imagined fusion with the source of nurture inevitably brings. Here, that source is the Suit, as stand-in for absent parents, and especially the absent mother.

The Richard action articulates these issues. Richard is a young man without prospects, an orphan who must make his way in the world. Jarndyce, under whose tutelage he is placed, sees his only hope for survival in finding a vocation by which to support himself. Richard's love for Ada and his engagement to her heighten the urgency of his doing so; indeed, his pursuit of a calling becomes the condition for his fulfilling his wish to marry Ada. His lack of tolerance for the monotony of available vocations hurls him into pursuit of what he takes to be his interest in the Suit. The pursuit of this interest consumes him with ever-greater virulence. His very being is said to be fatally blighted (378) by contact with the Suit; his blood is said to be poisoned (547) and his life is implicitly sucked out of him, by Vholes, the agent of the Suit. Richard is consumed by the intensity of his desire for what he imagines the Suit holds in store for him, and by the frustration of his effort to satisfy that desire. As a result, Richard dies, as Ada is about to bear his child.

The drama of Richard's destruction links him to all the victims with whom the novel is concerned, and especially to Jo, to Hawdon, and to Jenny's baby. More revealingly, it links him to Gridley and Miss Flite, in relation to whom we experience the full pain and pathos of the orphan condition, with its depth of yearning for an unattainable object and the intensity of the frustration and rage that it stirs. The saga of Richard's apprenticeships—first to a doctor then to a lawyer and finally to the military—takes up, moreover, the ideologically loaded theme of vocation that emerges in *David Copperfield,* and carries it further by exploring the impossibility of all the options available. *Copperfield* affirms the importance of finding a vocation and shows the possibility of identifying with it. *Bleak House,* exploring the reality of vocations, conveys a sense of the stultification that pursuit of a calling entails. It shows the dehumanizing effect of fusing personal identity with social role, so that the dyer's hand takes on the coloration of the dye itself (584), and therefore makes for a blurring of the distinction, so vital to Esther, of what is integral within the self and what is outside it. Finally, *Bleak House* shows how vocation makes for the stifling of individuality within the formalized professional role.

In effect, *Bleak House* develops even further Steerforth's sense of vocation as "Ixion's wheel." Although Esther implies that Richard's nemesis is his failure to apply himself, the representation of the world in the novel suggests that Richard nonetheless makes a good deal of sense when he inveighs against the monotony of life in a profession. The novel shows that without the intervention of something approaching grace, as with Woodcourt, professional men are constricted when they are not dehumanized by identification with their social and professional roles. This is driven home by the representation of a vast cast of characters, such as Smallweed, Guppy, Weavle, Vholes, Tulkinghorn, Kenge, and Bagnet, not to speak of the alphabetical noodles of Sir Leicester's world.

Richard cannot imbue the vocations he undertakes with a sense of meaning, and the vocations give him no ground for doing so. Altogether, the vocations as represented in the novel give no ground on which to project meaning or to satisfy vital desire.

If there is any viable emotional logic in the representation of the Suit as a monster, such logic resides in the reciprocity between the thwarted needs of its victims and the magical satisfactions that the Suit promises. It is through the lure of satisfaction that the Suit "draws" its victims and magnetizes them to it. Because the world of the novel does not nurture and cannot satisfy need or acknowledge desire, its victims tend to imagine that redemption can be achieved through the magical satisfaction promised by the pool of inheritance that the Suit is believed to contain.

In fact, the novel may be said to create the Suit by sluicing into it all the subjectivity banished from all the people in its ritualized, formalistic, repressive world. That subjectivity is rife with infantile need. The Suit figures, not only as a grotesquely ossified institution, but also as a demonically active subject, "the one subject that . . . resolve[s] . . . existence into itself" (612). In its demonic aspect, the Suit allures, then destroys, the desiring subjects who are drawn to it. Richard is sucked into the Suit not only because of his frustration in the realm of callings, but also because of deeper needs, whose nature is revealed by the terms in which the Suit is represented.

For Richard, like the other victims of the Suit, must be understood as an actively infantile subject, positioned in dramatic contrast to the passive, undemanding infants we are asked to pity elsewhere in the text. For those who, like Richard, demand satisfaction of their inexhaustible needs, the Suit assumes the shape of a composite, androgynous monster, which incorporates both a paternal presence in the person of the Lord Chancellor, and a maternal one, represented both by Lady Dedlock and the inheritance withheld by the Suit. Lady Dedlock, as linked with inheritance, is associated with the promise of nurture, which Lady Dedlock herself does not provide for her own child, but which the Suit is expected to provide. Chancery and Suit together are endlessly alluring to their dependents because of the unfulfilled needs they address. They hold out the promise of protection and nurture, but also, ultimately, they raise the spectre of extinction that the prospect of nurture gives rise to. By stirring the desire for a longed-for reunification with the imagined source of nurture, they threaten the negation of independent being—in effect, death—which results from the fusion implied by a return to the source.

The imaginative logic of this process is elucidated by the language and imagery of the novel. Very striking among the images used to characterize the Suit in its mythically demonic dimension are those which suggest the blurring, or even the absence, of a boundary line between object and subject, between Suit and suitor. Many of these images suggest the absence of physical or psychological integrity in the subject. The language of the novel suggests that the origin of these images is in mythical and unconscious fantasies implicit in the repressed psychic life of the ritualized characters. These fantasies are explicitly elucidated in the figure of Richard's legal advisor, Vholes, whose name suggests he is a burrowing rodent, but whose traits explicitly link him to dispeptically vampiric indulgences. These fantasies express the wish to merge into something outside the self: into something that, as Miss Flite's says of the suit itself, magnetically "draws" one out of oneself and absorbs one into it. Another, but closely related, order of images expressing transactions between Suit and suitor is connected, in Richard's case, with poisoning (547), rotting (548), tainting (581), and blighting (578)—images that resonate with the various pestilential fluids and oozings (blood, witch-ointment, slime) that fill the discourse of the third-person voice.

This constellation of images may be seen as oral, and they are connected in the psychoanalytic tradition to a fundamental ambivalence in the experience of nursing—of deriving the nurture that Richard would, symbolically, imbibe from the inheritance property he expects from the Suit. Taken together, they elaborate the content of the infantile wishes that pursuit of his inheritance stirs up in Richard. They transform inheritance property into tokens of the lost mother—the figure, in the guise of the suit, that stood behind "the curtain of Rick's cradle" (548). It is no accident that Vholes is Richard's lawyer, and that Vholes is directly identified as a vampire. In their vampiric form, and in the transfer of Vholes's vampirism to the Suit itself, this pattern of imagery expresses the inversion of the wish to swallow, to absorb, and finally to be merged with objects symbolic of the mother; these imaginings project the terror inscribed in the sense that one will be swallowed even as one swallows, that one will be eaten as one eats.

Vholes epitomizes both the contents of such a wish and illustrates how the novel uses the portrayal of characters to concretize these contents. Vholes is a literalized embodiment of the cannibal motif that recurs so frequently in Dickens's novels, with the additional fillip of vampirism. In his nature as man-eater, he is not as obliquely represented as Fagin with his toasting fork, leering at the Oliver who is imaged as a trembling lamb. He is, rather, a named vampire and cannibal. His presentation suggests that, insatiable, he feeds on the blood of his victims and that his predilections are those of a cannibal chieftain. The Richard who wants urgently to suck his inheritance up is drained lifeless by the lawyer he employs as the agent of his suckling.

What is being dramatized through these figures is the danger of being destroyed by the symbiosis toward which Richard aspires. The imagery linked to Richard suggests that he is in danger of being poisoned, infected, and tainted, by the very entity—person or breast—longed for in the fantasy of what stood "behind the curtain" of his cradle. These extrusions of orphan fear and orphan desire also reinforce the sense, conveyed through the third person, that contact, so humanly necessary and so infinitely desirable, contaminates and destroys; they affirm that human transactions of any sort are inimical to being—to the maintenance of independent, articulated form. To return to the mother and renew contact with her is to make contact with the presence that is most indispensable but also most contaminating, most poisonous, to the orphan imagination. The fact that the mother is "only" imagined—that she is merely a phantasmal presence, summoned by need—strengthens the pervasive sense of contamination that fills the discourse of the third-person voice and the imagination of the novel as a whole.

Only within Esther's sanitized world is a limited order of contact viable and activity possible. Elsewhere, threats both from the inner world and the world outside put powerful constraints on the possibilities of action. Indeed, the novel dramatizes the danger of both feeling and action in a way that is reminiscent of *Twist,* but that exceeds it by far. Richard's "depreciation" (548) brings to mind the image of life as the rubbing out of the images on coins. Similarly relevant is Esther's image of fishermen spinning themselves out; it occurs in Esther's account of her journey to visit Richard at Deal, where she finds him depleted by his hectic involvement with the Suit and already beginning to be eviscerated by that involvement.

By the evidence of the interlinked imagery of ingestion and contamination, Richard is destroyed by his most primitive pre-oedipal needs and the fears they generate. Not only is his life absorbed by the object of his imagining, but it is poisoned as well. Contact, even in the imagination, with object merely imagined, poisons and destroys. At the level of plot and psychological motivation, however, it is his need, on reaching manhood, to assert himself, that draws him on to his destruction; it is his insistence on taking his fate into his hands, and on mastering the Suit, that hurls him into the vortex of regressive needs that destroy him.

For it is a kind of reality principle—the sense of the world as a site of radical scarcity, and the brutal curtailment of desire which scarcity demands—that stirs up both the impulse actively to engage the world and the compulsion to lapse into a passivity that turns its back on the need to engage with it and struggle to find a place within it. The world represented in the novel and imagined by its characters is a world of dire scarcity. It is a world which, viewed from within the novel's perspective, must be thought of, in John Jarndyce's words, as "an indifferent parent" (122). From within his narcissistic euphoria Skimpole may celebrate Ada as a "child of the universe," but Jarndyce, with his insistent sobriety, must respond with the reality: that the universe is an indifferent parent. *Bleak House* shows us the magnitude of that indifference.

Bleak House, self-evidently, contains a multitude of parents who are indifferent and worse than that—from Mrs. Pardiggle and Mrs. Jellyby through Skimpole and, ultimately, Lady Dedlock. The inadequately parenting world, however, is, as the novel represents it, vastly generalized, so that the universe itself comes to be an indifferent parent. The indifference and the neglect are not just the work of a particular mother, who couldn't discern that her daughter was alive, not dead. Nor are they merely the consequence of that particular aspect of society that creates and harasses a Jo, or of the world of satisfaction-withholding vocations that throttle Richard's sense of the potentialities of his life.

The world as symbolized by the Suit is in fact something far more dynamic, far more demonic. The effects of the Suit, as we have perceived in the discourse of the third-person voice but also in the Richard action, are both psychic and apocalyptic. As unfolded through the Richard action, the lure of the Suit elicits compulsions that move people away from the present, into a realm of regressive needs that make action—and life—impossible. It also stirs radical imaginings that press toward a utopian reaching beyond the real. Such reaching is, the novel suggests, grounded on the one hand in a fierce appeal for justice, like Richard's conviction that "there is truth and justice somewhere in the case" (582) and like the third person's appeal for justice before the tribunal of "heaven and earth" (50). On the other hand the reaching is rooted in a primordial craving for nourishment. Because of the hopelessness of the effort at transcendence, as it is contemplated from within the crippling neediness that animates the imagination of the novel, such reaching and the transcendence toward which it aspires are virtually unimaginable.

Utopia is in fact a necessity of the imagination in *Bleak House,* and the novel articulates an interesting range of utopian images, but substantiates none of them, even as forceful images. All the images are revealing, as signs of the deprivation that animates the imagination of the novel. Skimpole's aversion to his profession, and to all professions because of the limitations they place on his imaginative possibilities, is an extreme version of Richard's response and has, as we noted earlier in this chapter, utopian implications. Similarly, Skimpole's conviction that there is a moral economy in the universe—his sense that everything has a purpose, that even slavery in America is useful as an item to titillate his imagination—is cognate with the voice's chiliastic conviction with regard to the vengeance that will be perpetrated by every cubic inch of infectious slime. Similarly, Skimpole's playful transformation of Richard into a poetic figure, who is the shepherd of classical pastoral, meshes with the third-person voice's ironic allusions to a golden age, which serves to dramatize the distance traversed by the world from the time sheep actually grazed in Lincoln's Inn's Field to the time their hides have been transformed into the parchments of the Chancery screeds and the tallow of Vholes's candles. Submerged within this discourse, there should be a vision of a golden age. Yet, as we noted earlier in connection with Skimpole, none of these pregnant images carries much imaginative force. Even the third-person voice cannot liberate enough energy to provide a more concrete vision of a better or more nurturing world or even a nurturing human relationship. It invokes heaven and earth, and it ironically assigns Jo a place with his Father Who Is In Heaven, but it cannot specify what heaven might be like.

The novel itself is in much the same plight. Utopia is a necessity of its imagination, but it has no utopian vision. To this extent, both the voice and the novel are like Esther, who cannot allow herself to imagine even her own desire, and certainly cannot set herself ambitious goals to strive toward. All Esther can do is manage to manage her own household, with no spillover into any of the other speakers' domains, except, of course, for the counsel of prudence her entire narrative implies.

Indeed, Esther's memoir portrays the workings of Esther's need to dissociate herself from feelings and fantasies rooted in her abandonment, including fantasies of succor. The Richard, or inheritance, action dramatizes the impossibility of such dissociation, and in doing so it engages the animating paradox of the novel. In Richard, it is the need to act to liberate himself from the past, for the sake of life in the real present and the real future, that—ironically—releases an irresistible tropism toward origins, toward the past, toward sustenance that comes from inheritance.

This paradox dramatically violates the classic *Bildung* pattern. Ordinarily, the protagonist of a novel of *Bildung,* like David Copperfield, reaches a crisis, usually of consciousness, and wills his way out of the obstructive circumstances of his early life. In doing so, he begins to make a place for himself in the world. With Richard, it is the very need to cut loose from the authority of a facilitating foster father, and actively to assert himself, which triggers his absorption by his own regressive craving for the endlessly alluring breast and all that it symbolizes. Unlike David, who is said to invest himself in real-world productive activity, and who feels that he carries his past into his future, mastering it as he does so, Richard is dragged back into the past by the very effort to move into the future. In this way, he validates his assertion that "there is no now for us suitors" (580). His relation to the times of his life bears home the meaning of how both narrators use grammatical tense to define their relation to the then, to the now, and to whatever it is that is destined to be in the spheres of their cramped existence. He imagines his own utopia, which is always a matter of the future, but like Skimpole and the third person, he cannot project a meaningful image of it.

The irony of the process by which Richard is dragged back into destruction by his primordial needs lies in the fact that the effort to be active gives rise to radical passivity, even as, throughout the novel, the desire for contact leads to contamination. The tension between activity and passivity in fact generates what is perhaps the most stinging irony of the novel. Of the two most active pursuits in the novel—Richard's pursuit of his interest in the Suit and Tulkinghorn/Bucket's pursuit of Lady Dedlock—the first activates in Richard a final, form-dissolving passivity; the other unmasks and destroys the figure who symbolizes the object of his essential desire: the seductive but absent mother.

The progress of Richard's deterioration involves a sucking out of his life by his craving for the nutriment the Suit might have given him, as signified by the vampiric predations of Vholes, the agent of the Suit. His regression also leads to a progressive fusion with the elusive object of his quest, which is portrayed as a voracious subject. Esther tries to confine the Suit within the bounds of her well-lighted, carefully cultivated, rationally ordered domesticities. Nevertheless, the Suit figures, even within her carefully controlled narrative, as a mythically irresistible monster. Indeed, within her narrative it comes to be depicted as a monster more horrific and more devastating, in its concrete effect on Richard, than the grotesque creature the third person makes of it.

Yet the striking fact is that, seen in the perspective of the Richard action, the two narratives again fuse. The Suit action, which is the Richard action, and the Lady Dedlock action occupy both narratives. The content of these narratives, as we have unraveled them, reflects the extent to which Esther's narrative and the third-person narrative are in substance a single narrative, animated by the same conflict. That conflict involves a clash between a regressive thrust toward deathlike passivity and an urgent need somehow to exercise the will to act. Both terms of the conflict have to do with inadequate nurture and unassuagable rage, and both are aspects of the same system of feeling—facets of the same person.

Richard's function in relation to the voices is decisive. His fate confirms the greater validity of the third-person voice's experience as compared to Esther's. As seen from Richard's incipiently utopian vantage point, the promise of the Suit is infinite, timeless, Edenic, and it serves to preclude any possible achievement of identity or meaning within the novel's world. In this perspective, what is buried in Richard, in his relation to the suit, are all the abandoned and deprived children in the novel, demanding their birthright. That birthright, rooted in the remote, unspecifiable past and pointing to an indefinite and elusive future, draws and uproots those who crave it from their present life; it makes for a postponement of present life and threatens to dissolve and contaminate any form their lives might have—even as the consuming rage of the third-person voice explodes any possibility of embodiment in any form its identity might take. Within this double bind, both meaningful action, to change the world, and warm personal contact, to satisfy the needs of the feeling subject, are highly problematic, when not wholly impossible.

Bleak House ends in an ostensibly affirmative way, with Esther fulfilling her motherhood, supported by both a loving husband and a doting Guardian. As most readers have agreed, however, the vital life of Bleak House lies elsewhere. It lies, as we hope we have convincingly shown, in its struggle with all that is implied by the explosiveness of the third-person narrative voice; in the constriction that informs and shapes Esther's narrative; and in the compulsive coherence of the actions and images that concretize the fear and the desires that inform the orphan condition. All these together collaborate to convey a sense of an end-stopped, unredeemable world, where both the psychic complexion of its characters and the nature of the relationships perceived and animated by them, preclude vital activity and happy endings—except, of course, within the terms of Esther's self-limited modes of self-containment.

The dead-end signified by the novel's underlying imaginative logic points forward to the still bleaker vision *Little Dorrit* projects. *Dorrit* probably constitutes the most devastating vision of sterility and negativity in the Dickens canon. Despite the profound fantasticality of the wish fulfillments inscribed in it—and the meagre figure of Amy constitutes the most radical embodiment of the fantasy of mothering in the entire Dickens corpus—*Little Dorrit* depicts a wasteland unmatched elsewhere in Dickens. That wasteland, in our reading, is the necessary terminus of the conflict we have been tracing.

5
Little Dorrit

BLEAK HOUSE DEPICTS A WORLD MOVING INTO AN IMPASSE. IN *LITTLE Dorrit,* the impasse has been reached. The complex process of Esther's self-formation and the vivid expressiveness of the third-person voice narrow here into the portrayal of Arthur Clennam's end-stopped development and of his regression into a deathly passivity that precludes any reaching down to creative levels of desire. It is told, moreover, not by voices that animate the reader's sense of possibilities, but rather by a narrowly bounded narrative presence whose tightness is congruous with the constraint of Clennam's inwardness. The world of the novel, moreover, reflects the devitalization both of the protagonist and the narrative voice. Yet the representation of that world is as rich in articulation as the most complex of Dickens's novels.

Little Dorrit's desperation arises from Dickens's sense of the impossibility of generating a coherent and energized identity, of the sort that David Copperfield is said to achieve and that *Bleak House* in effect despairs of. Arthur Clennam does move toward an ostensibly redemptive union with Little Dorrit. His marriage, however, is not a redemption, as it is sometimes taken to be, but rather a capitulation. It is a sinking into a compensatory fantasy of fusion with a mother figure, a fusion that empties the self of all possibility for action or integration. Far from successfully serving as "the Paraclete" who mediates between Clennam's depressed state and his possiblities of transcendence, Amy facilitates Clennam's lapse into utter passivity. Clennam's dilemma, moreover, is an extreme version of what afflicts all the victims of the orphan condition. He is beset by the difficulty of extricating himself from the depression into which he has fallen because of his inability either to exhume the desire he has repressed or to gain access to the fury to which the thwarting of his desire gives rise.

Clennam is an extreme variation on the ordinary *Bildung* figure. He is not an introspectively memoirizing ingenu—like

David Copperfield or Esther Summerson—telling of experience undergone on the way to ostensible selfhood, and providing us with vivid signs of what has had to be shut out of consciousness and has therefore been displaced and found expression elsewhere. Nor is he like Richard Carstone, who is energized by his need not only to assert his manhood, but also actively to enact his consuming regressive needs. He is, rather, a stymied, forty-year-old man, trying at once to unearth and to bury his past in a desperate effort to regenerate himself and ultimately failing to do either. The degree of regeneration that the novel seems to imply he gains is, moreover, not achieved through self-organization and renunciation as with David and Esther, or through a baffled reaching down to deeper strata of conflict and desire, as with Richard. Rather, it is achieved through an enactment of what is both the most blatant and the most masked version of the fantasy of passive nurture we have encountered so far. He realizes himself through union with a childlike figure who is virtually breastless—with Little Dorrit, who is symbolically all breast, all self-abnegating motherliness, in her ostensibly unstinting capacity to give.

Our reading sees Amy as part of a vision of reparative nurture, signifying both redemptive love and stultifying passivity. Both passivity and nurture are evident in the alignment of a pair of climactic scenes—one with her father, one with Clennam. In the course of the episode in which she consoles her helpless but outrageously exploitative father, she is directly associated with "that classical daughter . . . who ministered to her father in his prison as her mother had ministered to her" (273–74). Little Dorrit, we are told, "though of the unheroic modern stock and mere English, did much more in comforting her father's wasted heart upon her innocent breast, and turning to it a fountain of love and fidelity that never ran dry or waned through all his years of famine" (274). Amy here is linked to Euphrasia, the unboundedly loving daughter who quite literally nurses her father in his dire extremity: the extremity, in the Roman tale, of imminent death by starvation. Amy herself, as *Little Dorrit* portrays her, is diminutive, childlike, and markedly breastless. Her role, however, involves nursing that is both literal and potent, and is unmatched elsewhere in Dickens. The drama of the breast overflowing, proferred to the starving father, is all the more striking if we remember that Euphrasia's breast is one that the imagination of Europe portrayed with a concreteness and sensuality often almost pornographic.

nam serves to illuminate the scope of Clennam's long-standing depression, a depression that culminates in the enervation that besets him at the beginning of his quest. It also helps us make sense of the self-negation that marks his experience throughout. The images for Clennam's psychic and spiritual condition also cast light on his inability to apprehend the source of his underlying conflict. Clennam wants to unearth the past in the hope of freeing himself from it, but he cannot do so. His mother denies him access to the hidden facts of his personal history—chiefly, that he was born out of wedlock to a woman his father had loved—and he himself has no way of digging down to the vestiges of his lost desire, or even to the circumstances that led to suppression of desire. His inability to gain access to his experience and to come to grips with it is what lays the groundwork for his lapse into the stillness, verging on stagnation, of Amy's love.

To elucidate Clennam we have Mrs. Clennam. Mrs. Clennam, who has brought Arthur up as her own son and has functioned as his mother, is the representation of an extremely hostile, repressive, emasculating woman. Her stubborn brass-boundedness is the surface manifestation of her congealed fury; her paralysis signifies the self-jamming neutralization of her energies. With her stony headdress and her resemblance to Egyptian sculpture, she is a man-eating, Sphinxlike creature, and also a Gorgon who petrifies others as well as herself. Linked imaginatively to Mr. F's sqawking aunt, with her "stony reticule . . . as rigid as if it had been petrified by the Gorgon's head" (886), as well as, through her, to Mrs. Merdle's parrot, she radiates an aggressiveness that almost matches, in scale and intensity, her own imagination of vengeance.

Mrs. Clennam is endlessly associated with death. She is recurrently linked to Egyptian cults of the dead. Beyond that, "The Plagues of Egypt, much the dimmer for the fly and smoke plagues of London, . . . glazed upon the walls" (72). Her sofa, moreover, is like a catafalque, "black [and] bier-like," with a bolster "like the block at a state execution" (73); her room is airless like a tomb, and infused with the deadly dye of her mourner's crepe; time has stopped for her, as it will for Miss Havisham and as it inevitably does for the dead; and her version of the Calvinist creed negates all life-affirming impulses. She has dealt death to Arthur's childhood desires, not to speak of his single romantic attachment, denying him pleasure and fulfillment, and thus has denied him the instinctual grounds of the selfhood he seeks and, even at forty, cannot find.

5: LITTLE DORRIT

When Clennam replaces her father in the same
later scene, Amy adopts an identical posture towar
After she has addressed him by name and identifie
"your own poor child come back," we are told that, "
arm softly round his neck," she "laid his head upon
put a hand upon his head, and resting her cheek
hand, nursed him as lovingly, and God knows as inn
she had nursed her father when she had been but a l
ing all the care from others that she took of them" (8
nam revives, virtually resurrected from a sickness al
death, but our belief in his redemption is qualified l
that his salvation is also his negation as an autonomo

Indeed, a curiously ambiguous metaphor tells us
was, at that moment,

> [*his*] *vanishing point*.... [Her] figure ... was the centre of
> est of his life; it was the termination of everything that
> and pleasant in it; beyond there was nothing but mere
> darkened sky. (801–2)

The dominant metaphor is one of perspective; we h
"everything in its perspective led to her innocent figur
faceted, the metaphor bespeaks the centrality of Amy
nam's life; not only do all roads lead, in a manner of s
to Rome, but within the field of its reference, all thi
shape in terms of it.

The other side of the metaphor suggests darker mea
that Amy's bosom and the unstinting love she provides
empty Clennam of all content and dissolve him in her e
so that he vanishes at the very moment he should mat
Given the clarity with which the novel renders Clennar
chic history, it is clear that Clennam is in danger of los
psychic shape and is drained of will and active desire w
embraces Amy as the single source of meaning for his li

Altogether, Clennam's portrayal suggests an emotional (
ation that drives him to seek a mate who provides the n
which in effect undoes him. His encounter at the outse
London, with Mrs. Clennam, and with her house is an enco
with images of what we take to be his internal desolation, i
that point to the deprivation that is the source of his depre
In Mrs. Clennam we get a schematic portrait of as inte
version of an abandoning and, in this case, a hate-filled, c
dealing mother as we find in Dickens. The portrayal of Mrs.

Dickens portrays her, moreover, as an obsessively anal grotesque, not only in her accounting and in her brass-bound stubbornness, but also in her eating habits and all they suggest. Her meticulously laid out oysters, her numbered slices of toast, her sweating pats of creamy butter signify a self-consuming sexuality which has congealed into an obsessional negativity. At another level, she hoards money, garners thoughts of vengeance, and not only withholds the modest inheritance meant for Arthur's real mother, but also the release from his deadening past which he asks of her.

It is by such a figure that Clennam has been formed, and with such a figure that he must contend in seeking to make a life for himself in the ongoing action of the novel. In the present as in the past, she obstructs access to the objects of his desire, as well as to the springs of desire. In the present action of the novel, he seeks, without knowing it, the truth of his origins, even as he looks for the opportunity to rectify what turns out to be a gross injustice in relation to them. That truth is what she most vigorously withholds from him. Just as she would prefer to keep him bound to the counting house, so she would like to keep him trapped within the fictions of the life she imposed on him and within her system of moral accounting, where she plays God.

The truth itself—the bald facts of his life history—would do Clennam no good in terms of what ails him, namely, the persistent sense of desolating lifelessness. The pervasively depressive negativity of his life is horrifying: in his relation to his mother, and her glassy responses; in relation to Pet, for whom he feels he has no way of vying, so that we see him designating himself "Nothing," and longing to be carried away into oblivion, like the waters of the river he contemplates; in relation even to Doyce, through partnership with whom he seeks to realize the value of what remains of his-will-to-be—and of his patrimony; and of course, in the despair stirred in him by Flora Finching, to whom he had attached the one strand of hopeful memory out of his past.

Clennam's underlying paralysis is crippling. It is clear that it is a response to the negativity of his life's experience. Yet his capacity for absorbing blows without protest is not a matter of mere passivity or sheer weakness. Throughout, he responds to neglect and rejection with stoical dignity, breaking down only when a radical regression overtakes him. Clennam's resistance to his mother and to all that she represents is a powerful but passive resistance, not only rooted in the fear she has instilled in him, but also in a strength of character, which may be seen as an appropriately clenched response to her aggressiveness.

What marks Clennam from the beginning of the narrative is a stoical self-containment. He is firmly committed to avoiding active conflict with his mother, as with everyone else; he refuses a confrontational fight with her. Like Esther Summerson, Clennam will not and probably cannot be moved by strong passions of any sort. Although he believes in justice, truth, and virtue, he will not mount the barricades on their behalf. He will not breach the boundaries of a strict personal decorum, even to right the wrong he fears his family has perpetrated. Indeed, his quiet interest in Amy is first stirred by his fear that his mother's kindness to her is motivated by guilt for past misdeeds. Unlike a Tulkinghorn or a Bucket, however, he refuses to act or even to probe vigorously until he has clear evidence of the truth he seeks. At the same time, his quest for the hidden truth does bring him to Amy, suggesting that there is a subterranean link between what Mrs. Clennam withheld and withholds and what Amy can give—namely, the unconditional love whose absence is central to the orphan imagination. Its absence is the source of Clennam's debilitating depression.

Just as Clennam does not strike out actively for love, so he is not moved by vigorous anger. Again like Esther, he does not need to contain or restrain his anger, because his anger is inaccessible to him. It is at least as inaccessible as his active desire. Yet *Little Dorrit* suggests that this absent anger is an aspect of his continuing depression. It has no direct channel of expression, even as Esther's does not. At the same time, just as Esther's inaccessible anger and imagination find their outlet in the wild whirling of the third-person voice, so Clennam's still more occulted anger finds expression in the novel's moral vision and in the energies of aggression that fill its world. One facet of that aggression is expressed in the cold, rigorously controlled aggressiveness of the narrative voice, which, like the fury in the third-person narrative voice in *Oliver Twist*, but still more so, is expressed in a fierce exposure of what is wrong in the novel's world.

The link between Clennam's repressed needs and his mother's aggressive withholdingness becomes clear at the crisis of his life, when he takes the one bold move of which he seems capable after his break with the family business, namely, when he is infected with the plague of the Merdle speculation, and risks both his money and Doyce's in it. Like the victims of the Chancery Suit—Tom Jarndyce, Gridley, Miss Flite, and Richard—he is magnetized to the irresistible lure of unearned wealth and the nurture it symbolically affords. That moment is decisive for him, however; it effectively seals his fate. Within the underlying dynamic of his inner life, active desire can be stirred only by the lure of what was initially withheld. It is characteristic of the emotional and imaginative obstructedness of *Dorrit* that it gives us so little access to the concrete emotional process whereby his regressive desire is elicited. All we have is the vivid representation of his mother, the muting of Clennam himself, and his involvement in the Merdle Speculation—and alongside these, the drama of the tension between Amy's childlike lack of the overt signs of mature womanliness and her Euphrasia-like role in nursing both her father and Clennam.

And yet, the fact that Clennam sickens, falls into debt, and is thrown into debtors' prison conforms to the implied logic of his eviscerating passivity. That logic underlies the experience of the prototypical Dickens hero, from Oliver Twist through Richard Carstone. It is no surprise, therefore, that Clennam needs Amy, and that Amy not only figures, like Agnes for David, as the center of his life, but also as its vanishing point. She not only is a source of unfailing love and nurture, but is also a woman so disembodied sexually, so lacking in all independent desire, that she presents no threat to the emasculated male, but also, alas, no promise either. What she signifies, ultimately, is an ending more passive than Oliver's and as desolating as Richard's. Clennam, no more than Richard, can "begin the world"; we can no more give credence to his marriage as a vitalizing fulfillment than we can to the novel's feeble effort to suggest and even to depict Amy's development into a responsive woman. In her, Clennam gets what he needs, but as with all the passive victims of Dickens's imaginative world, the inaccessible rage at deprivation precludes his demanding anything more than subsidence into a crippling passivity.

Clennam's life turns out to be a wasteland as arid as the London Sunday to which he returns. That wasteland resides not only in his personal past and in the symbolic environment of his mother's house. It also permeates the entire world of the novel. Dickens has created that world by projecting upon it a vision of life rooted in Clennam's state of mind. What characterizes the novel as a whole is an unremitting sense of the world itself as wasteland—as a place where "there was nothing but mere waste and darkened sky" (802). That wasteland, in *Little Dorrit,* is recurrently envisioned as a prison.

Since the beginning, readers have borne witness to the power of the prison image that dominates *Little Dorrit.* What they have not sufficiently explored is the richness of the image and the resonance both of its visionary insight and of the canniness of the social psychology that it propounds. That insight reflects Dickens's agonizing consciousness of Clennam's plight, a plight that recapitulates in an extreme form the situation of all Dickens's afflicted orphan protagonists and carries to its logical conclusion the terms of the conflict that besets them all. The vision of life projected in *Little Dorrit* must be seen as the ultimate stage of Dickens's effort to envision through his protagonists the struggle to achieve a viable identity and to find a place in the world. That struggle is marked by a variety of elements, among them the powerful regressive tug of the needs that spring from abandonment; the repressed anger at the frustration of those needs; and the paralysis that ensues from succumbing to fantasies rooted in repressed rage.

The image of wasteland and prison is sustained by the density of the interlocking projections, many of them paranoid projections, that fill the world of the novel—that, ultimately, constitute it. *Little Dorrit* does not have a paranoid plot in the sense that *Oliver Twist* does; nothing palpable—not even the comic diabolism of Rigaud—converges terrifyingly on Clennam himself in the way that Fagin and the gallows converge on Oliver. Yet paranoid responses fill its action. *Little Dorrit* contains a vision of the social world as a set of mutually reinforcing projections rooted in hostility filled people such as Mrs. Clennam, Miss Wade, Merdle, Rigaud, and Gowan. "Society," with a capital "S," is seen to be a fetishizing monstrosity that compulsively worships unleavened clay barely emerged from the primordial slime; it is made up of a set of implicitly consensual fictions, such as those which willfully transform Merdle into a modern Midas and those which bind the Barnacles and the Merdles in a demented dance of mutually confirming claims to meaning and value. At the "highest" social level, the phantasmal falsifications that provide the social cement reside at the threshhold of consciousness, and are therefore consensual in the full sense of the word: that is, they are in the end sustained by deliberate choice. In the middle range, Mrs. Clennam's megalomanic constructs mesh with Rigaud's paranoid projections, with little consciousness on either side of the projective nature of their sense of reality, and no acknowledgment of what is going on. At the lower levels, there is virtually no sense of the nature and function of the projections that dominate the lives of the characters who fill them. The residents of Bleeding Heart Yard nonetheless unwittingly collude with Casby to sustain his patriarchal image, the expectations of Nandy mesh with the expectations of the workhouse, and the denizens of the Marshalsea, as we shall see in another context, confirm and create the prison walls out of their own need for enclosure, and none of them has an inkling of what they are doing. Yet the novel conveys a sense that they, too, in the end subliminally subscribe to the falsifications that sustain their lives.

Among the simpler and more transparent of the phantasmal projections in the novel is the wishfulness that drives John Chivery to pursue Amy Dorrit and that permits his mother, echoing and parodying the Merdle-centered marriage market, to assume that the conjoining of the scion of the house of the Father of the Lock with the daughter of the Father of the Marshalsea will produce a union to be envied. It is not only the unworldly Mrs. Chivery who nurtures fictions. Mrs. Merdle, we are told, lays Mrs. Gowan's fiction—the "polite" fiction that the Meagles connived to entrap Gowan into marriage to Pet—onto her snowy expanse of bosom and nurses it, quite deliberately. That Mrs. Merdle *nurses* fictions is deeply relevant, not least of all because the great Merdle swindle offers the limitless promise of gratuitous nurture. This is what makes it irresistibly seductive, appealing as it does to a universal need. It is no accident, as we have already noted, that Clennam succumbs to it as a prelude to his fall into debtor's prison and into the illness that precedes his recognition of his love for Amy and the release it ostensibly brings.

Like the Chancery Suit in *Bleak House,* the Merdle speculation derives its power by tapping into the unconscious needs of all the people who are drawn to it—in fact, of virtually everyone in the world of the novel. In that sense, it is a reification of those needs, achieving a life of its own, to allure and subvert endlessly. Although drawn from within the unconscious life of the denizens of the novel's world, it is cut off from them. It speaks, as though from the outside, to their deepest needs, and it does so through an unacknowledged set of nonetheless consensual fictions. The Speculation is not as vividly dramatized as the Chancery Suit in its effect on individual lives, and, therefore, it is endowed with a less richly concretized imaginative presence.

Its effect is more universal, however, addressing the urgencies of shared needs—here, the need to get something for nothing. Its power of attraction is so great that even the mechanically energized and compulsively calculative Pancks is sucked in.

The coercive allure of the Merdle speculation is the climactic instance of mass delusion in the novel. It is the culmination of the more decorous, more deliberate, more controlled dance of collusionary appearances which is, to begin with, the world of Society in the novel—the world of Bishop Bar and Brewer, of the Circumlocation Office, of Mrs. General, who puts her deadening Gloss on everything and robs everything of meaning and particularity with her generalizing varnish. The representation of Society, moreover, meshes with the treatment of the fictiveness, make-believe, and the falseness of virtually everything else that is the world of *Little Dorrit*.

Closely cognate with Society is The Circumlocution Office, which is reminscent of the Court of Chancery in the obscurity of its origins and the obfuscating deviousness of its proceedings. Its parasites, the appropriately named Barnacles, are close kin to the Parliamentary Boodles, Doddles, and Coodles of *Bleak House*, both in the lack of responsibility in their conduct of official affairs and in the blatancy of their self-interested manipulation of reality to achieve their own ends and baffle those of others. Their grotesque fictions, starting with the pretensions to an aristocratic habitation of Sir Tite Barnacle and his family, are even more transparent than those of Mrs. Merdle's magnanimity or Mrs. Gowan's gentility. Yet those fictions fix the consciousness of the novel's public world on themselves, and constitute an uncircumventable obstacle to change, progress, or justice.

In their paralytic rigidity and in the stultifyingness of their self-will, they serve as an inverted displacement of Clennam's slack will. Clennam is too clenched and too enervated to playact or otherwise to project himself into functional reciprocities with others who inhabit the public world. The Circumlocution Office and its minions are, for their part, past masters of make-believe, baffling, befuddling, and obstructing every constructive and creative impulse that arises in their domain. Doyle is only the extreme case of the stifling of energy and initiative that is the specialty of the Office. The stereotyped language—the creaking circumlocutions—of its agents is one sign of its petrifying willfulness.

Related to the cold, calculatingly fictive world of Society, the compulsive frenzy of the great Speculation, and the sclerotically stultifying bureaucracy of the Circumlocution Office is the less coercive set of fictions of people like Casby, the Patriarch, whose flowing hair and extreme unction of manner bamboozles almost everyone, until Pancks shears him of his patriarchal locks. Then there is the relatively minor but no less significant instance of the deliberate deception by the Virgin Ruggs, with her mulcting of her undesiring suitor for breach of promise—a deception and a mulcting that has its analogue not only in Gowan's self-conscious manipulation of the Meagles but also in Mrs. Gowan's pernicious fiction about the Meagles' conspiracy to entrap Gowan himself, not to speak of the fictions that govern Fanny's entrapment of Sparkler and the myriad fictions of the marriage market altogether.

Of slower growth but deep insidiousness are what Dickens calls the "traditions" of the Marshalsea and Bleeding Heart Yard. By this, he means the constellations of behaviors and beliefs that govern the lives of those who live in these humble and degrading places. Their legends of origin—for example, of why the Yard is named as it is, or what it means to be in the Marshalsea—are shown to spring up arbitrarily, it would seem out of nowhere. In fact, they grow out of the collusive shared imaginings of their denizens; there are ways of denying poverty, humiliation, and helplessness. What they believe about their history serves to mask the extent of their abandonment by the world and their desperate helplessness in the face of it. Both the inhabitants of Bleeding Heart Yard and the inmates of the Marshalsea have in effect been forgotten by the world, and they compensate for their desolation by generating myths. These myths constitute a shadow-world whose meaning no one wants to face. The anger that must color their existence is bypassed by the muffling fictions within which they live.

Subordinate to these public fictions are such arbitrary constructs as William Dorrit's feudal lordliness and the Plornish pastoral, not to speak of the make-believe in Amy's relationship with Maggy, the Meagles' domestic velleities, and the musings of Dr. Habbage, Mrs. Bangham, and the keeper of the three volumes of Birth, Marriage, and Burial in the church that abuts on the Marshalsea—all these being more or less deliberately agreed-upon fictions that permit reciprocity, communication, and persistence in the struggle to survive.

All these traditions must be read in the context of the blatantly paranoid projections of Dorrit, of Mrs. Clennam, of Miss Wade, of Gowan, of Rigaud, all of whom exemplify in various ways and degrees the disposition to project their antagonistic inwardness onto the world. Mr. Dorrit relentlessly plays out his drama of gentility in terms of the assumption that everyone is poised to pounce on every dropped inflection of his courtliness, and to expose him for the sham he is, as is revealed when, excruciatingly, he attacks Amy for appearing in public with "a Livery." Dickens subtly portrays how shame at the threat of being exposed in his lifelong submission to passive needs stirs a rage that rarely shows itself, but that flares up and is projected outward in situations like the one in which Amy "innocently" ends up "minister[ing] to him" like Euphrasia. Later, when he comes into his fortune and is surrounded by all the appurtenances of wealth, the terror mounts, of exposure for the lifelong debtor that he was; at that point, all his energy goes into warding off exposure. His pathetic collapse at Mrs. Merdle's Assembly in Rome involves a regression to a desired state he was terrified would emerge against his will and taint his honor—and this in spite of the fact that the whole world seems to have cared about nothing but his money and to have been committed to maintaining his fiction of gentility.

Miss Wade is a still more extreme case. Her nightmarish entrapment in her delusionary projections is the densest and the most revealing of the novel's projective systems. Miss Wade's *ressentiment* steeps her consciousness in self-contempt. She is, if we wish, the paradigmatic instance of the inability to deal with the self-hatred abandonment brings—that is, the tendency to assume that the object of rejection, namely herself, is responsible for the rejection, and must suffer the shame, guilt, and hostility that her sense of her culpability gives rise to. Unlike Mr. Dorrit, she cannot and will not transform her sense of shame and degradation into vanity and self-aggrandizement, with the appearance of benignity it achieves; unlike Esther Summerson, she will not erect an imaginary other—even a doll—to reciprocate need and desire, and then proceed to strive to "win" love by extending to all and sundry. Rather, she barricades herself within herself, cultivates her resentment, and displaces all her self-hatred onto others, dooming herself to the life of an outsider—to a nomad's life. The constitutents of her domicile—her very furniture and carpets—are said to lay themselves out in her room like a nomad's gear; her living space, is always contextualized in desolate, dead, eroded places like the Calais Meagles sees, or the house in London where we encounter her.

Miss Wade's lack of domesticity, of comfort of any sort, is an expression of emotional depletion. What characterizes Miss Wade is the deadness and death-dealing energy of her hate-filled subjectivity, a murderousness that she projects onto everyone who tries to make sympathetic contact with her. She not only alienates everyone, even in the end Tattycoram; she also fouls what should be her own nest. In *David Copperfield,* Dickens had equated Mr. Peggotty's home with his being, and Miss Wade's being is not viable. With the hatred that shapes it, it is a negation of being as Dickens sees it, trapping her in a state of paralytic deadness analogous to Mrs. Clennam's and characteristic of the novel's world. Both rigid and shaking with rage, she has little of the energizing fire of Rosa Dartle, whose lightning-flash scar signifies both the sexual violation and the emotional violence that torments and drives her. Betrayed in love by Gowan much as Rosa was betrayed by Steerforth, and festering with the humiliation of her dependency, Miss Wade represents a further extreme of Rosa's state: an extreme that coincides in its deadening effect with the paralytic deadness of the novel's world.

Miss Wade also epitomizes the reciprocity between subjectivity and the world; in her, we see how unself-conscious projection of a tormented inwardness generates a totalizing view of reality, a view that interlocks, in varying degrees, with other such more and less totalized views, eliciting in others the responses she needs to maintain her closed system of feelings. It also generates an environment appropriate to itself. In fact, she illuminates with great clarity a process enacted on a more heroic scale by Mrs. Clennam, who is probably the novel's most dramatic world maker and projector of inwardness, as well as the figure most vividly associated with death-dealing animosities.

Mrs. Clennam's place in this configuration is self-evident. She not only is manifestly megalomanic, but she is also transparently engaged in imposing her view on the world. The relation between subjectivity and vision is, in her case, highly dramatic, and it illuminates far more than herself. It casts light, among other things, on Dickens's view of the emotional and the imaginative roots of a decadent Calvinism.

The reciprocity between Mrs. Clennam's subjectivity and her environment is still more dense and generalizable than that of Miss Wade. Her deathliness is externalized everywhere. It is evident in every detail, not only of her person and room, but it extends itself to her house and her larger environment. It spreads from the bedposts on which guests might have impaled themselves to the withered trees seen from the windows of her house, to the City, and finally to the world—implicitly to the very cosmos, in which she and ultimately all the characters in the novel dwell. The stifling pentitential Sunday morning London to which Clennam returns not only is a displacement of his own depressiveness, but also an outgrowth of his mother's sense of life.

Indeed, Dickens makes it clear that in Mrs. Clennam he is giving us a derivation of a radical Calvinist vision. Mrs. Clennam's omnipotently punitive God is seen to be a fetishistic embodiment of her own vindictiveness. A part of the novel's impact stems from our recognition that the psychological process Dickens is depicting in Mrs. Clennam may well explain the broadly repressive cultural power of such a vision.

The nightmarishness of that vision resides in the reciprocity between the inner horror and outer deadness of Miss Wade and Mrs. Clennam. Readers have often remarked on the novel's equation of the world with a prison: how the images of prisons are ubiquitous, figuring everywhere, from the Great St Bernard to the Gowan residence in Venice to the Clennam house, not to speak of the actual prisons, such as the one in Marseilles where the story begins, or the workhouse and the Marshalsea. These images have been variously interpreted as referring to the prison house of society, of the self, and of man's condition in a fallen world. All these readings are valid, but they do not comprehend the larger implications of *Little Dorrit*'s vision of the world as prison.

We propose that the ultimate prison is the prison-without-walls of the reciprocal delusionary system—the interlocking network of conscious and unconscious fictions that is the "world." That world is rooted in and projected out of a multitude of isolated subjectivities. Out of them there springs an array of fantasies that mesh and in doing so, form the public world, with its elaborate hierarchical systems of rank, power, and self-aggrandizing recognition by others. We might expect that buying into such a shared world would bring one into contact with others and provide a comforting network of reciprocities. Instead, the extrusion of inwardness—of the fantasies that interact with the fantasies of others to form the common world—isolates the gridlocked individuals who make up society, and drives them still more deeply back into themselves. Indeed, the people within the novel have a tropism toward engulfment within the forms that constitute the common world. It is as though what they have projected out of themselves is at the same time a kind of cocoon into which they retreat. The characters of *Little Dorrit* seem to be absorbed in the womb of consensual fictions just as they might have been assimilated into the regressiveness of their own sensibilities. The prisons, in this perspective, are the womblike origin and end of the psychological states *Little Dorrit* engages. Those states encompass and mute an indigestible rage and humiliation, which can find no points of emergence into the light of clear consciousness.

The novel's informing fantasy, of regressive immobility, is palpably realized in the representations of the actual prisons in the novel. Thus, the Marshalsea, certainly the central prison image of *Little Dorrit,* is an "objective" reality—but it is also a representation of Mr. Dorrit's (but also Mrs. Bangham's and Dr. Habbage's, not to speak of Nandy's) needs and desires. Within them, the potential violence of rage and the vehemence of terror are transformed into the numbing grayness of paralytic passivity. Dr. Habbage's vision of the freedom that is to be found in the prison, and of the dead flies that characterize its life, is a perverse celebration of this paralysis and passivity. Doyce's stonewalling by the Circumlocution Office is one manifestation of the ghastly impact of the bureaucratic dead letter and of its part in the graying over of the world. Mr. Dorrit's wan courtliness is still another.

It is a phantasmal world that *Little Dorrit* represents. Afferty is a key figure for defining its problematics. In this world, where delusion and reality are interchangeable, she is explicitly represented as immersed in dreaming—dreaming things that turn out to be "real." What we are dealing with here is not a Keatsian celebration of imaginative activity, within which Adam generates his Eve by dreaming her, but rather a sense that reality is malleable and relative, haunted by the ghosts of memories and desires transformed by everyone's subjectivity into bizarre forms that are nonetheless accepted as real. Thus, Jeremiah Flintwich bamboozles Afferty, so that when she comes unexpectedly upon both Flintwinch brothers in the house, she believe his twin, Ephraim, to be no more than a dream. We come to feel that realities can be made to seem like dreams, and that dreams can become reality. This makes reality itself seem a strange and terrifying dream, whose deciphering is as mysterious and bewildering as the inner world from which dreams arise. This gives special force to the formulation by the narrative voice, uttered as Afferty contemplates the collapse of the Clennams' house, that she "had always been right in her facts and always wrong in the theories she deduced from them" (863). What the novel shows is how the world is all dead and disintegrating facts and all problematical interpretation, and how both facts and the interpretation of facts are part of a fabric of de-energizing delusion rooted in subjectivities both ineluctably locked into each other and excruciatingly cut off from each other.

What *Little Dorrit* also shows us is that the people who produce the facts of "reality" and then interpret them are themselves locked into conflicts that vitiate the possibilities of life: conflicts that involve repressed energy and devitalizing hostility. The defining condition of virtually all the more or less active characters is one of frictive, fratricidal rivalry, issuing in moral, if not literal, murder. It is surely no accident that Clennam associates the shaft of light linking the upper and lower storeys of Doyce's workshop with "the child's old picture book, where similar rays were the witnesses of Abel's murder" (312–13). The Cain and Abel association is, again, part of Clennam's repressed consciousness, but it is felt to be a truth about the world.

Nonetheless, the irony of this association is keen. We have no trouble recognizing the fratricidal Cain-and-Abel element in relationships such as those of Amy's siblings or of William and Frederick Dorrit or even of Rigaud and Cavaletto—and, if we admit doubles as brothers, of Arthur and Gowan, of Mrs. Clennam, Rigaud and Flintwinch, and, grotesquely, of Merdle and Mr. Dorrit. But what have Cain and Abel to do with Clennam and Doyce, whose partnership constitutes the most benignly constructive relationship in the novel? Why bring the primordial image of brother murder to bear on what the novel presents as the only constructive locale within its imagined world? Certainly nothing about the "objective" scene of the workshop where the partnership is effectuated would mandate this. Hence, the terrifying implication that in the end even the most benign collaboration and the most constructive enterprise is one of at least repressed murder, of those nearest and dearest to us.

Mr. Merdle epitomizes the process, pivotal to the novel's vision of life, of the murder that wells up from within, and of the way, though he has no visible access to his own aggression, he is the cause, through the Speculation, of incalculable destruction in the world of the novel. Merdle's suicide is the culmination of the depressiveness and the neutered inwardness that marks his character throughout. Fetishized idol of Society, master of the monied world, mover and shaker in everyone's mind, his dominant traits are lack of desire and an unleavened, dispirited clayey-ness of being. Sparkler, with his aristocratic pretensions, complains that Merdle carries the counting house into the drawing room and his wife complains of his lack of élan, in effect his lack of varnish, gloss, and empty reflection within the hall of mirrors that is Society. At the dinners that provide Society with all its heart desires, he eats barely 18 pence worth of food. Hands retracted in the cuffs that seem to take him into custody, he sits withdrawn in impenetrable dullness amidst the splendors of Mrs. Merdle's world. His marriage has been contracted to the snowy expanse of bosom that serves as a jewel-stand so splendid that even Black and Mortimer might covet it and that not only belongs to a vindictive Juno, but to a decapitating Judith. As for his marriage, the pleasures it may be assumed to afford are unimaginable.

The hangdog desolation that hovers about him reaches its climax in his terminal visit to Sparkler and Fanny, where Fanny's anger at her deformation by pregnancy and her boredom with being stuck at home epitomize the domestic bleakness that surrounds him throughout. The spectacle of his lifeless body in the bath, with its muddy ooze of blood, confirms the sense of deadness and abortedness that accompanies his figure throughout. The scatological associations of his name do nothing to lessen that effect,

It not only is Mr. Merdle who is seen to be emotionally sterile and without animating desire. No one in the novel is moved by authentic passion; the strongest active emotion that figures within it is that of rivalry and revenge, as in the case of Mrs. Clennam and Rigaud. Rigaud wants to avenge himself on society for not making him a gentleman. Gowan not only is Rigaud's ally, but also echoes Rigaud's resentment in a minor but meaningful way. Gowan's energy is invested in denigrating what he links to the world's failure to fulfill his expectations. He spurns the human, Clennam thinks, as he spurns stones with his foot, into the water, and he treats people, morally, much as he treats his dog physically. Fanny, with her fierce rivalrousness, pitting her embonpoint against the snowy reaches of Mrs. Merdle's jewel-stand, is a comic analogue of her mother-in-law. Miss Wade's indignant fist-shaking and Tattycoram's foot-stamping are further extrusions of this emotional state.

If characters are shown to lack vital desire, the world itself is represented as either illusory or lacking in allure. Venice, that opulent provocation to the European imagination, is seen by Amy as "[a] crowning unreality" (519), where the sunset "glowing on the buildings . . . made them look as if their strong walls were transparent" (520). Analogously, the Great St. Bernard, often the symbol of human intrepitude and of man's aspiration to the heights, is seen as a prisonlike mirage "dissolving into cloud. . . . as if the whole rugged edifice were filled with nothing else, and would collapse as soon as it had emptied itself" (484). As for Rome, we see it either as the scene of Mrs. Merdle's Assembly, that is, as a clone of her delusion-drenched London world, where dinner guests face each other at table insensible as the stone-faced houses on the street, or as the depressive scene—finally, of a funeral—that Mr. Dorrit sees on the road. That scene is reminiscent of what the reader has seen of London, when Clennam first returns, and proleptic of the dreariness of the Calais that Meagles will see when seeking Miss Wade and the documents that chronicle Clennam's origins.

Society, too, which is the scene of so much allure in nineteenth-century fiction, is—as evidenced by Mrs. Merdle's Assemblies—wholly de-eroticized, though full of rivalry. Society, to be sure, never constitutes for Dickens the kind of erotic field it does for Stendhal or Balzac. Yet the comedy of Weevle's fixation on the Gallery of British Beauties, like the representation of Lady Dedlock's disdainful domination of the World of Fashion, constitutes a strong if reductive analogue to the function of the Mmes. de Renals and the Baroness Von Nucigens of French fiction as the object of their lovers' desire. Indeed, there is a sense in which Lady Dedlock's tradeoff, whereby she gives up Hawdon and Esther for Sir Leicester, is a measure of the eros that can be invested—however misguidedly, from Dickens's point of view—in the Fashionable World.

No such desire plays itself out in Society, as represented in *Little Dorrit*. The snowy expanse of Mrs. Merdle's bosom is one measure of the erotic turnoff in the novel's representation of high society. Not Eros but rather Thanatos dominates the social world, as signified by the battle of the bosoms waged by Fanny against Mrs. Merdle's formidable bust. Whatever else these foregrounded breasts may signify in the imaginative economy of a novel that centers on Euphrasia's overflowing daughterhood, in this context they bespeak the mutual aggression that desire, as elicited by the allure of the Merdle money, activates. There *is* a sort of energy in the life of Society, and there is desire, but they transpose themselves into a death wish. Both energy and desire are channeled into fetishized forms and directed toward ossifying objects—toward Medusa-like women who, with all their difference from Mrs. Clennam and her widow's weeds, are imaginatively cognate with her in their ultimate stoniness. The tantalizing milk, not of human kindness, but rather of easy money is what infects the imagination of the whole world of the novel at the time of the great speculation craze. The primitive thirst for easy money drives men and women to destruction.

Yet even the Speculation is not endowed with the coercive allure the Chancery Suit holds for those who are destroyed by it. It is certainly not endowed with the sexualized glamor of the women Julien Sorel and Rastignac pursue and possess in *Pere Goriot* and *Le Rouge et le Noir*. Similarly, the Circumlocution office cannot match Chancery. It is characteristic of the thinness of imagined desire in *Little Dorrit* that Society itself is felt to be a gross abstraction, like a proper name with its upper case initial letter. It is abstracted, among other things, even from the density of potential desire in the people whose inner fantasy life generates it.

The entire world of the novel is marked by the thinness of the desire that creates it and fills it. The desolation not only of depressing scenes of dilapidation and disintegration, like London, the Clennam backyard, Calais, and Rome, but also of the whole imaginative world of the novel itself, springs from the absence of vital desire within it. This desolation, made up of so many scenes of traditional terror stripped of threat, of splendid illusion divested of allure, and of strenuous striving robbed of vitality, points in two directions. On the one hand, it points to the constellation of reified and fetishized traditions and consensuses that make up the world that humankind, as envisioned in *Little Dorrit,* inhabits. On the other, it points to the inner sphere of individual subjectivity. Everyone, or virtually everyone, in the novel is, ultimately, condemned to the numbness and the neutralization evoked by the external scenes and settings. No one, not even the narrative voice, is able to reach inward and downward to inner sources of vitalizing energy and conflict, or upward and outward to visions of life, splendor, or vitality. The grayness of the prison, the inertness of its inmates, the static quality of Amy herself, and the lifeless charade of Society finally epitomize the human condition as envisioned in this novel.

The world of the novel is represented as negative, negating and hostile. Perhaps the best image for the paranoia-reflecting and paranoia-inducing hostility it represents—and for the animosity vented in its projection—is the staring, glaring sun of the opening chapter, where the Great Eye of the World drives everything into hiding, implicitly imposing guilt and imprisonment on everyone. The motif of aggressive looking echoes through the novel: in the figuring of Merdle as the object gazed at by The Great Eye of the World; in the recurrent image of the goggling, ogling Sparkler, and his wobbly monocle; in the surrealistic image of the same Sparkler's lusterless eye in the window of a gondola, "like a knot in the glass" (550); in Merdle's terror of his butler's tyrannical gaze; in the image of Mrs. Merdle's dazzling jewel-stand of a bosom as the cynosure of all eyes, and especially as the object of Fanny's relentless rivalrousness; in the global representation of Society as a concatenation of obsessionally invidious watchers: as in the scene where the assembled company stares at the backs of Merdle and Sir Tite Barnacle of the Circumlocution Office as they back and forth meaninglessly, in the effort to let themselves maneuvre each other into a foregone conclusion; in the unfolding of the novel's plot, with its emphases on Rigaud's tracking of others, on Meagles's tracking of him, on Jeremiah and Mrs. Clennam's sparring-partners' surveillance of each other; and on Jeremiah's jailorlike scrutiny of Afferty and her every move—not to speak of Afferty's terrorized spying on him.

The novel represents a brutal world—a world so brutal, that the actual prison, the Marshalsea, seems by contrast a benign place. One striking dimension of the prison world is that, unlike the Circumlocution Office and the pecking order of Society, it is curiously lacking in formal structures of authority. Its "traditions" grow out of the needs of the inmates, and even the stringency of "the lock" seems more a part of a mellow tradition than a manifestation of an externally imposed system of retributive punishment. Indeed, life as it is actually lived within the Marshalsea would seem to make plausible Dr. Habbage's "philosophical" conviction that freedom exists only in the prison, that when you hit bottom and relax, having nothing to aspire toward and no energy to fight back, you are on top of the world.

Yet the ironizing perspectives of the novel undercut this sense of ease and freedom. Dorrit's ritual sense of himself as the Father of the Marshalsea and of its inhabitants as feudal tributaries exposes a hierarchical ordering as stringent and invidious as the Merdles' drawing room, and one as subject to unremitting surveillance—not by some overseeing authority, but, as in Society and Bleeding Heart Yard, by the anxiously interlocked consciousness of its denizens themselves. One of the most telling analogies in the novel is that drawn between the prison and Society: an analogy that is explicitly made when we are told that "this same society in which they lived [in Rome] greatly resembled a superior sort of Marshalsea" (565). In effect, the novel recurrently equates the two seemingly polarized conditions of prison and Society.

Clennam on the face of it belongs neither in Society nor in the prison. He neither participates in the frictive aggressiveness of the Merdle world nor seems eroded by the self-deludedness of the prison inmates. Yet he, in fact, comes to replace Mr. Dorrit in the prison, and he does so because of his one foray into the "great" world—namely, his hurling himself into the Merdle Speculation. It turns out as the plot of the novel unfolds that his locked-up subjectivity, with all its repressed desires and animosities, implicitly contains all the elements that make up the world. In addition to the fact that the whole novel enacts the contents of his unconscious, a great number of characters in the novel enact a relation to their past that is analogous to his. This is so in the sense that they, like Clennam, are controlled by the past, because they cannot deal with it. For what marks Clennam's quest is the hopelessness that springs from his inability to tap the wellsprings of his being. Clennam fails even to begin to resurrect the faintest vestige of the actual impulses that were repressed in his distant childhood. Yet we see him living out, somnambulistically, the self-negation implicit in it.

Clennam's complement in these matters is, of course, Amy. Amy, like Clennam, not only does not participate in the compulsive drama of projection and aggression which animates the world of the novel, but is linked to him by her inability either effectively to project or meaningfully to assault. Amy herself not only is Clennam's vanishing point, but a blank in and for herself. Although she has a highly specified life history, her history is the painfully self-limiting reality of her life in the prison and her repetition of that life in the world outside. Although she is represented as a tower of moral strength and fountain of nurturing generosity, she has little visible inner life. Represented as a center of stillness within the agitated aggressiveness of the novel's world, her own experience of that stillness is given no representation. Recurrently taking care of other people, and often "nursing" them from sickness to health, she not only is renunciatory in her behavior, as when she garners her meals at Mrs. Clennam's in order to feed her father. She is also profoundly inexpressive, except with regard to her tremulous yearning to sustain those who need her, and especially to protect her father and to spare him and herself exposure to the prying eyes of the world.

Amy's one venture into deliberate self-expression is the fairy tale. In the course of the chapter in which she tells Maggy her self-reflexive fairy tale, Dickens broaches the issue of fortune-telling—that is, of anticipating the future. He seems, at this point, on the verge of looking into her soul, or of having her do so; letting her tell her fairy tale, he gives her an opening for projecting her inwardness. By the end of that chapter, however, he gives up that hopeless task and leaves her inner life unrepresented.

This failed attempt takes the form of the tale she tells Maggy. There, she spins out a fantasy at some relative length, but the fantasy is a fantasy of absence, of a secret that is a shadow which eventually disappears. Even given the possibility of merely verbal wish fulfillment, perhaps analogous to the "chicking" of which Maggy dreams, she fizzles out completely. While she can materialize for Clennam as the realization of a dream—she appears in his doorway at the very moment he realizes the loss of his dream of Flora as his destiny and salvation—she herself cannot sustain a meaningful act of her own imagination. The Clennam she gets in the end is as much an opaque, phantasmal presence as she is herself, a presence through which she inarticulately projects and satisfies her own needs.

So lacking in articulateness, imagination, and animation—even in movement—is Amy, that Dickens must resort to a set of negative foils or mirrors to give us a positive sense of her presence. He surrounds her with a range of contrasting characters, and in this way he creates the illusionist impression that she is there. This is part of the imaginative function in the novel of Fanny, Pet, Flora, Mrs. Merdle, and Maggy and Mrs. Clennam, all of whom are contrasted with her. We may infer that the stillness—the tranquillity—she is meant to symbolize is the antithesis but also the derivative of the frustration and, in all but Maggy and Pet, the consuming fury of these women.

The juxtaposition of Amy with these women points to the fury that lies at the bottom of the orphan condition. It also suggests the way the irreparability of the wounds that generate the fury produces the endless versions of that condition, which are implicit in the fictions of everyone in the novel. All these characters reenact their basic experience of abandonment through their fantasies and through their fantasy-driven behavior. Hence, among other things, lies the ubiquitous isolation—the irredeemable solitude within the prison of their imagination—of everyone within that world.

Amy herself is part of a sort of somnambulistic action in which she and Clennam move toward each other like puppets, moved by the fantasy action that seems to destine them for each other. On the one hand, they serve as emblems of an otherworldly otherness that stands apart from the given world of the novel. On the other hand they are a replication of the passive fantasy of nurture that is the ultimate point both of departure and regression in the novel. As for Clennam, the very point of his representation is the irreparability of the emotional and imaginative stalemate that precludes self-generated movement or energetic activity.

Clennam's inability to disinter meaningfully either his true life history or to integrate what he does learn in an energizing way is reflected everywhere in the novel. Indeed, *Little Dorrit* engages directly with the themes implicit in his inability to integrate and animate his experience. It does so by creating a series of polarizations that are symptomatic of the novel's inability to imagine an experience of vitally lived life. The first of these dichotomies projects a sense of the unbridgeable gap between the fallen world of present life and any realm of transcendent values. The second foregrounds the distance between visions of a Golden Age of harmony and the present world of mechanical energies and pervasive Cain-and-Abel rivalry. The third articulates the impossibility of meaningfully relating past to present, and of evolving a vital identity by mediating the two. The fourth dramatizes the nightmare of distinguishing between fact and fiction and of allowing meaning to emerge. These motifs not only parallel Clennam's difficulty tuning in on himself, but also are central to the vision that springs from his root condition.

The fracture that separates the lower—the fallen—world from the higher reflects a traditional Christian dichotomy. From the bravura opening of the novel, with its drama of tension between the blazing sun and the world blinded by it, we are urged to perceive the distance between the fallen world and the world beyond, as well as between human beings and a "better order of beings." At the same time we are invited to listen to the dying echoes of an apocalyptic vision:

> The wide stare stared itself out for a while; the sun went down in a red, green, golden glory; the stars came out in the heavens and *the fire-flies mimicked them in the lower air, as man may feebly imitate the goodness of a better order of beings;* the long dusty roads and the interminable plains were in repose—and so deep a hush was on the sea, that it *scarcely whispered of the time when it shall give up its dead.* (53; our emphasis)

Death is central to another striking formulation of the distance between the fallen world and the world beyond. The death of William and Frederick Dorrit for a moment seems to overcome the insuperable gap between them:

> It was a moonlight night; but the moon rose late, being long past the full. When it was high in the peaceful firmament, it shone through half-closed lattice-blinds into the solemn room where the stumblings and wanderings of a life had so lately ended. Two quiet figures were within the room; . . . equally still and impassive, *equally removed by an untraversable distance from the teeming earth and all that it contains,* though soon to lie in it.
>
> One figure reposed upon the bed. The other, kneeling on the floor, drooped over it. . . . *The two brothers were before their Father; far beyond the twilight judgment of this world; high above its mists and obscurities.* (714–15; our emphasis)

In *Little Dorrit,* the realm of the Father is so remote, and man is so lacking in any Jacob's Ladder means of traversing the distance between His world and ours, that even the novel's most vivid hint of any possibility for redemption chiefly serves to reevoke the "untraversable" gap between the two.

The most extreme formulation of the possibility for transformation and redemption is embedded in one of the climactic scenes of the novel. As the energized Mrs. Clennam, accompanied by Amy, moves toward her house—which "heaved, surged outward, opened asunder in fifty places, collapsed and fell" (862)—we are treated to a vision of "one of those summer evenings when there is no greater darkness than a long twilight" (861), and we hear that

> the beauties of the sunset had not faded from the light films of cloud that lay at peace in the horizon. From a radiant centre, over the

whole length and breadth of the tranquil firmament great shoots of light streamed among the early stars, *like signs of the blessed late covenant of peace and hope that changed the crown of thorns into a glory.* (862; our emphasis)

Within the world of the novel, no such change is remotely conceivable, unless we were to view Amy as a successfully realized sacrificial figure. In her symbolic function, she is possibly intended to provide an image of mediation. In her actual presence in the novel, she succeeds only in drawing Clennam into the abyss of his own passivity. When Lionel Trilling speaks of Amy as the Paraclete, mediating between the upper world and the lower, he neglects a key configuration of images in the text. The Paraclete is traditionally associated with the dove which is the Holy Ghost. The birds of the novel suggest something very different. Think of the absurd Flora *Finch*ing, of Mrs. Merdle's grotesquely squawking parrot, and then of Amy feebly fluttering out of the Marshalsea gate.

Another major Christian trope foregrounds the distance between the higher and lower worlds. Life is spoken of in familiar Bunyanesque terms, as in the passage in which we hear of the voyage from which Clennam, the Meagleses, Miss Wade, and others are returning. Here the journey is transformed into a metaphor for all human life. Yet the metaphor points nowhere, just as the pilgrimage—presumably, from the worse world to the better—leads nowhere. The text tells us that

> The day passed on; and again the wide stare stared itself out; and the hot night was on Marseilles; and through it the caravan of the morning, all dispersed, went their appointed ways. And thus ever, by day and by night, under the sun and under the stars, climbing the dusty hills and toiling along the weary plains, journeying by land and journeying by sea, coming and going so strangely, . . . to act and react upon one another, move all we travellers through the pilgrimage of life. (67)

The journey leads nowhere meaningful—leads to a nowhere condition in which the meaning of the journey is not present. A variety of images, like the bedouin tents and the caravanserai with which Miss Wade's domicile is associated, reinforce the sense of aimless wanderings and of journeyings that are anything but pilgrimages with redemptive destinations. So do the images of the Dorrits' travels, in the Alps, and especially Mr. Dorrit's experience in the outskirts of Rome, where what he encounters is a grotesque priest shepherding a shabby funeral. This may also be taken to be a metaphor for the pointlessness of the novel's plot, which leads nowhere and produces nothing, consuming itself to a degree that the plot of no other Dickens novel does.

The irrelevance of the language of religious transcendence to the lives led by the people in the novel also serves to dramatize the absence, within their world, of authentic frames of reference beyond the self, through which to generate meaning or anchor value.

The Golden Age material in *Little Dorrit* elaborates the distance between any ideal world and the world of the novel, and it does so in ways that are closely linked to Clennam's personal quest. In the perspective of the mass of golden age references, it is surely meaningful that it is a *Flora*—named as a pagan nature goddess—who is the first personal object of Clennam's quest. It is equally meaningful that Flora is not a fecundating figure of nature; altogether, the novel stresses the inaccessibility of touchstones in nature for values in the present world.

For still more than *Bleak House*, *Little Dorrit* admits no focused imagination of visionary or utopian possibilities, and gives no meaningfully particularized way of imagining a better life in the present. Within the deadness and the deadliness of the *Dorrit* world, the very memory of a pastoral, Edenic past functions only as a measure of the death of vital aspiration; the most this memory can signify is a vague and weary yearning for something better, beyond the boundaries of present immurement. Pastoral images serve only to underscore the infinite sadness, verging on despair, of the vestiges that remain of a yearning for a better world. Indeed, even at their most positive, as in the representation of the pastoral field of the Chiverys' laundry-hung yard or in the portrayal of the Plornishes' living room, on whose walls a rural cottage has been painted, they ruefully mark the magnitude of the gap between the yearning and the actuality.

Value may be assigned to the garden cottage painted on the Plornishes' wall and to Mrs. Plornish's dutiful encouragement of her father's reedy singing. In the representation of the Plornishes, Nandy's plaintive—his *reedy*—strains as he renders Strephon's love or Phyllis's sound out as a rueful, affirmation of sorts. It does nothing, however, to qualify the anonymity and degrading poverty of Nandy and of his reduction to being one of the long line of undifferentiated coats made by fortune for the inmates of the workhouse. Nor does the field of stereotyped allusions to the pastoral tradition serve to do anything but highlight the hopeless impoverishment of the lives of the inhabitants of Bleeding Heart Yard and, for that matter, of the entire fallen world.

The arcadian imagery with which Dickens invests the Chivery aspirations dovetails with Romance figuration in the portrayal of John Chivery's aspirations to Amy's hand. Both images dramatize the pathetic self-deception involved. In John, we have the make-believe knight-errant and the languishing pastoral lover who obsessively contemplates suicide in composing lugubrious epitaphs for himself. With his plaintive affirmation of his "sacred spots," he is a dim, faded echo of the classical affirmations of Micawber and a mournful comment on Nandy's Strephon and Phyllis.

Yet even at their most positive, such evocations intimate, at best, the sadness of hopeless yearning, and the endlessness of such yearning. When Dickens feels for the Plornishes and the Chiverys, he feels for them because of the touching futility of their wishing and hoping—because of the vastness of the distance between anything implied by the imagery of literary arcadianism and the grimly prosaic reality in which they live: the distance as great as the distance that separates the crown of thorns transformed into a glory from the represented world of the novel.

Little Dorrit is fierce, however, in its handling of Mrs. Merdle's yearning for the natural order. Mrs. Merdle's Marie-Antoinettism, with its pretense of grief at being trammeled by the constraints of society, is one of Dickens's most powerful means for dramatizing the gap between society and a classical sense of nature, between the reality of Society's murderous invidiousness, with its meretricious falsifications, and the dream of universal love, where lions lie down with lambs. Mrs. Merdle, holding forth on the pain of having to relinquish her pastoral simplicity for the harshness of Society's judgments, is no more an image of natural feeling than she is of adequate nurture, the nurture one might have hoped, in some better world, would spring from her ample bosom. It is no accident that she takes, not a baby, but Mrs. Gowan's vicious fictions to nurse.

Indeed, all that can be found in the field of Mrs. Merdle's activity is rampant deception, faced with the highest General gloss, and sustained by the vicious Cain and Abel rivalries that mark

Fanny's relation both to her and to her bosom. As for the bosom itself, all it can be taken to symbolize within the larger realm of Society is the poisonous infusion of infectious fantasy it offers to the world at large: a fantasy of unearned wealth, promising the opportunity, not for ostensibly healing passivity, like Oliver's, or self-consuming effort, like Richard's, but the occasion for grazing in the field of varnished, mutually mirroring fictions that is Mrs. Merdle's domain.

For Dickens to put primitivist pastoral yearnings in Mrs. Merdle's mouth is to heighten his corrosive satiric assault on Society's pretensions. It is also to signify the magnitude of the distance between the two visions: the vision of a Golden Age and what is represented in the novel as an avowedly false and depravingly brutal present time. That distance is felt to be so great that the very fiction—the very idea—of Saturn's golden time is emptied of all usefully meaningful content, except as a ground for judging the present. In practice—in terms of any difference they might make to anyone's actual life as a touchstone to better things—the positives implicit in the Plornishes' tender treatment of Nandy or in Mrs. Chivery's solicitude for the fulfillment of John's romantic aspirations are as empty.

In the end, the Chiverys' dream for John and John's dreams for himself repeat and reinforce the hierarchical structures of value both within the Marshalsea and outside it. There is no escape from those structures of value, and no way of redeeming them.

The passivity of Nandy's idea of what he would do if a ship laden with gold should come his way dovetails with the passivity of the fantasy life evoked through the novel's representation of the Dorrits. If we track the logic of that representation, it turns out that the prison, like Amy herself, is the still place where fantasy can be played out, partly because active volition has no place within it. Yet when fantasy is liberated, all it can do is reproduce the condition it tries to escape. This is one of the points made through the fairy tale that Amy tells to amuse Maggie; within it, the absence that fills Amy's life in the prison is reproduced in the wish fulfillment world of the tale. Whatever transcendent associations she is haloed with, Amy, as we have just noted, has no accessible subjectivity, and she has nothing in herself to pose and pit against the world.

The third dichotomy is central to Clennam's experience: namely, the hopelessness of achieving a constructive relation between the past and the present, and the resulting impossibility of achieving any kind of growth or of finding a grounded meaning for life. This difficulty figures everywhere in the novel. Mrs. Clennam, Mr. Dorrit, Fanny, Flora, the Meagles, Tattycoram, Miss Wade, Gowan, and Rigaud are all engaged in variously obsessive, failed, and often comic efforts to deal with their past. No one succeeds in the effort. Clennam himself never learns the bare facts of his life history or comes to grips with their emotional implications. For most of the other characters, the past is something either to manipulate or to conceal. Yet despite all their effort to control the past, their past ultimately controls them. Their skewed relation to the past also contributes to the creation of the paranoid system of projections out of which the shared, illusion-filled world of the novel is made.

Indeed, throughout *Little Dorrit,* the past is at once so unavailable and so unusable, that it works like the repressed material of the Freudian unconscious. It works as a sort of mysterious machinery that moves things along to what are felt to be foreordained ends. Clennam is especially vulnerable to this process and so is Amy. It is their pasts that moves them like sleepwalking puppets toward their union.

Clennam's struggle to deal with the past has painfully ironic effects. He not only wants to right the wrongs that he fears were committed in the past, but also to use what he hopes to learn about his personal history to improve his life. Yet he not only never learns the truth about his birth, but it is Amy—his savior, ostensibly—who withholds it from him in the end, out of loyalty to his mother's wishes. Even if he had learned the truth, it would not have mattered, however, because his life has been worked out for him by his marriage to Amy and not through any revelation about the past. There is a sense in which that marriage has been foreordained by the "real" story of his life, namely, by his experience as the son of Mrs. Clennam, who has withheld, not only truth, but also love. It is the absence of her love and the palpability of her hate that determines Clennam's need for Amy.

As for the rest of the characters, they live out a variety of skewed relationships to the past. Some strive to disjoin their present from their past, or to obscure the relation between present and past; others tenaciously cling to the past, forcibly and inappropriately carrying it into the present. Some do both. Either way, they make it impossible to relate the two in a constructive way. This failure gives rise to many of the falsifications that constitute the field of interlocking fictions which makes up the common world of the novel.

The Mrs. Clennam action hinges on an obsessive effort simultaneously to suppress the past and to keep it alive. Both efforts are based on a denial of reality. Her interpretation of Mr. Clennam's "Do Not Forget" represents a refusal to forget or forgive the affront of her husband's love for Arthur's mother. In concealing the secret of Arthur's illegitimate birth, she not only obstructs his working out of its implications, but also feeds her own virulence. Ironically, her struggle with Rigaud to preserve her secret serves only to bring her secret to light and to force disclosure of what she has struggled to conceal. Yet the disclosure of this buried secret from the past has no significant effect on the present. Clennam is not only denied knowledge of it, but could not have used the knowledge if it had been revealed to him. For Mrs. Clennam herself the disclosure has no meaningful moral or psychological value. This holds true throughout all the plots of the novel; the disclosure of the secrets of the past in no way serves to transform the consciousness or the lives of the characters.

Mr. Dorrit's relation to the past is analogous to Mrs. Clennam's. He desperately tries to suppress the past but cannot escape it, and the restoration of his fortune is of no real use to him. Once he comes into his fortune, his energy is wholly invested in concealing his prison past. The shadow of the prison wall ineluctably pursues him, however, and finally overwhelms him—not from without, but from within. In the moment of his collapse, he reverts to the state of mind that characterized his Marshalsea past. In fact he again "becomes" the person he was then, grotesquely enacting the role of the Father of the Marshalsea, now in circumstances of tawdry splendor. This possession by a prior identity he assiduously sought to repress is based on a retentiveness that was also at play in his original process of accommodation to the Marshalsea, when he preserved vestigial forms of the gentility that marked his earlier life. It is also, in its way, analogous to the way the deprivations of Clennam's early life lead him to need Amy as his Euphrasia.

Like Mr. Dorrit and Mrs. Clennam, Amy clings to the past. Unchanging, she imports the sensibilities of her life in the Marshalsea into her life as an heiress. She remains loyal to the commitments that marked her life in the prison. Unlike her father and Mrs. Clennam, however, Amy has no wish either to conceal the past or to abandon it; if anything, she struggles to sustain it. Yet despite that contrast between her values and those of Mrs. Clennam and her father, she repeats their pattern of stubborn fixation on the past, and is not interested in liberating herself from it. Although the novel tries to represent a process of change in her as she becomes aware of her love for Clennam, and although it implies that she is moving toward the possibility of a vital relation to him, her emotional life is stuck in the desperate need to love and be loved. She is trapped within the patterns of nursing that are her essence. This is the case because she has no access to her own repressed subjectivity, and is never impelled to challenge or explore it.

In her relation to the past, Fanny is contrasted with Amy, but also with their father. Like her father, Fanny desperately wants to deny her life in prison. Here the motive is the wish to take up the life in Society that she has imagined for herself while still in the Marshalsea. Consummately accomplished in the nastiness of the World, Fanny makes a good fit with Society, and finds within it an arena for playing out both the real aggression and the make-believe gentility engendered by her life in prison. Yet the continuity of her life generates a vicious fiction: the fiction that the real past in prison, where she served her apprenticeship to Society, never existed.

Gowan neatly echoes Fanny in this, and provides a subtle contrast. His aristocratic past is both a fact and a fiction, but even its facts are largely fictitious. His expectations were never what he claims them to be. Yet he plays up his past as energetically as Fanny and Mr. Dorrit play it down; he builds his future life on the loss of a past that in fact only feebly existed—that seems to have existed in the modes of the make-believe world of Gypsy Bohemians to which his mother belongs.

Rigaud is not only Gowan's crony, but he is also an extreme version of everything Gowan represents. Unlike Gowan's, his past and his claims to gentility are absolute fictions. His project is to achieve both standing in the world and power that he and his ancestors never possessed, and in achieving it, to avenge himself for the humiliations he has undergone as an ordinary mortal. In seeking vengeance for the humiliations he has undergone, he is like Mrs. Clennam, sharing with her also the wish to destroy the whole world if he cannot achieve what he wants.

Indeed, Rigaud's effort to blackmail Mrs. Clennam by threatening to expose her real past puts in high relief his own lack of a significant past. It also suggests by juxtaposition the falsity of all the presumptions of authenticity put forward by people who, like the Barnacles, rest their claim to power and wealth on lineage. The bluster with which he enacts his gentlemanliness underscores the fictive nature of virtually all the claims to power and social position in the world of the novel. His effort to cash in on the evidence of the Clennam family history which he has illicitly acquired culminates in his disappearance in a cloud of dust. This not only confirms his origins in stage melodrama, but also the tenuousness of the fictions by which he lives. All his activity throws him back to the nothingness of his origins; in the end, he remains as ineffectual in the effort to move things along as the passively regressive characters.

Rigaud, Gowan, William and Fanny Dorrit, and Mrs. Clennam are deformed by their manipulation of the facts of their history. Clennam cannot integrate past into present, or project a future in terms of a meaningful past: these others are not interested in doing so. Clennam can find no way back to the parts of his experience that might be real and viable for him, and is therefore not able to imbue his experience with meaning. Hence, even the nihilism of Rigaud, who is so different from him in every way, shares with Clennam the inability to generate meaning for his life. Clennam cannot give meaning to his experience and to his residual desires. Nothing charges him with active desire, and nothing is charged for him with a desirability that might lead him on.

The final nightmare of this novel lies in the universal inability of its characters actively to deal with their past and thereby to generate meaning that can confer value on the effort to achieve identity and human connectedness. It not only is Clennam who cannot consolidate knowledge and experience and make use of them to forge a meaningful life, it is the world the novel represents. Everyone in the world of the novel is, ultimately, caught in violently erosive, entropic fields of debilitating weariness; all of them are victims of inner and outer forms of life-denying resentment or passive paralysis. All are trapped in a pervasive condition of negativity that makes it impossible to generate anything significant, anything original, anything new. Everyone is ceaselessly constructing themselves and their life stories, but no one can create a viable sense of experience out of the pieces of the lives they have actually lived.

Miss Wade's furious truthfulness, disclosed in the one direct autobiographical narrative in the novel, merely highlights how inaccessible she is to any positive use she might make of her life story. Even Doyce can find mechanical rules in nature on the basis of which to make useful objects, but can infuse no vitality into the world—not even to the extent that Rouncewell's energies can unconvincingly do so in the world of *Bleak House.*

Flora Finching epitomizes the problematics of generativity and of meaning in paradoxical ways. Despite her grotesqueness, Flora's own exuberance and the resounding energy of her representation make her a figure of surprising vitality in an overwhelmingly depressed world. Indeed, the vigor of her depiction allows Dickens to refract through her many of the governing issues of the novel: issues of meaning, of boundaries, of coherence, of time, and of generativity. He also uses her to reflect on his own creative process and on the life of the imagination itself.

Flora's salient characteristic is her unremitting need to breach boundaries. This is the more striking because in this she violates the prevailing imaginative and stylistic disposition of the novel. *Little Dorrit* is made up of a series of unresolvable polarizations, which are symptomatic of life in a world within which people cannot integrate their experience. That world is rendered by a narrative voice that sees things with stark, staring relentlessness, and renders them with cutting clarity. Everything about Flora, on the other hand, reflects a comic disposition to indiscriminate merging, fusing, mingling, intermingling combining, recombining. Flora grafts people onto each other and rides roughshod over linguistic categories; she mounts the past onto the present, the romantic onto the prosaic, and fantasy onto reality; and she magically transforms wishes into deeds. When she appears, "a singular combination of perfumes" is "diffused through the room, as if some lavender-water had been put by mistake in a brandy bottle" (680).

Her discourse endlessly breaches boundaries. In response to Mr. Dorrit's innocent assumption that Clennam and Co. is Mr. Clennam, Flora says, "It's a very different person indeed . . . with no limbs and wheels instead and the grimmest of women though his mother." Having created a strange new being, Flora adds, "And an old man besides" (683), and then wholly confounds Mr. Dorrit by

> dashing into a rapid analysis of Mr. Flintwich's cravat, and describing him, without the lightest boundary line of separation between his identity and Mrs. Clennam's, as a rusty screw in gaiters. Which compound of man and woman, no limbs, wheels, rusty screw, grimness

and gaiters, so completely stupefied Mr. Dorrit, that he was a spectacle to be pitied. (683)

What she does with language and with the details of reality, she does with time, blurring past into present and suffusing the present with the unfulfillable longing of the past:

> With these words and with a hasty gesture fraught with timid caution [. . .] poor Flora left herself at eighteen years of age [. . .]; and came to a full stop. . . .
> Or rather, she left about half of herself at eighteen years of age behind, and grafted the rest on to the relict of the late Mr F.; thus making a moral mermaid of herself." (196)

Despite the vigor of Flora's presence, in the end she reenacts the pervasive desolation of the novel. Her supreme fantasticality foregrounds the hopelessness of the mountings—of the montages—that she perpetrates and that she is. Like Mrs. Bayham Badger in *Bleak House,* she serves to dramatize a kind of bizarrely utopian possibility that Dickens plays with, of synthesizing the times of one's life, of integrating past and present in a way that overcomes the dichotomies that are so destructive in Clennam's experience. As with Mrs. Badger, the representation of her flounderings pinpoints the grotesqueness and impossiblity of such a synthesis. Mrs. Badger is grotesque in that the coexistence of all her husbands, living and dead, neutralizes Dr. Badger himself, and robs Mrs. Badger of her own present life; in this, she reproduces the disembodiment that marks the third-person narrative voice in *Bleak House,* whose special relation to time is one of the causes of its disembodiment.

Flora, for her part, not only is grotesque because of the traits that her portrayal mocks her for—her tippling, her blubberiness, and the hurtle of her compulsive talking—but also because of the pathetic hopelessness of the way she brings the past into the present, never confronting the gulf between them, and bridging them only through a denial of time and change. Hence, of course, she is not able to achieve a viable relation to either, or to achieve integration of what they mean to her. Indeed, her dizzying flights of language are shown to be rooted in the pain of the loss she underwent in being separated from Clennam and in her inability to cope with the pain, the anger, and the self-hatred-engendering humiliation of that loss.

No less hopeless is the way she muddles reality and fiction. Her sense of life is not mediated but rather controlled by the novels she has read; like Julia Mills in *David Copperfield,* she cannot distingush between her own life and that of the characters in the novels she has swallowed.

In this sense, Flora reproduces the plight of all the imaginers and fantasizers in the novel. The prison house of fictions that constitutes the represented world of the novel is crowded with figures who are either self-consciously or compulsively creating and emitting fantastic fictions. Mrs. Merdle and Mrs. Gowan's nursing of the fiction of Society; Mr. Merdle's magical power to make everyone believe in him as the new Midas, a power that seems all the more uncanny because he does nothing active to elicit that belief, but, on the face of it at least, is merely a screen on to which it can be projected; Mr. Casby's representation of himself as the benign patriarch exuding the milk of human kindness; Mr. Dorrit's collaboration with the Collegians in transmuting the sordid reality of the Marshalsea into a semblance of a tradition; Mrs. Clennam's creation from the ground of her own rage and guilt of a vengeful deity and her gorgonlike power to paralyze Clennam; Miss Ward's, Fanny's, and Tattycoram's paranoid projection of their rage and humiliation—all these are echoed in Flora's hilarious muddlings, from within which nothing of meaning or value can emerge. In virtually all these, moreover, the projections emanate from a history of humiliation, helplessness, and abandonment—from an unresolved relation to a past that has a stranglehold on them.

At the same time as it epitomizes the condition of her fellows in the prison house of wretchedness that is the novel, Flora's mode of thinking bears a close resemblance to features of Dickens's own creative process. There is a paradigmatic resemblance between Flora's brilliantly rendered linguistic absurdities and some of Dickens's most striking imaginative creations. Think, for example, of the relation between Flora's "screw in gaiters" as part of her shorthand for describing Jeremiah Flintwinch and Dickens's construction of the grotesque image of Flintwinch himself, with his cravat like a hangman's noose and his head all askew above it; or think of the affinity between the mud that collects at compound interest in the opening paragraph of *Bleak House* and the "compound of man and woman, no limbs, wheels, rusty screw, grimness and gaiters" (683) in Dickens's precis of Flora's account of the Clennam household.

However, what is pure comedy of confusion in Flora is for Dickens a purposeful synthesis of disparate elements so that the world may be revealed as a meaningful totality rather than as a splatter of discrete but dead and unintelligible structures. *Little Dorrit* itself is made up of such meaningful combinations of potentially muddled material. Think, for example, of all the boundaries Dickens must violate and how many disparate things he must bring together when he creates the vision of the world as a prison—how he must mount onto the central image of the Marshalsea the myriad literal and figurative prisons that fuse with it imaginatively: from the other literal prison in Marseilles to the workhouse to the bars in the windows of the ground floor of the Gowan household in Venice, which are vestiges of the bank that once occupied that floor, through the fog-bound mountain fastness of the Great St. Bernard and the self-generated jail of Mrs. Clennam, to the image of the sun over Marseilles as the jailor of all those who protect themselves from its assault by shuttering themselves into their houses. If we linger somewhat skeptically with this seemingly bizarre concatenation of places that signify the prison house of reciprocal projections that is the social world of the novel, we have a medley of images that is potentially as disorienting as Flora's discourse when, offering the fainting Amy her smelling salts,

> [She] hovered about her on a sofa, intermingling kind offices and incoherent scraps of conversation in a manner so confounding, that whether she pressed the Marshalsea to take a spoonful of unclaimed dividends, for it would do her good; or whether she congratulated Little Dorrit's father on coming into possession of a hundred thousand smelling bottles; or whether she explained that she put seventy-five thousand drops of spirits of lavender on fifty thousand pounds of lump sugar. (465)

The effect of Dickens's conflation of his widely disparate elements is of course the exact opposite of this. The entire novel is a brilliantly purposive and meaning-fraught representation of how and why it is impossible for anyone in its world to generate meaning or to act in positive and meaningful ways. Dickens deploys the Flora-dimension of his imagination to create the maddeningly coherent imaginative world of *Little Dorrit*. The novel itself, however, is in good part about the failure of imagination to work in positive, coherent, and generative ways. As we noted earlier, in our analysis of the paranoid and projective nature of the intersubjective world of the novel, *Little Dorrit,* more than any other Dickens novel, projects a world bursting with figures who are shown to be creating and projecting fantastic fictions.

These fictions are full of meaning in the imaginative field Dickens creates for them; in themselves, however, they are meaningful only as manifestation of the hopeless sterility of the world and of the characters' inability to make meaningful lives for themselves, or to relate to other people in constructive and rewarding ways.

Yet there is a sense in which even the copious creativity of Dickens himself is radically constrained in the making of *Dorrit.* The chief sign of this is the absence in the novel of representations of constructive psychic process or of any sense of a positive generativity. Flora is, in one sense, all process—so compulsively so, that we have no value-conferring exploration of her inwardness. Somewhat like the third-person voice in *Bleak House,* she has no center of self-confronting self-consciousness. She is all movement, all animation, all boundary breaking, but she has no way of taking hold of her inwardness, and integrating it, and the novel does nothing to elucidate its logic for us. Furthermore, Flora is not able to effectuate anything, apart from her facilitation of the neutralizing and neutering union of Clennam and Amy. Amy, on the other hand, is so rigidly contained within the forms of her own behavior that there is no bubbling up of her underlying inwardness, no exploration of her inner life. Far more than Esther, she has no access, even momentary, to whatever it is that moves her to be as she is and to behave as she does. And Clennam, as we have been saying, has a considerable range of memories, but no way of vivifying them or transforming them into grounds of action or a source of desire.

The meaningful energy and action of the novel are, in fact, concentrated in its narration, which, in fact, becomes the vehicle for expressing all the suppressed energy and anger of the characters. The narration combines several modalities that reflect the negativity and the weariness of spirit that informs the creation of the novel. It is, to begin with, full of assaultive energy in its disclosure of the negativity and the ungenerativeness of the world in the novel. As in *Oliver Twist,* but far more so, the third-person narrative operates with an aggressiveness that hammers out, as it were, the image of the reality that the novel projects. That image is a flattened, battered image, without the nuanced fluctuations of ordinary feeling-life. Its modalities in this respect are congruous with the battering mood of the opening chapter, which is as assaultive in its rendering of the brutality of the sunlight in Marseilles as the sunlight itself is said to be in relation to the world it shines on.

At the same time as it blurs and subdues the brutalized reality of the subjectivities it depicts, the narrative voice achieves a startling clarity in its representation of the world, even as it expresses a remoteness from what it is representing, as though it were located far away, where the sun shines, among the stars that look down on the straggling mortals on the earth below. Both the clarity and the remoteness are expressed in the abstractness of conceptualization within it. Society figures with an upper case "S"; the biblical Cain and Abel trope sums up human relationships; Amy is not a concretely conceived woman, but a symbol—Christlike redeemer in one perspective, Euphrasia in another.

At the same time, there is, cumulatively, a terrible resignation in the narrative voice. If the first chapter starts with the battering of the sun, it ends with the weary contemplation of humanity on its straggling pilgrimage to nowhere. If it tries, feebly, to redeem the dissolution of Clennam in Amy's embrace by figuring it as a redemption, it subsides by the end into the quiet irony of their "going down into" the turbulent, uncomprehending crowd.

There is also a numbing lack of process in the workings of the voice as well as in its representations of characters. If the third-person narrative voice in *Bleak House* is all churning process, the voice here is tight and rigid in its stance and tone. Everything in the novel is felt to be a fait accompli. Moreover, as there is no representation of process in the characters, so the voice admits no process in its own workings. It is, if we wish, in some respects analogous to Pancks, in the chug-chug-chug mechanicalness of its delineations—in its representations of character, of the intersubjective world, of the relations between people and their inner worlds.

It is as though the narrative voice, no less than Clennam, desperately needs the static, de-energized quietude of Amy for respite and solace—hence, the wan resignation of its evocations of what lies beyond the visible heavens, and the weariness of the tone in which it evokes the crown of thorns that became a glory. The dead-end that is *Dorrit* would also seem to be the dead-end of Dickens's searching, sometimes utopian imagination.

Hence, the wonder of Dickens's further work: Given the imaginative and emotional dead end that *Little Dorrit* monumentalizes, one is almost surprised to realize that Dickens completed three more novels, two of which are among the most admirable of his creations. Presumably, whatever the dead-endedness of *Dorrit,* Dickens mobilized renewed energies for what follows. Those energies find their best expression in *Great Expectations.*

Our own special interest in *Great Expectations* stems from the fresh perspective it provides on Dickens's vision of the orphan condition.

6
Great Expectations

STANDING NEAR THE END OF DICKENS'S TRAJECTORY AS A NOVELIST, *Great Expectations* provides a trenchant commentary upon all the novels that precede it, and with it, an energized response to the desperation of *Little Dorrit*. By a concerted act of control and liberation, it seems to master the disintegrative energies that shape *Little Dorrit,* and emerges as the most compact and coherent of Dickens's works. It also constitutes Dickens's most sharply focused treatment of the orphan condition.

The power of *Great Expectations* stems in good part from its uncanny access to its protagonist's inwardness and from its masterful articulation of that inwardness in vivid narrative terms. If *Little Dorrit* is made up of the endlessly displaced contents of Clennam's inchoate subjectivity, *Great Expectations* is the highly articulate externalization, in Pip's own words, of his life experience. Pip's narrative reaches back to what we must take to be his earliest coherent memory, and puts us in touch with the subjective resonance, in his discourse, of relatively coherent unconscious as well as conscious conflict.

In Pip's story, moreover, Dickens again engages the rawness of the experience of orphaning that fills his early work. Pip's infancy and childhood are not as brutally exposed as Oliver Twist's, but his narrative resonates to the primordial sense of abuse and violation that marked *Oliver Twist*. The great novels of the middle period—from *David Copperfield* through *Little Dorrit*—had brilliantly refined the moral and psychological insights of the early work, and they had projected the fantasy material that informs the orphan condition through remarkable structures of doubling and condensation. They had renounced, however, direct representation through their protagonists of the psychic and moral impact on the abandoned child of a violent and assaultive world.

Great Expectations restores to the center of interest the ineradicable experience of early deprivation, and it does so in a narrative that tracks the resonance of this experience through the entire trajectory of Pip's growth. It does so, moreover, within a narrative designed to represent how Pip strives to master the disruptive experience of his orphanhood, and how he emerges from it, not unscathed, but radically sad, human, and articulate. In portraying Pip, Dickens no longer abandons himself, as he did in the early novels, to an unself-conscious immersion in the orphan condition. Rather, he contemplates and represents it from within a keen consciousness of its hazards and of the need to master those hazards.

For Pip's story is not, to begin with, an account of his entrapment in the orphan condition, but rather of his movement toward a highly qualified sense of emergence from it. *Great Expectations* represents Pip's effort to overcome the batterings of his early life and the delusive expectations of his adolescent years. At the manifest level, the narrative vividly engages the moral conflict on which his narrative centers—that is, the conflict with regard to the shame and guilt he feels for the aspirations to gentility that led him to betray his best self in spurning Joe and yielding to the false allure of his expectations. At this level, the novel constitutes Pip's effort to recount the story of his liberation from the circumstances that victimized him in his early orphan life, but still more, of his struggle to free himself from his own passive wishes—operatively, from the wish, with which we are already all too familiar, to be freed, by coming into an inheritance, from the stress of striving in the world.

Pip's narrative conveys a sense of his emergence from the victimization of his childhood and the bafflement of his young manhood, and it does so within what is probably Dickens's most shapely narrative. *Great Expectations* achieves a classic formalization of Pip's development, and it does so with a clarity that exceeds almost anything else in Dickens's work. Its narrative is finely poised between its retrospective thrust and its forward movement; its structure turns on a series of recognitions and reversals as tightly wrought as classical tragedy. Pip's recognition of the pivotal people in his life—most dramatically, his identification of the returned Magwitch first as the convict in the graveyard and then as the source of his expectations—triggers a reversal, not only in objective knowledge, but also in the configuration of his inner life. The emphasis, finally, is not so much on the shock of recognition as on the way he deals with what has been recognized. On the face of it, Pip not only comes to see the source of his expectations, but also to see himself, with all his warts. The felicity of his language, the humor of his narrative, and the brilliant use of metaphor Dickens bestows on him suggest that he has indeed mastered the direst nightmares of his life and reached a point of insight and repose that reflects a partial liberation from the compulsive grip of his past.

Yet the forward movement of the action and the way it indeed renders Pip's liberation from the trammels of his external expectations do not in fact bear witness to a final redemption from the ineluctable dynamic of his orphanhood and of his victimization by it. Dickens's treatment of Pip's maturation through apparent renunciation of his passive expectations does not energize him or make for a more integrated personality. Rather, it leads to a loss of energy and a diminution of imaginative power. Pip does achieve a considerable degree of mastery over his experience, yet even at the end, he remains entrapped within the vicious circle of his orphan desires. He is not only sadder than we might wish, but he also continues to be sapped by the stresses of his unresolved orphan condition. Both the manifest point of emergence with which the novel provides him and the signs it gives us of the drift of his unconscious wishes bear witness to his continued domination by orphan desires.

The signs of Pip's orphanhood and of his sense of abandonment fill the novel's opening phase; they increasingly go underground as the narrative unfolds. The childhood scenes directly represent the brutality to which Pip remembers having been subjected in his early life; his discourse throughout is shot through with imagery that powerfully refracts fantasy material characteristic of early life. Much of this material is reminiscent of the images we enumerated in our chapter on *Oliver Twist,* where we noted how Oliver is terrorized by lethal threats that range from simple starvation to cannibalization by his famished bedmate. These images charge the first section of *Great Expectations* with a galvanizing imaginative energy. The galvanizating quality of the narrative subsides for a while when Pip moves into the London phase of his expectations, but the underlying grid of unresolved conflict shows both in details of the the narrative and in the overall structure of the fantasy that is inscribed in it.

It is the place of the orphan material in the text, with special attention to how it manifests itself in the later portions of the narrative, that we wish to track here. We want to show the masterfulness of Dickens's representation of the orphan condition and the way in which he fails to bring his protagonist to a point of emergence from it.

The basic facts of Pip's orphan condition are simple. We learn at the beginning that, like many of Dickens's heroes, he is the orphan absolute. He has never even glimpsed his parents, who exist for him only as figments of imagination—literally as images that he reads out of the letters on their tombstone. His solitude and isolation in the cemetery convey the desolateness of his life; his sense of how his parents actually looked suggests that he generates his images of them not only out of curiosity, but also out of the need for their companionship in his solitary state.

As his narrative unfolds, it emerges that he has had a number of surrogate parents and that all of them have functioned like archetypally threatening stepparents who intrude on him with various degrees of violence. His first stand-in parent is the sister who "brought [him] up by hand," hardhandedly flinging him like "a conjugal missile" and mauling him, physically and spiritually, at every turn. Mrs. Joe, who bears their mother's name, is unmitigatedly punitive. She heaps punishment on him for his very existence, dressing him in "Sunday penitentials" and making him feel that a "policeman accoucheur" had delivered him into his wretched life. One of his later parent figures is a vengeance-seeking, witchlike woman; the other is a convicted criminal. Both of them are represented as springing on him— Magwitch, with violence that is both physical and emotional; Miss Havisham, with an effect of emotional and imaginative violence hard to match even in Dickens.

The external "facts" of Pip's terror-ridden childhood are matched by his subjective experience of not only being intruded upon by an array of particular parent figures, but also by the world at large. Pip's narrative suggests that he has experienced the world as mobilized for an incessant assault on him. His discourse is in fact shot through with images of literal bodily invasion. Magwitch himself lurches at him from behind a tombstone in the opening scene, and Pip imagines him as an intrusion from the world of the dead. The young man with whom Magwitch threatens Pip in the graveyard will, Magwitch threatens, imbrue his hands in his blood and tear out his heart and liver. Pip feels that Estella dips her hands in his heart's blood.

Such incursions are complemented by images of goring, associated with animals, such as the looming cows of the opening segment, the locution that has Mrs. Joe on the "*ram*-page," and the naming of the Blue *Boar*. This sort of intrusion has its counterpart in images of crushing, as in Pip's comparing the imminence of Magwitch's return with the falling of a slab of marble on the sultan in *The Arabian Nights*.

Sheer physical threat—the threat of utter annihilation—takes a still more extreme form in Pip's evocation of the threat of being eaten alive. Cannibal intrusions, where others bite into you and consume you, are rendered here with greater directness than even Vholes's voracious metaphoric consumption of Richard in *Bleak House*. It is striking how the vigor with which the imagination of this child, whose ravenous infant experience of not being nurtured must have made him endlessly imagine that he is eating others, proliferates scenarios in which others eat him. At the very beginning, Magwitch's cannibal threat of the young man who tears out your heart and liver is amplified by the sight of Magwitch himself ravening like a dog on the food Pip steals for him. It is further elaborated, on a vast and hilarious scale, by Pumblechook's disquisition on Ingratitude, with "Porker" standing in for the terrified Pip, so that Pip feels that he is under threat of being eaten for his sins. Pumblechook's Porker homily has its echo at the end of the novel, when his own mouth is stuffed with "flowering annuals"—something whose cannibal tincture we take in only when we realize that the "flowering annuals" are not plants in exuberant flower, but rather the seeds (or *pip*s) of such plants!

Pip's evocation of the fear that he will be eaten is reinforced by the recurrent sense that he has been handled like food. The language of his discourse suggests he has lived with the continuing fantasy that processes of food preparation are repeatedly performed on him. Explicitly or implicitly, he is grated, pierced, pricked, kneaded, trussed, and, as already cited, crushed. His anxiety about being treated as food is echoed in a variety of ways. It is refracted in his report of Miss Havisham's vision of her relatives battening on her when she is laid out on the table where her rotted wedding cake is on display and where frantic vermin scuttle night and day. Cannibal atrocities lurk in the scene where Pip lets Wemmick's Aged Parent's sausage burst into flame as he toasts it, and then learns the sausage comes from the slaughter of Wemmick's well-tended pig, whose loin is to be consumed at supper.

The phantasmagoria of being eaten is elaborated through a ramified series of situations that involve resistance to ingestion. This is expressed in representations of horrendous gaggings and chokings that suggest a proliferated nightmare of feeding. These must be taken as displacements of the experience Pip must have undergone in the course of being force-fed—we hear that he has been dosed on tar-water—and then gagging on what is crammed into him. That Mrs. Joe's breasts are never in evidence is no surprise; she has, after all, brought Pip up "by hand," and one of the salient aspects of the novel is the absence in it of the breasts that figure so centrally in, say, *Little Dorrit*. Hence, there is high drama in the fact that Mrs. Joe's nutmeg-grated cheeks are complemented by a bib bristling with pins and needles, which get into the bread and butter that is dealt out to Pip. Such pins and needles recur at the Pockets', where Baby is given the needle case to play with, and everyone is hysterical about the danger of its choking.

The experience of choking is, in fact, a recurrent motif in the novel, and represents one of the more racking horrors within it. It is palpably present from the early scene of Mr. Pumblechook's cruelly hilarious choking on the tar-water Pip has put in the brandy bottle through his choking on the mouthful of flowering annuals which is his final comeuppance. Joe only fears Pip may choke on the chunk of bread he has secreted in his trouser leg for Magwitch, who eventually does bolt it with the other food Pip brings him. In the context of all the novel's other instances of choking, we take it to be a further example of the radical threat Pip feels from the possibility of choking on his food or suffocating for lack of air.

Hence, the powerful imaginative impact of the plaster casts in Jaggers's office, with their evocation of the agony of strangulation on the gallows. The presence of the casts, in turn, pumps further gasping horror into the opening chapter's image of the gibbet on the horizon. It is not surprising, therefore, to learn, in the final unraveling of the novel's plot, that Molly, with her powerfully muscular arms, has strangled her rival to death. The click in Magwitch's throat in the initial encounter is part of this fantasy field, in the sense that it suggests the possibility of strangulation from things fatally stuck in the throat. Pip's notion of Estella as Sleeping Beauty, with himself as Prince Charming, who will liberate her from lifelessness in the grass-choked castle, joins this battery of images, for the Sleeping Beauty of the fairy tale has choked on a piece of apple fed her by her wicked stepmother. And Compeyson dies in the river while held in Magwitch's strangulating grip.

The novel's images of eating and being eaten are reinforced and their subjective reverberation is amplified by a fantasy—generally registered as fantasy rather than as palpable experience—of invasive, flesh-consuming vermin, which not only gnaw their way into your body, but decompose it. During his hallucination-ridden night at the Hummums—a night ushered in by Herbert's imperative, "Don't go home"—Pip feels threatened by the blue-bottle flies from the butcher's, the ear-wigs from the market (ear-wigs being maggots supposed to enter the brain through the ears), and grubs from the country, which he imagines in the bed. Such invasive, flesh-consuming, and life-polluting vermin mesh imaginatively with the beetles and spiders scurrying on the table Miss Havisham anticipates being laid out upon, but also with a still more terrifying image, elicited in the course of Pip's first visit to Satis House, of Miss Havisham, in her yellowed wedding dress, as a corpse, that disintegrates on exposure to air.

These images link, in turn, with the radical sense of decay and disintegration with which the marshes are associated, but that is also implicit in the fermentation that must be imagined to have taken place in the Havisham brewery. These associations are further amplified through the heaps of rotting casks that fill the yard at Satis House. This line of associations culminates in the climactic episode in which Orlick threatens Pip with literal bodily dissolution in the limepit. The "Jack," who so bizarrely intrudes on the escape party's sojourn at the riverside, marsh-imbrued inn dovetails with this range of images. He is represented as a slime-clad figure who arises from the river mud, which reminds Pip of the marshes of his childhood, and his physical presence reinforces our sense that Orlick's slouching figure seems to come from and fade into the marshes. The image of a toy boat that is invoked during the Jack episode contributes to an overriding sense of the world emerging from the primordial slime. That image is also caught up in the imaginings stirred by Magwitch and Compeyson's life-and-death struggle in the river's murky depths.

The novel, in short, abounds in nightmarish images of passings out of life into death, but also of still more bizarre eruptions of death into life. Foremost among these are the ghosts and the ghostly presences that mysteriously return from the land of the dead to the precincts of the living. Such presences range from the imagined figures of Pip's parents, as Pip envisions them in the opening scene, to the hilarious but deeply meaningful presence of the ghost of Hamlet's father in Wopsle's London performance. In form at least, most of the ghosts are less primordial than the invasive ear-wigs, the rotting corpses, and the dissolving bodies of Pip's narrative, but they are no less insistent in refracting Pip's preoccupation with comings-into-being and passings-out-of-being.

Not surprisingly, this Pip, who is much obsessed with death, is also preoccupied with birth. Pip's fantasies of origin may be said to be presided over by the magisterially resonant opening scene of the novel. There, Pip not only conjures images of his dead and buried parents, but also in effect represents the birth of his consciousness of himself as a separate being. This takes place in the course of an assault upon him by a figure—that is, by Magwitch—which he takes to be a specter in a setting where he conflates the world of death with an epoch-making moment of birth. Within that scene, the red lines of the setting sun and the fact that the episode takes place on Christmas Eve, marking Christ's nativity, reinforce the sense that we are witnessing a birth as well as a generative nightmare of death and dying. The opening represents Pip's discovery of "the identity of things" through his discovery of the separateness of things. That discovery is expressed in terms of Pip's having discovered that the steeple was the steeple, as opposed to the bundle of shivers that was himself. It is surely no accident that in the experience of this prototypical orphan, who feels, in a sense, that he has had to generate himself, this discovery is couched, in part, in an image of birth. Nor is it surprising that this birth is induced by bleeding horizons and a moment when, turned upside-down by Magwitch, he loses all sense of differentiation between self and world, as though he is on the verge of a mysterious parturition out of the undifferentiated marsh slime. That parturition, however, is in effect the opposite equivalent of the realities of disintegration and death in the marsh. It is as though Pip's emphasis on his emergent consciousness of himself as a discrete entity is in part a buffer against the danger of dissolving back into the slime.

Pip, in fact, lives with an eerie set of fantasies that imply a two-way traffic between the world of the living and the world of the dead. This is rooted in the tenuousness of his sense of his own place in the world and of the infirm boundaries of his own being. His problematical sense of his own boundaries is reinforced by the intense moral and psychological punishment he undergoes, and especially by the manipulation to which he is subjected. Handled by others, pommeled by others, kneaded by others, his boundaries are both incessantly breached and recurrently redefined though such breaching.

Manipulation is, in fact, at the heart of the novel's moral and psychological concerns. Here the fantasy material we have been tracking is reinforced by the external events of the narrative. Throughout *Great Expectations,* manipulation operates at many levels. It starts with Magwitch's physically turning him upside down and the violence of Mrs. Joe's having "brought him up by hand," and it culminates in the impact on him of his entanglement in the intricate plot of the novel. Pip is not only psychologically manipulated by those who initially infused into him his ineradicable sense of guilt, but also by the series of figures who are involved in his expectations. Jaggers's accusingly hurled finger plays an obvious part in amplifying his guilt. So does Magwitch, who has sent the guilt-provoking Jaggers to lure him into the process of becoming a gentleman. Miss Havisham, who entices him into his involvement with Estella at the price of his loyalty to Joe, plays a no less dastardly part in driving him ever deeper into the morass of guilt and betrayal.

Miss Havisham's project of avenging herself on men is achieved by her manipulative use first of Estella and then of Pip himself in relation to Estella. Magwitch's determination to "make" himself a gentleman, so as to compensate for the way his social inferiority has subordinated him to Compeyson and made the courts believe Compeyson's lies about him, has the same motive. He uses Pip, instrumentally, to achieve his own ends.

Here the radically infantile, largely preoedipal fantasies of bodily invasion, boundary breaching, and finally fusing with others meshes meaningfully—and brilliantly—with the novel's moral and thematic interests. *Great Expectations* is, at one level, "about" the ethic of instrumentality. Not only Magwitch and Miss Havisham but also Jaggers and the legal system use others to achieve their ends and in the end dehumanize them by doing so. That dehumanization dovetails with the experience of battering, invasion, and cannibalization that are at work at the level of Pip's infantile fantasies and reinforces his childish fears of being undone.

The interplay between primordial fantasy and the moral and thematic aspects of the novel is in fact one of the striking achievements of *Great Expectations,* and it manifests itself in fine details throughout the text. Pumblechook's Porker homily, for example, centers on a theme of ingratitude—Pip's ostensible ingratitude—but the conflation of Pip and the Porker implies a radical cannibal fantasy: the fantasy that Pip might, like the Porker, be served up, to be eaten, at Christmas. Indeed, the scene of the Christmas dinner early in the novel strikes a clangorous gong of guilt, especially because it is the first dramatized scene in which Mrs. Joe's densely reported guilt provocation is directly presented. That guilt is recurrently amplified by Jaggers's endlessly accusing finger and by the inquisitions to which he subjects Pip. It is further impressed on him by the pervasive presence in Pip's London experience of Newgate, with its threat of hanging and its invasively contaminating smut. The smut, as perceived in a moment when he is waiting to meet Estella in town, stirs up Pip's shame with regard to his plebian origins, but is also linked to all the other invasive aspects of Pip's life, including the grubs and the earwigs of his night at the Hummums.

Guilt, in fact, cruelly pursues Pip through all the stages of his journey, joining other excruciating emotions to make his moral life a misery. It operates almost diabolically, in consort with the shame about his humble origins that Miss Havisham and Estella deliberately elicit in him, to create the central moral dilemma of his development. The human agents of his torture manipulate him in such a way that he is caught in a vicious circle, within which only guilt-provoking denial of his origins can seem to free him from the shame of those origins, while the guilt triggered by that denial elicits further shame because Pip experiences it as betrayal—and especially betrayal of his bond of love and loyalty to Joe. Even Magwitch's partly benign wish to make a gentleman of him enters into this circuit, by feeding the ambition that Satis House has stirred in him. In this way, Pip becomes subject to further shame, as the action unfolds, for his ingratitude to his new benefactor.

Miss Havisham's deliberate moral sadism, as she teases him with the distant, frigid star of an Estella, strengthens the vicious circle in which Pip is trapped. Here, as elsewhere, the violence directed at him elicits emotions that deepen his entrapment, in this case, emotions that spring from his ineradicable experience of his orphan condition: craving for love, frustration at the inaccessibility of that love, and repressed fury at the perpetrators of the abandonment that is at the heart of his experience. It is his fury, in fact, that ultimately shapes Pip's destiny and that constitutes the pivot of his struggle, first to liberate himself from the frustrating relationships that characterize his early life and then to experience something akin to love, in himself, and for others. This, in fact, is what he is shown to achieve, in a limited and self-deceptive way, in the course of his final reconciliation with Miss Havisham, with Magwitch, and with Joe.

The poignant sadness of the novel's ending in fact stems from the magnitude of the distance he has traveled toward liberation from the nightmare of the orphan condition and from his inability to move still further from it. In the end, all he can achieve is the capacity to *nurse* Magwitch, to be nursed by Herbert and by Joe, to forgive Miss Havisham, and to reconcile himself to a life with love, without marriage, without children, without deeply meaningful work. Pip travels a vast distance, even as Dickens has traveled a vast distance, in his own struggle with his orphan imagination—a distance whose magnitude should be measured in terms of the difference between Pip's ending and Oliver Twist's. In the end, however, Pip—and Dickens with him—remains sheathed within the integuments of the rage that, unconsciously, is inscribed in his narrative of his movement beyond it.

Indeed, so profound is the determining power of Pip's orphan condition, that, despite the maturational thrust of the story, and the movement to ever-higher levels of consciousness as well as to more complex relationships with the people who surround him, Pip never fully leaves behind him the early fantasies that figure throughout his narrative. These fantasies permeate the discourse in which he tells us of how he has, on the face of it at least, moved from the state of entrapment in passive expectations to a position of relative freedom from within which he recounts the history of his life. From within that discourse, we are pained to learn of how in the present of the telling—from within his seemingly liberated vantage point—he preserves his infantile sense of the interpenetration of life and death, of the living and of the dead, as well as of his endlessly vulnerable self and the relentlessly invasive others. The very texture of his narrative bears witness to the vividness with which he still envisions these things, and the events he reports are marked by the contents of the fantasies that have impelled him throughout.

This vividness shows itself, among other things, in his fantasies of birth, of coming into being. This radical fantasy finds its key expression in his feeling that he has, in a sense, generated himself. It finds expression in the startling statement of the novel's first sentence: that he named himself, and generated, on his "infant tongue," a name that deviates from his real name. Related to the fantasy of self-generation and self-naming is the sustained enactment, from the beginning of his story, of the need, which he shares with Esther Summerson, to mother those who have played a part in his orphaning—that is, to nurture the parents, or the characters who stand in for the parents, who have, in fact (or at least in his fantasy), failed to nurture him. As with Esther, this reversal not only constitutes a reversal of the impulse toward vengeance, but also a compensation, through identification, for the nurture that he himself has never received.

It is striking, in this regard, that it is Pip who feeds Magwitch at the beginning of the novel and nurses him in the end. In relation to Miss Havisham, he overcomes, as it were, the frustration of the "broken meats" he eats at her house through the identificatory protectiveness he shows when he risks his life in the effort to save her as she goes up in flames. In both cases, Pip reverses roles with the surrogate parents who have played a central part in shaping his experience, and assumes responsiblity for them—as Esther Summerson assumes responsiblity for Lady Dedlock—in ways they never did for him.

These role reversals are part of the maturation that Pip tells us he has undergone and that Dickens imagines for him. Pip's narrative suggests that they are part of the development that frees him from his bondage to his debilitating expectations and from the guilt and shame they generate. As part of his struggle toward liberation, it shows us how he comes to relate to Magwitch and Miss Havisham as people with a life and a life-history of their own, and how he deals with them compassionately, with something akin to love, from within his own hard-earned autonomy. Indeed, his autonomy seems to be expressed in the representation of his reconciliation to them. The plot of the novel is carefully structured to give him the chance to respond empathically to Miss Havisham's remorse at the grief she has caused both Estella and him and to relate compassionately to Magwitch as an appropriate object of sympathy and even identification. Magwitch proves to be an orphan who has suffered experiences very like Pip's own, at a level still deeper and more destructive than his. Although Magwitch's life story may be read—and certainly in part is—as a projection of Pip's sense of his own life, it also constitutes the story of a separate life, to which Pip, in fact, is able to extend in imagination and in feeling.

The signs of maturation are striking throughout. Most of all, the first-person narrative, rooted in the assumption that he himself is recounting the story of his life, sustains the impression of massive growth. The narrative itself, with its finely forged account of the closely interrelated stages of Pip's development, and with the rich play of humor that informs it, suggests that Pip has reached a point of control and of insight that attests his emergence, not only from the iron grip of his orphan sensibility, but also into a ripely "philosophic" view of his life.

At the same time, the narrative shows signs that Pip's emergence is at most partial. It not only suggests that Pip, but also Dickens, have struggled heroically to overcome the orphan condition, but that they are still mired within it. A curious (and decisive) detail in his narrative suggests this. We are thinking of the moment when he contemplates the horror of the mere possibility of his being beholden to Magwitch for his expectations and are referring to the analogy that Pip then draws between his story and that of Frankenstein.

The Frankenstein reference occurs when Pip is contemplating Magwitch, and beginning to identify him—that is, when he is beginning to grasp the possibility of his being beholden to Magwitch rather than to Miss Havisham for his expectations. If this is the case, he must face the possibility that he may be the creature of Magwitch's will, as the monster is the creature of "that student."

This, for him, is a horrendous possibility, and at a variety of levels. "Objectively," it not only threatens him with the prospect that Miss Havisham has not destined him for marriage to his beloved Estella, but also with an origin more degrading than his real one. To be the "creature" of what he thinks is a condemned murderer and confirmed low-life is still worse than to be the child of his sister and the blacksmith at the forge, and to be still more unworthy than ever of the well-bred, ladylike Estella.

At the feeling and fantasy level, other threats are invoked by the association. The Frankenstein story hinges on the fabrication of a living creature from the parts of a dead one—that is, on the possibility, so vivid in the child-Pip's imagination, of traversing the boundaries between life and death, between the organic and the mechanical, and between the past and the present. Such violations are accomplished elsewhere within his narrative by the creepy-crawly things of Miss Havisham's shuttered chamber and the canopy bed's swarming wildlife, as well as by all the instances of ingestion, incorporation, and regurgitation with which the text is filled. They are also implied by the uncanny recurrence of events, perceptions, and people that loom suddenly out of storm or mist, bringing back raw pieces of experience that have not stayed in their place—or in their time—in the course of Pip's ongoing life and that are constantly being resurrected in the process of telling his story. These include recurrences as disparate as Pip's glimpse of the convict with the file, and the startling appearance of Compeyson in the theater as Pip contemplates Wopsle in the role of Hamlet's father's ghost. One such climactic recurrence is Magwitch's materialization at Pip's lodgings when he comes to London—a materialization that in fact gives rise to the Frankenstein reference.

Although it figures only once, that reference resonates with an extraordinary range of fantasies projected within the text. It not only echoes, to start with, the sense that Pip has of being a lay figure in Wopsle's staging of *George Barnwell,* but also in the real life activity of the adults who surround him. It also amplifies in a radical way the sense that he himself is a creature made out of clothing or other random bits and pieces—a fantasy that is confirmed in Pip's account of the sojourn at the inn during the escape episode toward the end of the novel. There, Pip recounts in some detail how the Jack is, quite ghoulishly, made up of items of clothing scavenged piecemeal from drowned sailors. The fantasy of being compounded of random elements finds expression, at the moral and sociological level, in the idea that Magwitch can in fact *make* a gentleman of Pip. Just as the monster is the projection, as it were, of the student's—that is, of Frankenstein's—generative imagination, so Pip may be seen as a creature projected from the imagination of his benefactors and controlled by their will. *This* notion is the more terrifying because it coincides with, and reinforces, our sense that so much of Pip's life has been manipulated by the plot of the novel whose narrative he recounts.

The Frankenstein reference, in its concrete formulation within the text, has a more startling field of reference, however. The text itself, by what seems to be a slip of reference, reverses the direction of the manipulation that it is dramatizing and makes Magwitch Pip's creation rather than Pip Magwitch's. Pip says, as he contemplates Magwitch and all that is implied by his eruption into his life that night, that "the imaginary student pursued by the misshapen creature he had impiously made was not more wretched than I" (354). If Pip is "that" student, then Magwitch must be Pip's "creature"!

This "slip" confirms the hypothesis that we have already put forward: Pip's benefactors may well not be an objective reality but rather some sort of projection. It implies that Pip's narrative, or at least part of it, is a complex, if unconscious, strategy, to help him cope with the stresses of his life within his own version of the orphan condition.

This transgression of boundaries is startling—more spine-tingling at the imaginative and moral level than the ghosts and the maggots of Pip's fantasy life. It functions on the narrative as well as on the psychological plane to reverse much of the manifest drift of the novel. It suggests that Pip's touching account of his life may be read as a fantasy, or at least a fantasy-ridden, projection-drenched vision, which is rooted in his experience but which transforms the realities of his life, such as they may have been, into the terms of his orphan sensibility. Seen in this way, his narrative is an interpretation of his actual experience, within which it is difficult to distinguish fantasy from reality, yet which bears home on us with hallucinatory immediacy the essence of Pip's experience and the intractability of the conflicts Pip, like his creator, is struggling to overcome.

Thus, the seemingly innocuous Frankenstein reference is crucial for understanding the novel and for elucidating the way in which it negotiates the tension between its representation of Pip's growth and development and its refraction of elements in Pip's inner life that undermine that development. The Frankenstein "slip" subverts the relatively unilinear developmental thrust of Pip's story. In doing so, it elucidates what readers in recent decades have come to regard as the text's most controversial crux—namely, the question of whether Pip really takes himself in hand, and emerges from the matrix of his expectations, or whether his ostensible maturation is largely a sort of whistling in the dark—or, worse than that, a self-aggrandizing self-exculpation? And if it is the latter, what is being vindicated?

Our view falls somewhere between the two positions. We think that Pip is ultimately still trapped in his orphan condition, but that, having valiantly striven to overcome it, his entrapment is partial, though crippling. The chief sign of its partiality, despite the strides he has taken toward relative autonomy, is his unwitting indulgence of the furious orphan's ultimate fantasy—the wish-fulfillment fantasy of avenging himself on the surrogates for parents who, as he perceived them, abandoned him, and by abandoning him, have exposed him to the nightmares of his life. In this reading, there is, finally, no affirmably objective "world" in the novel; in this perspective, the entire novel is a structure of multiple interlayered fantasies which work and rework the inaccessible reality from which they spring. Within those fantasies, Pip first projects his images of nightmarish parenting into a variety of figures, and then disposes of them, against his conscious will and judgment, to satisfy an implacable need for vengeance.

In this reading, Mrs. Joe, Miss Havisham, Magwitch, Pumblechook, and Jaggers are not to be apprehended as reliable representations of real people. They are, rather, to be taken as Pip's projected images of the people who have, in his experience of them, tormented him. They take shape in his narrative as representations of what is, in fact, his highly subjective experience. The characters he depicts may have literally, or in biographical fact, been Mrs. Joe, Miss Havisham, and Magwitch, but their representation is determined by the dynamics of Pip's inner life and not by their real-world qualities. Their fate, moreover, is a representation of Pip's wishes with regard to them, as well as to himself, rather than of anything that has happened in the real world.

There are strong traces of Pip's aggressive imaginings. These include the moment when Pip imagines that he sees Miss Havisham hanging in the decayed brewery; the episode in which Pip is co-opted by Wopsle into playing the wretched apprentice George Barnwell, who kills his uncle and benefactor; the recurrent allusions to Hamlet, who must kill his stepfather to avenge his father; and the doublings in his text, like the one that makes Orlick Pip's surrogate in clobbering Mrs. Joe. In this reading, it not only is Orlick who, as Julian Moynahan pointed out long ago, serves as Pip's surrogate in disposing of Mrs. Joe. Instead, all the elements in the novel are subordinated to a plot that objectifies and externalizes's Pip's vindictive needs, much in the way that in *Bleak House* the plot of Lady Dedlock's pursuit and death is shaped by the wishes of Esther and the third-person narrative voice.

In this light, the entire novel may be viewed as an expression of Pip's way of experiencing the world, and of his fantasy-ridden way of dealing with it, rather than as an account of what really happened to him. Indeed, it may be seen as a means for fulfilling his ultimate wishes. Thus, for example, Mrs. Joe, Magwitch, and Miss Havisham figure both as Pip's persecutors and as his victims. Their characterization and the behavior attributed to them express Pip's sense of how they treated him, and their fate is the result of his rage at the suffering he felt he underwent at their hands. In this perspective, what he suffers because of them is, ultimately, the manifestation of his experience of his orphan condition, as realized through these agents of his fate as an orphaned and therefore abandoned child.

Understood in this way, both Magwitch's pathetic death, with Pip loyally nursing him, and Miss Havisham's gruesome conflagration, with Pip's desperate, self-mutilating effort to save her, serve a double function. They satisfy Pip's wish to avenge himself on them, but they serve his no less urgent wish to redeem himself through love, or tenderness, from experiencing guilt for killing them.

Within this construction, the ultimate (but also the original) manipulator in the novel is Pip himself, whose narrative of his life rewrites his story in a way that transforms everything to his advantage. First he creates figures who, much like the images he forms of his parents while contemplating their tombstone in the isolated cemetery, fill some part of the terrible loneliness of his orphan condition. Then, to express how he experienced that condition, he makes of his substitute parents a series of harrowing grotesques that conform to what must have been his sense of his battered childhood and of the people who battered him.

The parent figures he creates are not single, but multiple and mixed; he may be taken to split and recombine the elements of his experience and his fantasy, and he does so through a variety of figures. For mother, he first projects an initial surrogate, in the shape of Mrs. Joe; for father, we get Joe, who is not as grotesque as his wife, but who is a caricature of the wished-for tenderness Pip needs and imagines. Then, doubling them, he projects Miss Havisham and Magwitch—the one, consistently threatening, to begin with, like Mrs. Joe; the other, more ambivalent, because he embodies elements of tenderness, like Joe, and of a terrifyingness that must be taken to be modeled on the intrinsic terror that dominates Pip's vulnerable self. Indeed, through Joe from the beginning, and increasingly through Magwitch as the narrative moves on, he struggles to realize an image of redeeming love that can counter the initial terror, using the comfort he derives from that image as a way of escaping the horror of the basic situation and of the emotions it elicits.

Having shaped the pivotal figures of his narrative, and given them scope for violent action upon him, he then stages their destruction. This, too, serves to express the stresses of his inner life, fulfilling his own underlying needs—his need, finally, for vengeance. Then, he redeems himself for having done so, by imagining and representing the forgiveness and, in Magwitch's case, even the love he can extend to them. Both moves—the destruction of the parent figures and the self-exoneration through reconciliaton with them—are part of the process whereby Pip avoids experiencing the full pain of losing his parents, that is, the loss that exposed him to the horrors of the orphan condition and to inexpressible anguish of his own grief and rage at the torment he has undergone.

This is, by any standard, a radical reading of the novel, and it raises several questions. There is the immediate question of how we establish the boundary between fantasy and reality in a text that purports to tell us about the reality of Pip's life as it unfolds but that turns out to be not only full of fantasy, but in fact wholly determined by fantasy. Our reading holds that *Great Expectations* is a complexly interlayered structure of fantasy within which it is difficult to decide what, if anything, within it is "real."

This question, to be sure, only makes explicit, in an extreme form, something that, it seems to us, has always challenged readers. One of *Great Expectations'* great charms but also one of its greatest difficulties is its pervasive fantasy atmosphere—the sense that Satis House is something out of a nightmare, as are Magwitch's intrusion on Pip in the graveyard and Pip's struggle with Orlick near the lime pit. Even the beautifully modulated and exciting race down the river, for Magwitch's freedom, has a hallucinated quality. Our reading offers a way of understanding the fantastic, often hallucinatory, quality of the experience rendered in the novel; it allows us to interpret and give meaning to its blurring of the distinction between fantasy and reality, even though it does not give us adequate tools for separating what we might take to be the "reality" of Pip's life as it was lived from the fantasy projected through his account of it.

Intertwined with the difficulty of distinguishing between fantasy and reality is the question of whose fantasy we are talking about. Should we think of it as Pip's fantasy? Or as Dickens's? Pip is, after all, an image out of Dickens's fantasy world, and his inner life is generated out of Dickens's own. This is a problem in all fiction, but it is intensified by this novel's powerful fantasy elements and because of the congruity between those elements here and the fantasies that pervade and sustain the other novels.

Great Expectations echoes many of the patterns we enumerated in our Introduction and which we have traced through the novels. Striking among these are the absence in Pip, as in Oliver Twist and in David Copperfield, of direct signs of the aggression we might expect to find in him. His aggression is displaced, as it is displaced in *Oliver Twist* and *David Copperfield,* into doubles and into the plot of the novel itself. As in *Bleak House,* moreover, much of the aggression is displaced into the style of the telling.

Great Expectations, of course, differs from the earlier novels in several major ways. Here, Dickens does for once endow his protagonist with an ample subjectivity and dramatizes the imaginative resonance of his experience, and he does so in an unprecedented way and degree by giving Pip a voice that is very much Pip's own and by dramatizing his struggle to come to grips with his experience in ways that are unmatched in the earlier works. At the same time, *Great Expectations* does reproduce many of the recurrent difficulties of Dickens's treatment of the orphan condition, including, as we have just said, a characteristic pattern of splittings and displacements.

These difficulties are particularly acute here because of the doubleness of the novel's emphases. On the one hand, *Great Expectations* sustains the impression that Pip has, in some meaningful way, come through for himself. On the other, it allows him to shape his narrative in ways that satisfy his vindictive feelings toward his surrogate parents, whom he perceives as his tormentors, and then lets him whitewash himself by ministering to them. Dickens, by plotting the novel as he does, by putting in Pip's mouth the words that he utters, seems to support his self-exculpation.

Beyond this, it is after all, Dickens, not Pip, who has imagined the death of Magwitch and Miss Havisham, as well as of Mrs. Joe. It is Dickens, moreover, who generates and, on the face of things at least, subscribes to Pip's self-absolution, and this, among other things, by creating the impression that Pip has indeed emerged from the haze of his expectations, even though his emergence neither invigorates him nor opens further possibilities for living. Dickens, in short, seems to be more than usually caught up in his ambivalence toward the orphan condition and his sense of how to master it; the very elements that seem to carry him beyond his achievement in the other novels in fact intensify the sense of the similarities between *Great Expectations* and those novels.

How are we to understand the mixed impression we have of Dickens's relation to Pip? It seems to us that in shaping Pip's story as he does, Dickens is reenacting the vicious circle of orphan imaginings that we laid out at the beginning of this study. More than that. It seems to us that in Pip Dickens retraces, as we have noted, the dynamic that has controlled his development from *David Copperfield* through *Little Dorrit,* though he does this at a different level and with different emphases.

Thematically, Dickens's project in *Great Expectations* is to carry Pip beyond the pale of his passive expectations and to give his reader a sense of Pip's relative empowerment as an independent agent—as a more or less full-fledged person who lives, works, and acts in the world. This serves Dickens's manifest theme, which is the importance of work and striving as the ground of life. It is this theme that generates the resistance, and with it the surge of imaginative energy, that fill the novels which follow *David Copperfield.* Pip's ostensible emergence from his expectations into a working life represents a renewed affirmation on Dickens's part of the *Copperfield* imperative of activity in the world and of earning one's place within it.

Here, that affirmation lacks the ideological urgency of David Copperfield's credo, and as a result, *Great Expectations* lacks the tortuousness that makes for its subversion in *Bleak House* and *Little Dorrit.* In *Great Expectations,* Dickens does affirm the imperative of work—of activity in the world—and rejects the passivity of Pip's expectations, and with it, the inheritance fantasy that supports it. Here, he does not subvert the work ethic by foregrounding the nightmarish repressiveness of the distorted Calvinist stringencies of a Miss Barbary or a Mrs. Clennam. Though Mrs. Joe and Pumblechook speak for a view of children akin to that of Miss Barbary and Mrs. Clennam, Pip is given a distance on them that the earlier protagonists lack, a distance that reflects a measure of internal balance.

And yet, much like *Bleak House, Great Expectations* contains a teeming subjectivity that is analogous to the seething inwardness that Esther Summerson struggles to keep under control and that erupts so explosively in the discourse of the third-person counterpart narrative voice. It is this subjectivity that rustles and heaves within Pip's discourse and that may be taken as a response both to the realities of his abandonment and the renunciation of his passive expectations. It is the play of this subjectivity within him that generates the opulent particularization of the orphan experience that he conveys in his narrative, a particularization that may be understood to be nourished both by his original orphan fantasies and by his struggle, in his narrative, to come to grips with those fantasies.

The subversive, or undigested, part of this subjectivity is cognate with the surging rage that informs the third-person narrative voice in *Bleak House* and the narrative voice in *Little Dorrit.* Here, the rage finds its open expression in the nuanced energy of Pip's humor, and its covert outlet in the vengeance that Pip ultimately takes on the manifestly negative parent figures in the novel. As with *Bleak House* and *Little Dorrit,* we take both the rage and its venting through the characters, the plots, the narrators, and the language of the novel to be a manifestation of Dickens's continuing participation in the feeling life of his orphaned and abandoned protagonist. We take it that his continuing capacity to empathize with his protagonist's strategies for deflecting the weakness, the helplessness, and the vulnerability of the orphan condition leads him to identify, at least partially, with Pip's enactment of his vengeance as a way of warding off the intolerable experience of the loss he has undergone. Indeed, we take it that it is out of his struggle with his own identifications that Dickens achieves the splendid representation of the orphan condition that is *Great Expectations.*

It is a question, to what extent Dickens is aware of the intricate play of identifications that marks his treatment of Pip. We take it that he is deeply aware of the bind Pip is in and of the price of Pip's inability to face the deepest level of the conflicts that his orphan condition has generated in him. Yet we think that he also participates in Pip's unself-consciously self-deceiving emphasis on his reconciliation with Magwitch and Miss Havisham. Indeed, we think that it is to justify his own affirmations that he painstakingly constructs the moving scenes of reconciliation that have made many readers feel that Pip has really grown up. We are thinking of the powerful representation of Pip's acceptance of Magwitch first as a kindred spirit and then as a kind of spiritual father, a representation that finds its climax in the courtroom scene which Dorothy Van Ghent celebrates for symbolizing a kind of redemption from the splits and animosities that have filled Pip throughout—and of the scene in which he responds to Miss Havisham's plea to forgive her.

Yet we also believe that Dickens is aware of the problematical nature of Pip's seeming affirmations. This shows itself in his representation of the imaginative and emotional depletion Pip suffers at the end. In depicting that depletion, he shows, moreover, a profound understanding of the dynamics of the projective imagination, as they play themselves out in Pip, and of its place in vitalizing or failing to vitalize the individual and his world. One measure of his understanding is the novel's treatment of the nature of projection itself and of the place of imagination in the lives of the characters who fill Pip's narrative.

One of the more extraordinary aspects of *Great Expectations* is the depth and consistency of its representation of the workings of the projective imagination. Central to its vision of life is the notion that imagination, like the projections that spring from it, is rooted in abandonment, victimization, helplessness, and humiliation, in extreme situations of powerlessness, vulnerability, and loss. *Great Expectations* suggests that imaginative creativity itself is rooted in the desolation of the self: here, emphatically, the orphan self, with its complex history of loss and of the need at one and the same time to reexperience the anguish of that loss and to circumvent the full impact of loss itself. It also insists that the price of such creativity is the loss of contact with reality and the depletion that the self undergoes because of that further loss.

It is one of the striking things about *Great Expectations* that so many characters in the novel confirm the sense of the vivid but problematical life of the imagination that is conveyed through Pip. Their lives and environments are imaginative constructs that are rooted in deprivation. For them, renunciation of the fantasies projected in the forms their lives take leads to an attenuation of their sense of being. The moment they move beyond the compulsiveness, verging on automatism, that leads them to enact to the fullest the grotesqueness of their lives in the story, they lose energy, force, and intensity. At the same time, life within the worlds that their projected inwardness creates for them is endlessly thwarting, though it is vivid. This is so because their worlds lack suitable objects of desire or the possibility of relating to such objects in life-affirming ways.

Miss Havisham's world—that is, Satis House, when Pip enters it, and all the elements of its representation—proves to be the elaborate product of her imagination. Through it, she lives out her virulent hatred of men, which, in turn, is a reflex of her mortal humiliation by Compeyson when he jilted her at the altar; through it, she also punishes herself, but also wards off every possibility of life-giving interaction with the world. Magwitch's effort to "make" a gentleman also may be seen as the outcome of his own life history. It is his mode of imagining a way out of the mortifying bondage and degradation within a state of orphanhood and abandonment that first marginalizes and then criminalizes him. Similarly, Wemmick's castle, with its grotesque appurtenances, may be regarded as the imaginative product of the embattlement he feels within a world that demands that he suppress all his empathic and compassionate feelings and treat his fellows as the source of nothing but portable property. And Mrs. Joe's obsessional account of the troubles Pip has caused her would seem to be her own way of generating a livable world. Her querulous aggression not only creates the ambience in which Pip must grow, but also generates an environment that convinces her of her own validity and vitality.

Even Joe fictionalizes. Joe is the character in the novel who is least given to imagining, and his productive labor is represented on the whole as the direct—the virtually unmediated—outcome of his pleasure in making things. But his memorial couplet to his father is in fact a compensatory construct, designed to whitewash the brutality and the drunkenness that not only led to Joe's childhood battering and to the death of his mother, but also to the illiteracy that continues to mar his life.

In effect, *Great Expectations* lays out an anatomy of fantasy and imagination that is analogous to what we found in *Little Dorrit*. In both, reality comes to be perceived as a system of reciprocal projections of fantasies rooted in the psychic needs of everyone who participates in the field of relationships that is under scrutiny. *Great Expectations* may be said to go deeper than *Little Dorrit* in the way that it enages more fully the particular life history of the characters whose losses have spurred their imagination. It suggests that although fantasy and imagination may be rich in projected life, they distort reality and diminish the scope of experience. Indeed, it entertains the notion that what is imagined can be regarded as lies, which is how Joe designates Pip's account of the wonders of his first visit to Satis House.

Joe's formulation is, of course, comically reductive. Its relevance is confirmed, however, in the way the novel suggests that fantasy distances and ultimately strips its objects of their independent reality, and shows how it constitutes a manipulation that makes love impossible. The life of the imagination does not repair loss by augmenting the images of its objects. Rather, it leads to a greater loss—the loss of the reality of the person with whom the fantasizer is interacting. It, therefore, also leads to a depletion of the self, because the self must enter into viable relationships with others to live with some degree of fullness.

Pip's account of his infatuation with Estella reinforces this view of the projective imagination. It encompasses an etiology of both fantasy and of the projections it nurtures and it dramatizes the dynamics of his entrapment within projective systems. Pip's lyrical "rhapsody," on losing her, particularizes the projective nature of his love. It illustrates how his imagination, seeking her in her absence, extrudes an image of her out of his head into the world in a way that is different from his experience of her when she was present to him as herself.

In his rhapsody, Pip sees her everywhere, because her presence informs all vistas; he reads her in a variety of circumstances and objects. It is as though his loss of her and the emptiness he experiences because of the absence of response from outside himself is the condition for his forming of an image of her, within himself, which is then projected onto the world outside. At the linguistic level, it is as though the "broken words" he utters with the gushing of the heart's blood caused by her loss generate the gorgeously articulated language of the rhapsody itself. Here, the sort of inarticulateness that makes Daniel Peggotty bleed from the mouth at the loss of Emily is superseded in Pip by the gift of transforming pain first into images and actions and then into words. This transformation may be taken as a metonymy for the entire process of Pip's use of language as a way of dealing with his experience.

The irony of Pip's virtually magical command of language—and Dickens gives him a curtailed version of the full range of his own extravagant verbal resources—is that language, even in Pip's mouth, cannot transform either his inner or his outer reality. In the last analysis, there is no way for Pip to retrieve Estella by rhapsodizing about her or to transmute his orphan condition into anything more than the story he tells. In the end, Herbert's warning to Pip as they plan Magwitch's escape, when he writes "Don't go home," enunciates the terrible truth of Pip's condition, namely, that there is no way back to the point of origin and no way to rectify the nightmare of the experience the original abandonment gave rise to. There is no way to go home, certainly no way to retrieve it through language.

Indeed, the Hummums episode, in which Pip finds sanctuary for the night in a hotel that bears the name of a Turkish bath, where he undergoes the hallucinatory envisioning of the grubs, the blue-bottles, and the ear-wigs, concludes with an exercise in the effort to achieve control through language. There, Pip conjugates the imperative "Don't go home" as though he can control it and transform it in terms of his desire. Clearly, he cannot succeed, because he is stranded within his ineradicable wish to go back to the home he never had. Indeed, his verbal prestidigitations are rooted in the impossibility of reaching back across the boundary between past and present, as well as between self and world, that is the condition for language.

Estella is central to the etiology of the wishes that are linked to Pip's nostalgia for what he never had, as well as to the role of both fantasy and language in his relation to what he longs for. We take it that Estella is, for Pip, essentially a stand-in for his absent and, therefore, from his point of view, his cruelly abandoning mother. She is a representation of the essential meaning for him of the unimaginable mother whom we nonetheless see Pip imagining, in the opening scene, to be sickly and freckled, on the tenuous but richly imaginative basis of the lettering on her gravestone. Between the moment when Pip imagines his mother and the moment Estella appears on the scene, we encounter other mother images. We have had the harsh and elaborately imagined figure of Mrs. Joe, with Joe himself as a kind of filler for the maternality that is absent in his wife. Then we have the no less forceful and far more bizarre image of Miss Havisham, with Magwitch as an anomalous but relatively maternal figure. Finally, we have the solitary and unadorned presence of Estella, who is the incarnation of absent motherliness.

Estella too undergoes modulations in the course of Pip's experience of her. First, there is an actively cruel child Estella, who openly mocks and torments Pip. Then there is a passively but tormentingly unresponsive Estella whom he courts in the course of his basic training as a gentleman. Finally, there is the Estella who removes herself from the sphere of Pip's expectations by plighting her troth to Drummle. This last Estella, who is the Estella of the rhapsody, is the most remote of these figures; indeed, she is, like his real and original mother, finally lost to him. It is, therefore, no surprise that Pip sees her everywhere, as he dimly "saw" his mother by reading her out of the letters on her grave. In both cases, we see him displacing the image in his head onto what is out there, in the world—objectifying, as it were, what has existed within his imagination and expressing its reality in words.

All the images, however, and finally the changing image of Estella, represent the crystallization of a fixed, inner image of a hostile, abandoning mother. It is presumably the craving for that mother that initially fixes Pip on Estella—on the remote, starlike, coldly bejewelled Estella—and thus facilitates Miss Havisham's sustained manipulation of him through her. It is, explicitly, Estella's remoteness and unattainability that fixes him on his adoration of her, on his yearning for her, and on the impossibility of achieving a virile assertiveness toward her.

Pip's rhapsody follows the sequence of events in which Estella separates herself from Pip. Because he has more or less effectively internalized the separation, she becomes a kind of blank screen onto which he displaces his feelings, rather than a presumably concrete person onto whose present characteristics he projects his inner needs. That she has come to be what he himself perceives as a blank, rather than an ostensibly active agent, suggests that he has created or at least accepted a boundary between himself and her in response to the boundary she has drawn by marrying Drummle. Because he has established this boundary, however provisional it may be, he can contemplate the reality of her absence by rhapsodizing about her. But in doing so, he is implicitly recognizing—or Dickens, at least, is recognizing—that as Pip's fantasy image, onto which he projected his own needs, she was never really there, as herself, out there, on the other side of the boundary that has come to mark and therefore to define the limits of his existence within himself.

That boundary, which not only should separate Pip from Estella, but also from the world, provides, as it were, a membrane that contains such selfhood as he can achieve. We might expect that its firming up would serve to generate a space within Pip where his consolidation of his own sense of being would facilitate a richer life for himself. We might imagine that on a firmer ground of selfhood, he might reach outward, and even project outward, in a more rewarding and less eviscerating way: that he might reinvest the energy of imagination and desire in more suitable objects.

The reality is different. Dickens's representation of Pip's experience, as distinct from the anatomy of projection for which it is the vehicle, cleaves to the immediacies of his orphan plight, so that the violation of the boundary betweeen himself and the world is in fact the heart of the novel's most palpable vitality. Much of the story's energy, starting with the powerful opening scene, stems from Pip's rendering of how the line that separates him from the world is breached, and how it is recurrently restored in all its fragility, only to be disrupted again. It is as though the novel's imaginative dynamism derives from the two-way traffic across that line. Brutal reality intrudes on Pip in a way that confirms his sense of its relentless invasiveness and in response his fantasy fares forth again with equivalent force. In doing so, it generates the field of projections that the novel portrays and that is, in effect, the novel. Dickens's/Pip's very struggle to overcome this process and to emerge from the field of battering and of projection that defines Pip's essential experience only deepens his entrapment within it.

Not surprisingly, the novel begins with the traffic across the tenuous bounds of Pip's identity. Magwitch, lurching from among the graves whose boundary Pip has already crossed when he generates his image of his dead parents, violently turns him over, so that the world goes topsy-turvey, and he loses whatever tentative sense of self he had already achieved. Integral to the drama of that scene is the restoration, after Magwitch has turned him right side up, of his consciousness that the world-out-there is really out there and not him, while the bundle of shivers, as distinct from the steeple, is in fact him. His stunning disorientation when Magwitch suddenly tips him over serves to bear home to him the nightmarish reality of his being just that: a bundle of shivers and, for the moment, nothing more.

From that point on, Pip's most vivid experience springs from the great variety of breachings, at different psychic and moral levels, of the boundaries of his selfhood, but also of his continuous existence in time. Throughout the novel, the past erupts into the present, even as his inwardness is extruded into the world outside. The resolution of the novel, entailing Pip's very partial emergence from some of his childhood vulnerabilities, makes for a curtailed liberation from the threat of violent incursions and disruptive manipulation. His liberation, such as it may be, is accompanied, however, by a loss of intensity. As he moves toward the end of his story, he not only loses the teasing sight of Estella in every vista and every prospect, he loses every sense of prospect, in the other sense of the word, of things to look forward to, to strive toward—of the expectations that he has in fact renounced.

Indeed, by the end, Pip has not only renounced the expectation of property and the dream of being a gentleman; he has also renounced the hope for a meaningful future. We feel, as he contemplates Joe and Biddy's domestic happiness, that he cannot envision for himself any sort of love, or marriage, or parenthood, and that he is not likely to generate any other sort of dreams or ambitions. For Pip, by the end of his trajectory through his tale, seems no longer to have any way to mobilize his imagination in ways that could invest the outside world with vitality and meaning.

The sense of dreariness that informs the present time from within which Pip tells his story may seem to be a correlative of the apparently contradictory impulses that govern the end of the novel. On the one hand, it springs from the backfiring of the maturation Dickens allows him, and of the renunciation of the wish-fulfillment fantasies that Dickens himself seems to have achieved in failing to provide him with an Agnes or an Amy, to sustain even the illusion of a "happy ending" in any form. Instead of being energized by this renunciation, however, Pip undergoes an emotional and imaginative emptying out. On the other hand, the dreariness and the sense of hopelessness of the ending may be understood to have been determined by Pip's enactment, in his story, of the murderous fantasy with which Dickens indulges him, and by the undermining of his sense of self-identity because of it.

These impulses are not contradictory, of course. It is Dickens's renunciation of the fantasy of his hero's restoration to the comfort of a mother-woman like Agnes or Amy that unleashes the culminating wish fulfillment of the novel. Pip, finally, enacts the prototypical orphan fantasy of avenging himself for his deprivations by destroying the perpetrators of the abandonment that is at the root of the deprivations. The price of such liberation from his hauntings and his regressive longings as Pip may be said to have achieved is, therefore, his virulent enactment of the fantasies bred out of those longings, namely, his "killing off" of Magwitch and Miss Havisham. Unconsciously to indulge wish fulfillments such as these is to guarantee the attenuation of his sense of being. You cannot liquidate your parents without liquidating the better part of yourself.

This is the case in spite of the fact that Pip seems to have achieved a great deal by the end. He has, as we have just noted, in fact been freed from his bondage to Estella, and he has concomitantly freed all the major characters in the drama of his upbringing from the iron grip of the grotesqueness his fantasy has imposed on them. Magwitch especially has undergone a dramatic softening and humanization, so that, liberated from the fantastic mold in which the child-Pip had cast him, he has become an object of sympathy. Even Miss Havisham has become a pitiable victim as well as a reprehensible victimizer. The price of Pip's letting go of these figures as objects of his childhood fantasy, however, is their destruction and with it an augmented sense of emptiness within himself: an emptiness that no longer generates images or actions. Rather, it leaves him deeply solitary—a mere witness of the lives of others rather than the hero of his own.

What remains for him, it would seem, is the capacity to tell his story. Its telling, as we interpret it, reflects the fact that he clings to the desires that control that part of his narrative which is a story of unconscious revenge and a no less unconscious self-exculpation. By the time of the telling—that is, by the time his story is all retrospect—he seems able to energize himself only through the semblance of control that the telling affords him through the reliving, by reimagining, his experience in the course of his narrative. The control he achieves, limited though it is, exacts a terrible price—the price of the further attenuation he undergoes by the end of his story. This attenuation is caused both by the ostensible renunciation of fantasy and projection and by the survival within him of the unexplored emotions, of pain and loss, that inform his entire life and that, ultimately, generate his culminating fantasy of retaliation.

Pip's narrative is not, of course, directly focused on the unconscious processes we have been describing, and its manifest emphasis is his emergence from, and not his continuing entanglement in, the vicious circle of orphan desire. Nor does *Great Expectations* directly address the issues with which we have been dealing in our discussion of his motives for narrative. *Great Expectations* in fact contains no scene of writing and never directly explores Pip's reasons for telling his story.

Yet it seems to us that the memoir of Pip's life that constitutes the novel represents an effort to master the primordial terrors of his earliest experience and to contain the continuing threat of regression into the engulfing terrors of the orphan condition. It seems to us that, like David Copperfield's story or Esther Summerson's part of *Bleak House,* Pip's narrative must be read as an effort to achieve a sense of the coherence of his experience, with a view to containing the disruptive energy of his conscious and unconscious life as well as to imposing some order upon the elusiveness, the treacherousness, and the instability of his experience. No less pressing, we take it, is the need to shore up such identity as he has achieved by the end of his narrative, but also the need to conceal from himself as well as from his readers what we take to be the ultimate horror of his narrative, namely, the fact that it is so largely an externalization of his tormented inwardness and an occasion for indulging in a wish-fulfillment fantasy that obstructs and obviates any chance of final emergence into some fullness of life and being.

Pip's continuing entrapment can be elucidated by two closely related elements in his personal history: the kind of men and women who figure in the course of his growing up and how Dickens places him in relation to them. The alignment of gender roles and the modes of Pip's internalizing them—or rather, his way of refusing to internalize them—have a strong bearing on the absence of any sort of full-blown assertiveness in his personality and on the immobility that characterizes his life at the end.

The male figures that Pip must deal with in the course of his growing up are, ultimately, victims, and both embody what Pip (and Dickens) perceive as feminine traits. Joe is a powerful figure—a muscular smith, who is, Pip tells us, gentle as a woman, and his relationship with Pip is tender and often maternal. Magwitch starts out as a powerfully threatening figure, but he, too, relates to Pip with a spark of tender love and a gruff but tender nurturingness. Even in the graveyard, at the beginning, when he very nearly scares the wits out of Pip, Magwitch, as he later tells Pip, identified with him as a person analogous to himself— as the little boy Magwitch whose first consciousness of himself is of standing alone and nameless in a turnip field, wondering about the names of the birds. In the course of his long struggle to "make" Pip, to transform him into "his" gentleman, moreover, his conscious motive was affection for the child who had fed him, who had not tattled on him, and who had in fact saved his life. For his part, Pip's relationship with this curious father figure is an implicitly maternal one. It starts out with Pip feeding him and ends up with his nursing him, albeit to his death. In this, Pip's nursing echoes Joe's tender relation to him, both in his childhood and in the course of his recovery from the illness that follows Magwitch's death.

Dickens in effect gives Pip a pair of father figures who provide no models for channeling or transforming aggression in socially effective ways. Both are deeply nonassertive figures; both are, ultimately, victims of early abandonment or abuse. On the other hand, the mothers who figure in his development serve as models for the venting of aggression, but not for channeling or transforming it. Pip, in any case, gags on their modes of being; by the evidence of his narrative, he refuses to internalize their modes of operation, though he does accept the burden of the guilt they inflict on him.

In this respect, he provides, as we have suggested earlier in this chapter, an interesting contrast to Esther Summerson, who takes in and acts upon the moralism of her surrogate mother, only modifying its violence, and directing it chiefly at herself. Her style of self-organization, of ordering time, and of recording experience reflects this internalization. Pip's very mode of discourse refuses the moralism of Mrs. Joe and her cohorts and shows no signs of Esther's rigid self-constraint. Even when he is tormented by shame with regard to his blackened fingernails or his naming of Jacks, he suffers from the shame, but does not actively mobilize himself, as Esther does, to judge himself cruelly in terms of it. There is, in fact, no institutionalization, within the narrating Pip—that is, within the adult Pip—of the predatory conscience that is at work in Esther.

The polarization of possibilities for dealing with one's aggression—on the one hand, to incorporate it like Esther, and effectuate it against oneself and to vent it, like Mrs. Joe and Miss Barbary; and on the other hand to deflect it altogether—is close to the core of the difficulty that haunts the entire body of Dickens's work. Both poles obviate the possibility of mediating aggression and channeling it in constructive ways. Dickens, in effect, exempts Pip from the stresses of crucial processes of development that must be undergone if one is to mature and be able to harness one's aggression for a vigorous life. Although he represents a Pip who is striving, even in his narrative, to bring together his present and his past, and to integrate the poles of his experience, Pip achieves no integration of his desperate need for love or of the rage that its absence generates in him. Pip is not provided with the escape hatch of an inheritance or with the equally debilitating comfort of the mother-wife Dickens provides for David and Clennam, but he also does not reach the point where he can mediate the active and the passive, or the aggressive and the regressive aspects of his personality and experience.

Pip's relation to his anger, and his failure to confront it or to integrate it, may be illuminated in terms of *Great Expectations*' treatment of property and inheritance, as these bear upon questions of identity formation. We have been speaking of Pip's affinity with Joe and Magwitch, and there is a sense in which he may be seen, willy-nilly, to have absorbed them, or at least relevant aspects of them, into the amiable but passive side of himself. There is another sense, though—the sense evoked by all the gaggings and chokings in which the novel abounds—in which Pip refuses to internalize them, even as he refuses to internalize the mother figures he depicts.

Pip's refusal to retain Magwitch's wallet, or to claim his property in Australia, entails a refusal of inheritance. Specifically, it reflects a refusal to accept any aspect of the heritage that comes from the active, masculine Magwitch—a refusal that is the more dramatic because so much of his fantasy life has been caught up in his Miss Havisham/Estella expectations. In effect, this refusal of property is another version of his self-naming; Pip, in a sense, insists on generating himself, on being autochthonous. As we have suggested in dealing with Pip's fantasies of birth, the orphan in him would like wholly to generate himself. He despairs of doing this, however, not chiefly because he knows it is impossible, but because he needs to refuse what comes to him from those who have come before him and betrayed him so horrendously—even as, in another dimension of his being, he has needed so desperately to swallow what they offer.

So radical is Pip's operative refusal to incorporate origins that he rejects even Wemmick's version of inheritance: the version that insists on the portability of property, on its absolute separability from its sources. Wemmick dissociates the mourning rings he wears and the "gifts" he amasses from the reality of the people who bestow them and from the world of violence from which they derive. Wemmick's relation to portable property is based on a disjunction analogous to the dissociation of his Walworth emotions from his Little Britain emotions. His psychic and moral split is designed, in all realms to which it applies, to prevent seepage from one realm into another. Past and present are meant to be airtight too, as are death and life; to place any of the terms of these dichotomies in relation to each other is to place himself and the poles of his experience in danger of dissolution through intercontamination.

The primary "moral" of the Wemmick story in general, and its relevance to the issues of Pip's development, is that the realms dichotomized in Wemmick's structuring of his reality are not dissociable. The violence of Little Britain and the Newgate world wells up in the Walworth world in a great variety of indirect but meaningful ways. Like Grimwig's eruptions in *Oliver Twist* or Boythorn's in *Bleak House,* the comic poppings-off of Wemmick's Walworth cannon signify the penetration of the violence of the one world into the other. Even the drama of gentle attentiveness to the Aged Parent involves an implicit enslavement, not unlike the imprisonments of Newgate; the flaring up of the Aged Parent's sausage, as Pip toasts it, may be taken to be emblematic of an oedipal eruptiveness within that fortified realm of filial devotion and bucolic innocence. Similarly, it is implicit that what comes with portable property cannot be dissociated from that property. Violence, death on the gallows, blackmail, and the smut that rubs off on Pip—all these are implicit in Wemmick's funerary paraphernalia and the portable property that is linked to it.

Pip vigorously distances himself from Wemmick's dichotomizations. His refusal of Wemmick's advice, to hold on to Magwitch's wallet and the riches it contains, represents an implicit recognition of the impossibility of dichotomizing one's existence. Dickens's elaboration of the Wemmick material serves to drive home this moral; his representation of Pip's growth and development seems designed to suggest the need for achieving a more integrated identity.

Yet in the end Pip lives with an inner split as subversive as Wemmick's. We refer to the split between the aggression he has not yet digested and the amiable tone of his narrative, with its brilliant play of language and its elegaic resolvedness, even when the experience it represents is full of violence and terror. No less dramatic is the gap between the true sources of his bedevilment and the consciousness of himself that is refracted through his discourse. Although he refuses Wemmick's deeply problematical portable property solution to the problem of how to incorporate his past in his present—of how to lodge his antecedents, which are his heritage from the past in his emergent identity—he can find no alternative way to integrate the conflicting terms of his experience. He does refuse to appropriate what remains of his anticipated inheritance, and he formally renounces the desires linked to the fantasy of inheritance. Yet the question remains of where the heritage—the desires and the angers—of his early life has gone, and to what extent his depletedness at the end of his story is a function of their repression—of his inability to incorporate, in whatever way is available to him, what comes from his past.

What does remain for Pip is the capacity to look back. His retrospection has a sharp double edge, analogous to the doubleness of the fantasy projections it contains. On the one hand, Pip energizes himself by reexperiencing the vivid but terrifying nightmare of his early life, and he enacts the underlying needs of his orphan existence through the wish fulfillments of his narrative. He also tempers his early experience and the terrors it entails with the filter of language, of humor, and of the firmly forged structure of his narrative. He generates a simulacrum of identity through the language and the structure in which he casts his story. His narrative revivifies his experience for himself and for us. It cannot, however, revitalize him through its telling. His story, like all stories, is, after all, a passing thing. And the content of his story, with its unself-conscious reenactment of his unassimilated aggression, guarantees that he can find no way of mobilizing his energy and his imagination for action in the world.

It is part of the achievement of *Great Expectations* that it will not let Pip get away with the illusion that he has freed himself from the iron grip of orphanhood and abandonment. Although Pip would like to think that he has laid the ghosts of the past, they are too palpably present for this to be the case. The ghosts of the past cannot be tamed; they rise up with every movement of Pip's psyche and of Pip's tongue—with every stroke of Dickens's pen, as it gives tongue to "Pip"'s experience. These ghosts are not merely the literal ghosts of the narrative, like the comic presence of the ghost of Hamlet's father in Wopsle's grotesque performance, or the all too palpable, all too real, "ghost" that is Compeyson in the theater. They are also the ineluctable and unexorcizable ghosts of Pip's (but also of Dickens's) ineradicable orphan experience: the residue of the pain, the desire, and the anger that generate the fantasies that control Pip's life.

Hence, the power of the strangely haunting, pervasively haunted narrative that is the novel, which ends up giving us a Pip who no longer lives within the world of the projections that fill his story, and who cannot mobilize desire to engage a world—his present world—that is no longer energized by those projections. All he can do in the depleted state into which he emerges after his story has "ended" is regale us with that story and its account of the world as it once was for him.

Pip's narrative may be seen to provide a paradigm for the story of Dickens's life, work, and development. More valiantly than the protagonist that he so brilliantly shapes here, into whom he infuses so much of his own energy of imagination, Dickens has struggled with his own beleaguerment within his own version of the orphan condition. Like Pip, he has striven to batter his way out of it, and he has ultimately failed to emerge from it. Even here, in *Great Expectations,* he cannot bring his hero out of his orphan floundering, though he has striven heroically to salvage a life and an identity for him. From within that striving he has forged the powerful novel that Pip inhabits.

The ultimate source of Dickens's version of the orphan condition is, as we noted in our Introduction, impossible to determine. Much of it is doubtless shaped by his experience of having been abandoned to the blacking warehouse at an early age—an experience that he recurrently translated, in his fiction, into the more radical state of orphanhood. As we noted in the Introduction, however, the compendious imaginings of that condition, and of the images that can be generated from its conflicts, must be rooted in far earlier experience—finally, in the unassuaged terrors of his very early life. Clearly, he knew its anguish on his pulses, and, like Pip, never came clear of it, though he made much of it, in every sense of the word—especially, like Pip, by telling stories generated from within it.

That telling gives rise to the coruscating body of his work, within which he has delineated the plight and the agony of the orphaned and the abandoned with an intensity that no other novelist approaches. Dickens's novels not only involve us in the anguish of the orphan condition. They also, as we noted at the outset, project a rage for justice and an appeal for compassion rarely matched in literature.

7
A Bibliographic Overview

IN SETTING OUT OUR VIEW OF DICKENS'S WORK, WE HAVE PRETTY largely sidestepped the rich and ramified literature on Dickens. In what follows, we address several issues and spheres of discourse that seem worth further exposition. One is the biographical evidence with regard to Dickens's relation to the problems of orphanhood and abandonment. Another is the historical background of the orphan theme. A third is the Dickens discourse in recent decades—the discourse that follows on the "classical positions" with which we deal in the Introduction.

1. *The Biographical Evidence.* Since Foster's *Life,* which appeared within six years of Dickens's death, biographies have placed greater and lesser emphasis on the autobiographical fragment that Forster embedded in his text. Over the past century and a quarter, Dickens scholars have variously related to his experience in the blacking warehouse his passionate involvement with issues of social justice as well as the centrality to his work of situations of loss, bereavement, abandonment, and orphaning. Especially since Edmund Wilson's "The Two Scrooges," biographers have increasingly stressed as a decisive element in Dickens's development the experience of declassing and identity blurring that he underwent at Warren's. Indeed, with growing consciousness of the complexity of Dickens's sensibility and experience, and of the desperation and frenzy that underlay the exuberance celebrated by late nineteenth-century hagiography, the impact on Dickens's life of his relegation to Warren's blacking factory has held an increasingly central place in the effort to factor the dynamics of his inner life and of his relation to the outer world.

Indeed, the biographical sources of Dickens's radical sense of abandonment have been richly elaborated and explored by scores of his biographers and by critics of his work. Utilizing primarily the fragment of the autobiography in Foster's biography and the autobiographical elements in *David Copperfield,* the major biographers of the past half century—J. Edgar Johnson, Norman and Jean Mackenzie, Fred Kaplan, and Peter Ackroyd—have largely succeeded in demonstrating the centrality for his work of his experience of the traumatic collapse of his childhood world with the bankruptcy and incarceration of his father and his own proletarianization in Warren's blacking factory.

There have been dissenting views, of course. One of the more dramatic of these is Alexander Welsh's *From Copyright to Copperfield.* Welsh's revisionist reading proposes that Dickens's later character was not determined by experience of the blacking factory, but rather that the autobiographical fragment, with its sad tale of abandonment to the ravages of the blacking experience, was a fabrication designed to allay the bad conscience Dickens came to be afflicted by in the course of the copyright battle he had waged before first the autobiographical fragment and then *David Copperfield* were written.

The great majority of readers take the traditional view, however, and we hold to it as well. We hold to it, however, with the complication that we have come to believe that the trauma of the blacking warehouse must have been grafted onto far earlier experiences—onto preoedipal configurations that in fact shape decisive elements in his life and work and that lay the groundwork for the resonance of the blacking episode. Having tracked through the novels the pattern of fantasies that inform the Dickens world, we have been persuaded that they cannot be derived exclusively from the traumatic experiences Dickens underwent at the age of twelve, but must be rooted in deep-seated infantile experience. The reason is our sense of the ubiquity and determining power of these fantasies.

It must be acknowledged, however, that the biographical evidence that would allow us directly to derive Dickens's sense of abandonment from earlier experience is elusive and at best fragmentary. Indeed, the material directly available from the hard biographical sources is very like the evidence we have garnered from the novels themselves. It is material that expresses what we take to be Dickens's radical anxieties and his infantile desires exclusively through metaphor and dramatized situations. This material must be interpreted to reach the position we argue in this study.

The evidence available is more or less as follows. Scanning the biographical record, we learn that Dickens's adult memory, recalling what may well have been his most jolting geographic wrench—the trip, at the age of ten from his beloved Chatham to the dreaded world of London—reflects deep trauma. He writes that he was "packed like game" (Ackroyd, 55), suggesting the ubiquitous presence of a fantasy that translates all loss and injury into the root fantasy of being hunted and slaughtered and then sold to be eaten. A similar metaphor figures in his account of being taken in childhood to a lying-in where he saw the corpses of four dead infants laid out on a cloth. He writes that the spectacle reminded him of "pigs' feet as they are usually displayed at a neat tripe shop." This transformation, even in childhood, as he remembered it, of the spectacle of death into what he later spoke of, when referring to himself, as "boy-slaughter" (Kaplan, 28), constitutes suggestive evidence of the presence in Dickens himself as child of a very fragile sense of self, of blurred boundary lines between fantasy and reality, and of doubt about the integrity of the self and the stability of the world: doubts that are reminiscent of what is represented in the first chapter of *Great Expectation,* when Pip, turned topsy-turvy, learns the "identity of things." It suggests, again, that the radical experience of abandonment at the age of twelve must have been preceded by substantial parental failures in mediating his process of separation from them, of individuation as himself.

And indeed, Dickens expressed very clearly in adult life his sense that he was a neglected child, a "not overly-particularly taken-care-of boy" (Mackenzie, 8). "My parents," he said, "were of the sort whose care at best soon ends" (Kaplan, 134). Although we know very little about his early childhood—how the constant moving from house to house affected him or how the ever-tightening noose of debt and the threat of ensuing bankruptcy were translated into a sense of his parents' failure to nurture—it seems to us that there is a link between the endless evidence in his writings of such failure in the experience of his characters and his actual experience as a child.

The persistence of his tendency to imagine experience in terms of radical infantile fantasies finds more direct expression in his translation of his anger at being financially exploited in adult life by his parents and siblings into a vision of how "all of them, look upon me as something to be plucked and torn to pieces for their advantage. They have no idea of, or care for, my existence in any other light" (Ackroyd, 395). He also calls his family "blood-petitioners" (Kaplan, 158), a phrase that lines up with the sense of "boyslaughter."

Kaplan sums up all of this in his analysis of the Dickens image of the dead babies as pigs' feet neatly lined up in a tripe shop. "Many of his most potent descriptions of death and dying associate the bodies of the dead with food for the living.... From childhood on he became obsessed with cannibalism, with images and scenes of human beings ingesting other human beings, of people being transformed into food, and also with the act of eating, both as a festival and as Thyestes' feast" (Kaplan, 29).

Despite the lack of hard and fast direct evidence about neglect in early childhood, biographers, at least since Edgar Johnson's monumental two-volume study of 1952, have increasingly tended to postulate a problematic relationship between Dickens and his mother, and they have variously pointed to evidence of hostility rooted in experience that long antedates the resentment stirred by the fact that, in Dickens's own words in the autobiographical fragment, "I never afterwards forgot, I never shall forget, I never can forget that my mother was warm for my being sent back" to Warren's (Ackroyd, 95).

Angus Wilson and Fred Kaplan, among Dickens's major interpreters and biographers, are especially explicit about the problematics of the relationship between Dickens and his mother; both stress the workings of what we call orphan fantasies within his imaginative life and within his fiction. In a review of Kaplan's book, John Bayley singles Kaplan out for praise with regard to the emphasis he places on the cannibal motifs in the fiction, but regrets that he does not make more of it than he does—though as the passage from Kaplan we have just quoted should show, Kaplan goes very far in stressing the centrality of the motif.

Material that serves to reinforce Kaplan's stress on cannibalism was in fact copiously exhumed some few years later in Harry Stone's *The Night Side of Dickens: Cannibalism, Passion, Necessity,* though it is not interpreted by Stone himself. Even in its raw state, however, it offers a cornucopia of details for readers like us who are concerned with the configuration of such fantasies in Dickens's imagination. Our own readings bear witness to the resonance of such material within the field of preoedipal fantasy, and its usefulness for making sense of a great variety of elements in the novels. Stone extends the field of reference not only by reading all the novels, instead of just our five, but also by fine-tooth-combing everything Dickens wrote—journalism, stories, novels—for evidence of the cannibal preoccupation.

Whatever the plenitude or the dearth of evidence for such disruptive early experiences or relationships that Dickens may have undergone, there has been an increasing tendency, in the past decade or so, to stress such determinative early experience. Thus, Gwen Watkins, in *Dickens in Search of Himself,* argues, in largely Jungian terms, that Dickens was unloved as a child, so that his personality developed in terms of a split between a true and a false self, while his work recapitulates the problem by endlessly generating plots that center on doubles, mysteries, and violence. More recently, and working within a more object relations-centered frame of reference, Natalie McKnight, writing in a feminist vein that turns attention to issues of relationships between mothers and their children, argues that Dickens's "conscious [as opposed to deeper, unconscious] complaints against his mother [cannot] satisfactorily explain the battalion of wretched mothers who frequent his fiction" (178). Not only does Dickens, in her view, make mothers suffer and consistently batter women in general, but he also reflects, in his representation of women, signs of the terror she assumes he experienced in the face of them. This is manifested, according to McKnight, in both his work and his life. Even his idealized, angelic women, like Agnes and Amy Dorrit, bear the stigmata of his anxiety: "They must not venture into assertiveness, lest they begin to seem like mothers" (180). McKnight also attributes Dickens's growing resentment of his wife and finally his ultimate rejection of her to the fact that she increasingly showed the signs of her motherhood, signs that were not only repellent, but deeply threatening even to the adult Dickens.

To be sure, such readings as McKnight's, much like our own, arise from consideration of the play of elements in the writings themselves. There is, again, no strong concrete biographical evidence to confirm them. Nonetheless, we hope that our extrapolation of these elements in the chapters of this book provides adequate evidence for our thesis and that arguments like those of Watkins and McKnight serve only to deepen and buttress our own. We should note, moreover, that even in life, where there is irrefutable external evidence and even direct memory of early bereavement, abandonment, and deprivation, the subjective resonance of preoedipal experience is of the sort we find for Dickens. Even in the lives of living people, evidence for the reverberation of early grief reverberates in images, associations, and fantasy material that yield results largely through interpretation and reconstruction.

2. *Historical Perspectives.* We must ask, in the context of our foregrounding of the place of orphans and orphaning in Dickens's texts, what the historical reality was—to what extent Dickens's recurrent representations of abandonment and destitution, and especially of children, was a reality, and to what extent it was the product of his passionate imagination, or at least colored by that imagination. It seems appropriate further to ask why Dickens's readers were so susceptible to the vision of neglect and abandonment he unfurled.

Looking at the evidence amassed over the past decades, much of it excavated from the material gathered in Dickens's own time by Parliamentary committees and researchers such as Mayhew, one earnestly wishes what he shows us were at least in part his invention. Though clearly colored by the tincture his genius gave it, the reality was as least as harrowing as its depiction in the novels. Indeed, unmollified by the aesthetic shaping Dickens gave it, it is often still more harrowing.

The fate of the orphaned, abandoned, and vagrant child throughout the early and middle part of the nineteenth century was most often death by disease. In the 1840s, of every 1,000 births only 522 children survived until the age of five. For the poorest children, the mortality rate was catastrophic. It is estimated that in the slums in the East End of London four out of five poor infants died before they reached their fifth year. (For discussion of the condition of poor and orphaned children see Pinchbeck and Hewitt.) Among the children of the poor, those who survived faced an average mortality age of twenty-two. The abandoned child typically lived by casual labor, as a prisoner in jails, or as an inmate of the brutal system of workhouse incarceration instituted by the Poor Law of 1834 (Longmate).

The fate of children was only part of the nightmare of a pestilence-ridden city whose nightmarishness Dickens evoked but could not, even in his most feverish conjurations, particularize to the end. Ackroyd's biography conveys the quality of life in the city Dickens lived in and wrote about:

> What sewers existed were already falling apart.... Gutters in the middle of the street were used as avenues for excrement and urine until they were stopped up in a court or alley.... The Fleet Ditch

which ran beside Holborn Hill was no more than an open sewer which emptied out into the Thames, as did two hundred other sewers, so that during the hot summer of 1858 . . . the stench of the great river became insupportable and it was recorded at the time that ". . . the sewerage of nearly three million people had been brought to seethe and ferment under a burning sun, in a vast and open cloaca lying in their midst. . . ."

There was another and equally insidious threat to the health of the citizens—it came from the burial grounds in the city which were now overflowing and in which the bodies were piled high upon each other, sometimes breaking through the soil and emitting noxious gases which poisoned or even killed those who were in the vicinity. . . . The soil was "saturated, absolutely saturated with human putrescence." It was common for those who worked among the tombs literally to pick up the pieces of the overflowing dead and burn them. One graveyard worker reported that "I have been up to my knees in human flesh by jumping on the bodies so as to cram them into the least possible space at the bottom of the graves in which fresh bodies were afterwards placed."

And so disease spread like a stain. There were four epidemics of cholera within Dickens' own lifetime and, besides these mortal visitations, there were periodic and regular outbreaks of typhus, typhoid fever, epidemic diarrhoea, dysentery, smallpox and a variety of ailments which were classified only as "fevers." Between November and December of 1847, 500,000 people were infected with typhus fever out of a population of 2,100,000, and it seemed to many that London was indeed becoming what *The Lancet* described as a "doomed city." The average age of mortality in the capital was 27, . . . and in 1839 almost half the funerals in London were of children under the age of 10." (Ackroyd, 383–84)

Dickens's representation of Jo the crossing sweeper imaginatively refracts and interprets the realities of the London streets, even as Tom All Alone's reflects the ultimate reality of the most egregious London slums; the graveyard where Hawdon and then finally Jo and Lady Dedlock are buried epitomizes the plague-ridden final resting places of the indigent, and often even the nonindigent, poor—as our citations from Ackroyed clearly show.

Focusing on the issue of orphaning alone, Eileen Simpson, in her eminently readable and moving *Orphans: Real and Imaginary,* surveys the conditions that led to the multiplication of orphans in Victorian cities. She not only sketches the causes for the increase in their numbers, but also tracks how traditional ways of providing for them broke down, so that their wretched derelict life in the byways of the towns, including their tendency to form gangs that threatened the equanimity of the evermore ascendant middle classes, led them to penetrate the consciousness of those classes. Part of her emphasis is the way that the reformist impulse was stirred, not by charitable concern alone, but also by threat, much in the way that much of the concern with the homeless in contemporary cities reflects a sense of danger to bourgeois life more than it reflects concern with the plight of those condemned to life in the streets.

The reality was horrendous, and historians have amply documented it. They have not been satisfied with documentation, however. Students both of Dickens and of Victorian culture have begun to investigate the reasons for the attention paid to that reality and to the forms the attention took. In modern times, as we have noted, both biographical and critical discourse attribute Dickens's susceptibilities to his trials in the blacking warehouse, and historians have pointed to the objective conditions that assaulted the sensibilities, the consciousness, and the consciences of contemporaries exposed to the horrors of the mid-nineteenth-century city.

Yet already in the discussions that marked the centennial year of Dickens's death, Angus Wilson, himself finely attuned to the biographical grounds of Dickens's sensibilities, noted that other dimensions must be considered, among them the cultural status of childhood in his time. More recently, in *Dickens and the Grown-up Child,* Malcolm Andrews takes up Wilson's challenge, writing that because "we have become so used to the topos of the neglected child in Victorian England, and to seeing this as a social problem endemic in the period, . . . there has been comparatively little exploration of the extent to which this topos functions as a metaphor for the neglected *internalized child.* Middle class Victorian culture encouraged the maturing male systematically to betray and abandon his own childhood" (180).

Andrews argues that heightening the guilt and compassion that liberal Victorians felt about class and family attitudes that lead to the suffering of the young were "memories of the psychic abandonment of their own childhood, an ordeal which has become the rite of passage for all those who strove to establish a secure position in the 'advancing culture' of nineteenth century England" (180). Ackroyd notes the phenomenon: "[I]n the death of Little Nell there was a threnody for the gentler and more innocent part of themselves which in actual existence had to be discarded in the 'struggle' or 'battle of life'" (327).

The subjective predispositions of which Andrews speaks must have conspired with still another culturally determined element that we have intermittently noted in the course of our book. We mean the sharp focus on children and childhood that begins to find its culmination in the nineteenth century, and the contradictions that beset it within the middle-class family—contradictions no less dire than the one Uriah Heep complains of in the self-justifying diatribe that follows his unmasking, when he complains of the clash in his upbringing between the notion that work is a blessing and the conviction that work is a curse.

Philippe Ariès and other historians have shown how the "discourse of childhood" emerged only in the eighteenth century—at the earliest at the end of the seventeenth. That discourse, as it evolved in middle-class English culture from the eighteenth into the nineteenth century—traced by Peter Coveney and Penny Brown—was marked by tugs in two directions, one Rousseauan, the other Calvinist.

The Rousseauan strain stressed the intrinsic potentialities of the child, potentialities that, if properly nurtured, would grow into fullness and fulfillment as naturally as the acorn grows into the oak. This view harmonized with the Rousseauan appeal to mothers to nurse their own babies, and accorded with the emergence of the nuclear family, with its tendency toward child-centeredness, as the dominant mode for the middle classes. Its effect, historians think, was to stimulate the child's expectations, and to bond it evermore closely to its parents, especially its mother. The upshot was an endless horizon of expectations, concurrent with the liberal political program guaranteeing the individual "life, liberty and the [endless] pursuit of [limitless] happiness."

The second pull, and especially in England, was in the direction of an essentially Calvinist vision of the depravity of man, and consequently of the child, fulfilling the biblical notion that "the disposition of man's heart is evil from his youth," and mandating a penitential repressiveness from infancy onward. We recognize this in the punitive guilt-provoking propensities of Dickensian mothers (or, in both cases, stand-in mothers) such as Mrs. Clennam and Mrs. Joe. Such repressiveness and the punitiveness that accompanies it have real-world underpinnings and a clear teleology within Victorian culture. Both punitiveness and repressiveness subserve the Victorian work ethic; they fuel the psychological motor of the Samuel Smilesian and Horatio Algeresque imagination; and they reinforce the dynamic Andrews is describing, both by fixing the individual, especially the male individual, on childhood desire even while alienating the individual from it.

We assume that in cultural terms, these contradictions, in their various incarnations, were intensified by a pervasive real-world anxiety about social standing, but also about survival, to which people were subject. That anxiety, which was lived out with such intensity by Dickens at twelve, was bred by the prospect of being cast out of one's relatively safe niche of aspiration and middle-class striving into the pestilential plague spots the orphaned, the abandoned, and the derelict inhabited. John Dickens's waystation on the path to such casting-out was the debtor's prison; Charles Dickens's was the blacking factory.

3. *The Critical Discourse.* Having aleady placed ourselves, in our Introduction, within what we take to be the classical positions on Dickens, we now wish to contextualize our work within a range of contemporary, largely postmodernist discourse.

Although our strategies of reading share much with postmodernism as a whole, the thrust of our reading is very different. Postmodernist discourse has largely subordinated consideration of Dickens himself and of his novels, taken singly and taken as a body of coherent work, to radical recontextualization of the work. It has done so to illuminate it from a variety of perspectives, historical and linguistic. We, for our part, though we hold the historical and linguistic issues in high respect, insist, for the sake of interpretation, on the centrality of Dickens himself— of his conscious and unconscious life, and of his sense of experience in shaping the form and substance of his fiction. As we say at the very outset, we do not focus on these things because of interest in Dickens as a particular human being, but rather because of a conviction that Dickens's work is Dickens's own and must be understood in terms that consider his place in generating that work.

Our insistence on this has a sharp polemical edge. We believe that, after all is said and done, particular people are the locus of cultural creativity. We believe that whatever determinations shape individuals and the contents of their consciousness, it is individuals who meaningfully filter and focus their experience. However individuals are "constructed," it is the nodes of consciousness that are individuals that generate meaningful perspectives on the realities that surround them.

This is an important issue. The discourse that contextualizes Dickens virtually out of existence is a discourse that in principle celebrates, not only the "death of the author," in the manner of Foucault and Barthes, but also insists on the demise of the individual as a category relevant to cultural discourse, except as an object of skeptical inquiry. Indeed, the discourse of postmodernism savages the humanist tradition that places the individual at the center of its consideration. It tends to regard the individual as at best a necessary bourgeois fiction, at worst as an arbitrary delusion cultivated to trap human subjects within the forms of bourgeois life and striving, a delusion that is then co-opted for a variety of social and political needs. In the course of its polemic against "humanism," postmodernist discourse has in fact reified the Romantic notion of the self, interpeting it as a fixity—as an "essentialized" *donnee* that is equated with the "platonic" notion of the immortal soul. Having created this straw man, it proceeds to deconstruct it by showing the socially constructed nature both of the abstract notion of the self and of the particular selves that have existed in history.

This is not the place further to reason or ground our own view. Let it suffice to say that we define ourselves within the terms of the position we take. These terms are rooted in a conception of the human psyche that arises from classical psychoanalytic notions of human development, as elaborated but also modified by object relations theory.

In this, we differ radically even (or perhaps especially) from the postmodernist theoretical and literary-critical discourse that has grown up in and around psychoanalysis. Postmodernist psychoanalytic criticism, even as practiced by some of the most scintillating and aggressive of its representatives, has displaced its emphasis from the Dickens as an individual who lived in history and from the characters Dickens created to analysis of the "unconscious" of the text, to the unconscious transactions between the text and its readers, and to the play of signification within the text. In this, it has developed along lines that run parallel to the very interesting and productive neohistoricist, neomarxist, and feminist work, which has focused on the immanent logic by which the novels have worked out the perplexities faced in Victorian culture with regard to personal, domestic, familial, social issues. Like these other approaches, it tends to lose touch with the substantive realities of the work in and for itself, and, therefore, from our point of view, with what is most valuable in literature.

Yet all these approaches, including the psychoanalytic, have been surprisingly effective in their interrogation of hitherto unexplored aspects of Dickens's work and especially in the interpretation of its salient formal features. There is an irony here. Formalism, almost as much as "humanism," is a favored whipping boy of postmodernism, yet the discourse of postmodernism illuminates formal elements more effectively than most earlier approaches.

Thus, the neo-Marxist Terry Eagleton elucidates the very blankness or shallowness or pallor of the Dickens protagonist in a way that is very different from our own, but that vigorously engages this striking phenemenon as earlier critics did not. In this, he follows T. A. Jackson, the precursor of all later Marxist criticism, who proposed that Dickens's "flat" characters reflected the way people in his time had been flattened by oppression and that his tendency to caricaturistic representation refracts how capitalist development had distorted those caught up in its toils. Eagleton, who has digested the lessons of structuralist and deconstructionist criticism, refines such observations, working from a strong biographical base. As S. D. Trezises writes,

> Eagleton picks up Jackson's location of Dickens on the precarious petit-bourgeois rung of the social ladder, able to look down as well as up, and shows how this leads to the presence of both the dominant and the dominated in his work. Eagleton juxtaposes the nature of the culturally barren bourgeois class with the central but strangely anonymous middle class protagonists in Dickens' novels (e.g., Clennam and Jarndyce), so colorless and so unmemorable by contrast with the eccentrics and monsters on the apparent periphery of the plot, where the secret life of the novels flourishes. (133)

The most sophisticated neo-Marxist studies, such as those of Frederick Jameson, have cut across many traditional discourses to link socioeconomic, psychonalytic, Derridean, and literary parameters in unprecedented ways. So has the feminist discourse that has often been closely related to it. Over the past twenty-five years or so, the second wave of feminism has come to grips with hitherto elusive elements of the Dickens corpus. Initially concerned with sociohistorical issues, such as the conception of women and their representation in Victorian culture in general and in Dickens in particular, it has also done splendid work in illuminating the thrust and tenor of Dickens's art. Among other things, it has cast light on the logic underlying the articulation of his plots from within the stereotypic marriage and other plots of Victorian popular culture, and has explored some reasons—reasons very different from those we adduce—for its grotesque and caricaturistic treatment of character. It has also engaged some of the cultural patterns that have determined major aspects of Dickens's vision.

By the midseventies, feminist critics and historians were indicting the patriarchy as an outthrust of capitalism, and attributing the Victorian polarization of male and female roles to the complex politics of accommodation to the given world. In "Making—and Re-making—History: Another Look at Patriarchy," Judith Newton studies the ideological aspect of the reconstruction of the roles of women in society; in *Half Savage and Half Free: Women and Rural Radicalism in the Nineteenth-Century Novel,* Judith Weissman traces the transformation of women's roles from that of workers in an agricultural economy to that of tending their men.

Later works, however, relate such sociological and sociocultural issues to the patterning of materials in fiction. In *Desire and Domestic Fiction: A Political History of the Novel,* Nancy Armstrong ponders how the plotting of Victorian Fiction constructs the consciousness and roles of women in family and society, with emphasis on how relations between men and women were shaped in terms of shifts in power relations in society. The shaping in question was one that stressed personal attachment, psychological development, and romantic love as substitutes for social and economic power. This, of course, is reflected in the representation of women in Dickens and other Victorian writers. In *Uneven Developments: The Ideological Work of Gender in Mid-Victorian England,* Mary Poovey explores how the discourses of law, medicine, and literature executed the "work" of containing anxieties about the presence and power of women, "both provid[ing] individual readers with an image of what identity was and creat[ing] a subject position that reproduced that kind of identity in the individual reader" (89).

In a powerful analysis of *Dombey and Son* but with reference to a wide range of other Dickens texts, Lynda Zwynger uses deconstructionist, psychoanalytic, and feminist strategies to map the impact of "the daughter's seduction" on the overall configuration of language and action in the novels. No less trenchant are Eve Kosofsky Sedgwick's discussion of various Dickens works in her wide-ranging anatomies of the treatment of sexualities in literature.

We want especially to stress the feminist approaches here because our own discourse functions in a seemingly gender-blind way, subsuming some of the most difficult figures of women under the rubrics of mother and nurturer or as orphans who suffer from the *absence* of nurturing mothers. Obviously, there are grave gender issues in Dickens—issues that we touch upon only in passing, as in our consideration of the relation between Agnes as Angel in the House and David Copperfield as implicit Devil in the Marketplace (p. 72 above). They are still more marginal to our general argument than, say, the ideological and economic issues in *David Copperfield* or the "theory" of social relations that is implicit in the representation of the paranoias that fill the world of *Little Dorrit.*

In retrospect, it seems to us that, had we been so disposed, we might well have linked to the feminist issues the recurrent vindictiveness toward mothers that are felt to have abandoned their children, as in the running down of Lady Dedlock by that composite orphan, Esther, and the third-person voice. Such themes self-evidently intersect with feminist and other cultural issues. Indeed, one of the more recent readings of *Bleak House* (Jasmine Yong Hall) interprets the pursuit and exposure of Esther's mother much in the way we do, with a view to interrogating "What Is Troubling about Esther," though it tilts its interpretation in a very different direction.

Social and cultural teleologies like those which have intrigued feminist readers also figure powerfully in Foucauldian work, but here, too, interesting light is shed on the inner life of the novels themselves, and—ironically, again—on their formal articulation. In *The Novel and the Police,* D. A. Miller traces the way the conventions of the novel serve to reinforce social surveillance. He demonstrate the workings of the system of social surveillance to enforce values and repression in a variety of Dickens's novels—notably, *Oliver Twist, David Copperfield,* and *Bleak House.* He works from an assumption of reciprocal collusion between the novel's role in creating in the reader an illusion of autonomous selfhood and its function as an agency policing individual consciousness on behalf of the society.

As with the work of most of the writers we mention here, Miller's book is chiefly concerned with systemic elements within Victorian culture, and not with the working of Dickens's art or sensibility. Yet as with many of the other studies surveyed here, Miller makes striking sense—sense that is very different from ours—of the characterizing marks of the fiction—in Miller's case, the recurrence of plots that are concerned with mysteries and their solution, as well as with the entire range of issues linked to detection, spying, and other peephole preoccupations, not to speak of the doublings and repetitions that chime with each other, and of the macabre, often hallucinatory, effect of the plots as a whole. It is also peculiarly apt in unraveling the intricacies of language—of the punning, of the play on names, and of the ornate rhetorical structures of discourse.

Close reading of the verbal texture of the novels is, in fact, one of the achievements of postmodernist engagement with Dickens. As part of a radical decentering process, postmodernism, following deconstruction and the structural analysis that it supplanted, not only deflects attention from Dickens, the ostensible "source" of his "texts," but also from the texts' manifest modes of self-organization: from their thematic patterning, from the articulation of their plots as vehicles for their themes, and from the treatment of characters as "sites" of consciousness and meaning. In doing so, they have on the whole foregrounded other elements—often largely the element of language, not as a vehicle for manifest meaning, but as a manifestation of underlying currents and trends, including very often the issue of language itself. They have, in effect, more or less consistently allegorized Dickens in innovative ways—ways that tend to make of his novels' allegories of reading itself, rather than discourses that engage the world.

Perhaps the most dramatic of these allegorizations is J. Hillis Miller's introduction to the Penguin edition of *Bleak House*. Miller extricates a great variety of elements having to do with representation, documentation, and naming to establish his thesis: that *Bleak House* is ultimately and radically about semiosis, that is, about the problematics of meaning as generated through language.

In doing so, however, he loses—or so it seems to us—the substance of the novel, and we would read "substance" as Kenneth Burke used to read it—etymologically, to stress *what lies beneath*. In fact, by our lights, he loses the essential focus and meaning of the novels. The same can be said for a wide variety of readings, some of which are dazzling in their ingenuity, which have appeared over the past twenty-five years.

Among the more striking of these is Willian Cohen's verbally and interpretively pyrotechnical essay on "Manual Conduct in *Great Expectations*," whose title epitomizes both the brilliance and the deflectiveness of this particular piece of reading. In it,

Cohen offers a "cultural" reading of the novel that tracks what its author takes to be the displacement of repressed sexuality onto the only visible part, apart from the face, of the sheathed human beings who lived in the high Victorian era, namely, the hands. His reading is concerned with a phenomenon that we have never seen adequately interpreted—that is, omnipresence of hands in the text, including the emphasis on the affinity between Molly's manual gestures and Estella's, and its place in unraveling a major piece of the novel's tangled skein of plotting.

The manual conduct in question is, of course, masturbation, and the essay is concerned with the fact that in Victorian culture,

> even as sexuality is unspeakable, ... it is everywhere being spoken.... [In the novel], the placement of hands remains a secret, but like all secrets it wants to be told.... The novel ... encrypts sexuality not in its plot or announced attention, but in its margins, at the seemingly incidental movements of its figurative language.... In a genre that forbids ... observation of genitals in action, the manual code gives voice to what cannot otherwise be spoken. (221)

Cohen's essay is an extreme instance of decentered reading, and it is all too easy to mock. In its excessiveness, however, it carries to an extreme the tendency in postmodernist interpretation which we are describing—that is, the tendency to lose track of the vital centers of gravity of the works that are studied. It seems to us—and this is, again, the pith and thrust of our argument in this essay—that there is an order of priority and even of causality in the generation and the retrieval of literary works and that however we may want and even need to recontextualize them, we pay a price for our recontextualization.

There is no reason to limit treatment of literary work to the context that is their author. As cultural evidence, no text should be spared scrutiny—in every possible direction. Yet there is a perspective in which particular works and bodies of work need to be conceived in terms of themselves. Our own emphasis, for the sake of this study, is on the fact that *Dickens* lived his life and wrote his works, and what is in them refracts the substance of his experience. We have been concerned with exploring the conflicts he was subject to, the obstacles he confronted, and the gifts he brought to his confrontation with the world that shape and determine his novels. As we understand him and his work, his conscious and unconscious struggle with himself, his public, and the issues he bravely confronted are reflected in everything he wrote, but always in terms of a grid of conflicts that colored his entire being.

This book is—has been—an effort to define that grid, without denigrating the other levels of consciousness and striving that mark it. Indeed, we would hope that our work will serve others further to contextualize its insights—literarily, psychoanalytically, feministically, historically, sociologically, and linguistically. Most of all, we would wish that someone would take up our work and use it to elucidate the one thing in Dickens that we have neglected altogether—namely, his humor. On this, there is much to say, from our perspective, about how humor both serves to deflect and to reflect or express the emotional perpexities of the orphan condition. We have, alas, been too intent on elucidating other things, and because our time is up for the moment, we must leave this issue for others to tackle.

References

Ackroyd, Peter. 1990 *Dickens.* New York: HarperCollins.

Andrews, Malcolm. 1994. *Dickens and the Grown-up Child.* Houndsmills & London: Macmillan.

Aries, Philippe. 1962. *Centuries of Childhood.* New York: Knopf.

Armstrong, Nancy. 1987. *Desire and Domestic Fiction: A Political History of the Novel.* New York: Oxford University Press.

Auerbach, Nina. 1975. "Incarnations of the Orphan." *English Literary History* 42:395–419.

Barthes, Roland. 1977. "The Death of the Author." In *Image, Music, Text.* New York: Hill and Wang.

Brontë, Emily. 1965. *Wuthering Heights.* Edited by D. Daiches. Harmondsworth, England: Penguin.

Brown, Penny. 1993. *The Captured World: The Child and Childhood in Nineteenth-Century Women's Writing in England.* New York: St. Martin's Press.

Chase, Karen. 1984. *Eros and Psyche: The Representation of Personality in Charlotte Bronte, Charles Dickens and George Eliot.* New York: Methuen.

Cohen, William. 1993. "Manual Conduct in *Great Expectations.*" *English Literary History* 60:217–59.

Coveney, Peter. 1967. *The Image of Childhood: The Industrial Society.* Harmondsworth, England: Penguin.

Daleski, H. M. 1970. *Dickens and the Art of Analogy.* London: Faber and Faber.

Dickens, Charles. 1971. *Bleak House.* Edited by Norman Page. Harmondsworth, England: Penguin.

———. 1966. *David Copperfield.* Edited by Trevor Blount. Harmondsworth, England: Penguin.

———. 1965. *Great Expectations.* Edited by Angus Calder. Harmondsworth, England: Penguin.

———. 1967. *Little Dorrit.* Edited by John Holloway. Harmondsworth, England: Penguin.

———. 1966. *Oliver Twist.* Edited by Peter Fairclough. Harmondsworth, England: Penguin.

Eagleton, Terry. 1980. *Criticism and Ideology: A Study in Marxist Theory.* London: Verso.

Foucault, Michel. 1979. "What Is an Author." In *Textual Strategies and Perspectives: Post-Structuralist Criticism.* Edited by Josue V. Harari. Ithaca, New York: Cornell.

Frank, Lawrence. 1984. *Charles Dickens and the Romantic Self.* Lincoln: University of Nebraska.

Frye, Northrop. 1963. *The Well-Tempered Critic.* Bloomington: Indiana University Press.

Hall, Jasmine Yong. "What's Troubling about Esther: Narrating, Policing and Resisting Arrest." *Dickens Studies Annual* 22 (1993): 171–93.

House, Humphrey. 1960. *The Dickens World.* London: Oxford.

Jackson, T. A. 1937. *Charles Dickens: The Progress of a Radical.* London: Lawrence & Wishart.

Jameson, Frederick. 1983. *The Political Unconscious.* London: Methuen.

Johnson, J. Edgar. 1952. *Charles Dickens: His Tragedy and Triumph.* 2 vols. New York: Simon and Schuster.

Kaplan, Fred. 1988. *Dickens: A Biography.* New York: William Morrow & Co.

Kucich, John. 1987. *Repression in Victorian Fiction: Charlotte Bronte, George Eliot and Charles Dickens.* Berkeley: University of California Press.

Lanham, Richard A. 1976. *The Motives of Eloquence: Literary Rhetoric in the Renaissance.* New Haven & London: Yale.

Longmate, Norman. 1974. *The Workhouse.* New York: St. Martin's Press.

Lukács, Georg. 1964. *Studies in European Realism.* Introd. Alfred Kazin. New York: Grosset and Dunlap.

———. 1971. *Theory of the Novel.* Translated by Anna Bostock. Cambridge, Mass.: MIT Press.

Mackenzie, Norman, and Jean Mackenzie. 1979. *Dickens: A Life.* Oxford: Oxford University Press.

Marcus, Steven. 1965. *Dickens from Pickwick to Dombey.* London: Chatto & Windus.

McKnight, Natalie. 1944. "Making Mother Suffer and Other Fun in Dickens." *Dickens Quarterly* 11, no. 4 (December).

Miller, D. A. 1988. *The Novel and the Police.* Berkeley: University of California.

Miller, J. Hillis. 1958. *Charles Dickens: The World Of His Novels.* Cambridge, Mass.: Harvard.

———. 1963. *The Disappearance of God: Five Nineteenth Century Writers.* Cambridge, Mass.: Harvard.

———. 1972. "Introduction," to *Bleak House.* Harmondsworth, England: Penguin.

Musselwhite, David. 1987. *Partings Welded Together: Politics, and Desire in the Novel.* London: Methuen.

Newton, Judith. 1984. "Making—and Re-making—History: Another Look at Patriarchy." *Tulsa Studies in Women's Literature* 3:125–41.

Orwell, George. 1954. *Eight Essays.* New York: Viking.

Pinchbeck, Ivy, and Margaret Hewitt. 1973. *Children in English Society.* London: Routledge and Kegan Paul.

Poovey, Mary. 1989. *Uneven Developments: The Ideological Work of Gender in Mid-Victorian England.* Chicago: University of Chicago.

Sadoff, Diane. 1982. *Monsters of Affection: Dickens, Eliot and Bronte on Fatherhood.* Baltimore: Johns Hopkins.

Schwarzbach, F. S. 1979. *Dickens and the City*. London: Athlone Press.

Simpson, Eileen. 1987. *Orphans: Real and Imaginary*. London: Weidenfeld and Nicholson.

Slater, Michael, ed. 1970. *Dickens 1970: Centenary Essays*. London: Chapman and Hall.

Stone, Harry. 1994. *The Night Side of Dickens: Cannibalism, Passion, Necessity*. Columbus: Ohio University Press.

Trezises, S. D. 1994. "Dickens and Marxism." *Dickens Quarterly* 11, 127–35 3 (September).

Trilling, Lionel. 1955. "*Little Dorrit*," *The Opposing Self: Nine Essays*. New York: Viking.

Van Ghent, Dorothy. 1950. "The Dickens World: A View from Todgers." *Sewanee Review* LVIII: 419–38.

Watkins, Gwen. 1987. *Dickens in Search of Himself*. London: Macmillan.

Weissman, Judith. 1987. *Half Savage and Half Free: Women and Rural Radicalism in the Nineteenth-Century Novel*. Middletown, Conn.: Wesleyan.

Welsh, Alexander. 1987. *From Copyright to Copperfield: The Identity of Dickens*. Cambridge, Mass.: Harvard.

Wilson, Edmund. 1954. "The Two Scrooges." In *Eight Essays*. New York: Doubleday.

Wilson, Angus. 1970. *The World of Charles Dickens*. New York: Viking Press.

———. 1970. "Dickens on Children and Childhood." In *Dickens 1970: Centenary Essays*. Edited by Michael Slater. London: Chapman & Hall.

Wordsworth, William. *The Prelude* (1850 version).

Zwerdling, Alex. 1973. "Esther Summerson Rehabilitated." *PMLA* 88 (May): 523–40.

Zwynger, Lynda. 1991. *Daughters, Fathers, and the Novel*. Madison: University of Wisconsin Press.

Index

Abandonment, and Dickens, 16, 25, 49–50, 201–2, 205; effect of, 12, 14, 22, 138, 149; experience of, 86–87, 187, 189; historical aspect of, 206, 208; rage at, 26, 43, 175; and third-person voice, 98–99, 103, 107
Ackroyd, Peter, 202, 203, 206–7, 208
Aggression, 35, 132, 142, 144, 195–96, 198; displacement of, 18, 38, 67–68, 184, 199
Agnes Wickfield, 60–61, 68, 73, 77, 83; as mother figure, 84, 193, 205, 214; naming of, 71–72; and sexuality, 69
Amy Dorrit, 130, 132, 137, 148, 156–57; and Clennam, 135, 149, 155, 163; and fusion fantasy, 127, 129; and motherhood, 126, 193, 205; and nursing, 128–29; stillness of, 145, 147, 154; as symbol, 128, 133, 138, 151, 164
Andrews, Malcolm, 208, 209–10
Angel in the House, 72, 214
Aries, Phillipe, 209
Armstrong, Nancy, 213
Auerbach, Nina, 12–13

Barthes, Roland, 211
Betsy Trotwood, 59–61, 64–65, 83 (*see* Boundaries)
Biblical imagery, Cain and Abel, 142, 149, 164, 209; David and Uriah, 71–72
Bildung, 21, 115; and Arthur Clennam, 127; and David Copperfield, 56, 62; and Richard Carstone, 87, 117, 124
Blacking, 26–27, 48–50, 200, 201–2, 208
Blake, William, 29
Bleak House, 20, 21–22, 23, 49, 81; in contrast to *David Copperfield,* 85;

and interpretation, 214, 215; and narrative voice, 18, 27, 31, 64, 164; and subjectivity, 185, 186
body, 36, 45, 93, 111–12, 172; of mother, 20–21, 48,
boundaries, blurring of, 93–94, 120; breaching of, 51, 76, 159–62 (*see* Flora Finching), 173–74, 192 aintaining, 89, 91–92, 132; and narrative, 21, 101, 162, 180; need for, 59–61 (*see* Betsy Trotwood)
Brontë, Emily, 30; *Wuthering Heights,* 30
Brown, Penny, 209
Burke, Kenneth, 215

Calvinism, 130, 139–40, 185, 209
Cannibalism: Dickens, 204–5; in *Great Expectations,* 170–72, 174–75; in *Oliver Twist,* 35–38, 43, 44, 46; and Vholes, 121
Character, 28–29, 58–59, 64, 69, 100–101; in criticism, 212–13, 215
Chase, Karen, 28, 88
childhood: Victorian preoccupation with, 19, 208–9
Christian imagery, 23, 42, 110, 137, 149–50; Christ analogues, 71, 99, 164, 173; Paraclete, 127, 151
Circumlocution Office, 136–37
Clennam, 14, 22–23, 132, 134–35, 144; and Amy, 129, 133, 146–49, 164, as Bildung figure, 127–28, depression of, 15, 130, 140; and Flora, 152, 160, 163; and fratricide, 142; passivity of, 127, 131, 136, 147, 151; and relation to past, 154–56, 158
Cohen, William, 215–16
Coveney, Peter, 209

David Copperfield, 19, 20–21, 139, 184, 214; in contrast to *Bleak*

221

House, 85, 86, 93; and identity, 20–21, 31, 54; as turning point, 17; and vocation, 118
David Copperfield, 18, 20–21, 59–60; and aggression, 67–68; biblical analogue, 71–72; doubles of, 64–65, 68, 72–75, 77–78, 84, 115; identity of, 61–62, 83; and values, 56–58, 70–71, 76–77, 80–81, 85
death imagery, 22, 54; in *Bleak House*, 99, 106, 109–10; and Dickens, 203–4, 207 in *Great Expectations*, 172–73; in *Little Dorrit*, 130, 139–40, 150; in *Oliver Twist*, 40–41
depression, 77, 127, 129–32
detection, 107, 215
disease, 15, 95, 109–12, 206–7
displacement; in *Bleak House*, 87, 100, 115; in *David Copperfield*, 64, 68, 72–73, 77, 84; in *Great Expectations*, 184, 190; in *Little Dorrit*, 132, 140; in *Oliver Twist*, 18, 34–35, 43, 54
Dombey and Son, 55–56, 213
Dostoevsky, Fyodor, 25
doubles, 83, 107; in *David Copperfield*, 20, 64–65, 68, 77, 84–85, 115; and Dickens, 205; in *Little Dorrit*, 142
dreams, 42, 51–52, 94–96, 141–42, 148; and David Copperfield, 70, 77,

Eagelton, Terry, 212
Eliot, George, 28
Esther Summerson, 15, 86–100; feminist issues, 347; and formalization 112–16; her fulfillment, 126; and guilt, 14; and mothering, 176; splitting from third person 18, 21, 99–100; vs. Pip, 196, 316–17

Fagin, 17–18, 51–53; and cannibalism, 35–38, 44–45, 121; and marketplace, 26, 40; and violence, 33, 34, 43, 64
fantasy: anatomy of, 135–42, 186–94 (*see also* Projection); of being eaten, 35–37, 44, 172–75, 203–4 (*see* Cannibalism); of birth, 176–77; Dickens's use of, 159–60; feebleness of, 40, 42, 51; of Frankenstein, 178–80; fusion and restoration, 15,

17, 117–18, 121, 128 (*see* Fusion); of imprisonment, 148, 161; of inheritance, 20–21, 32–33, 47–48, 117, 197–98, 203; of omnipotence, 107; regressive immobility, 140, 141, 154; vs. reality, 12, 91, 193, 204
feminism, 72, 205, 211, 212–14
Flora Finching, 131, 148, 155; affinity with Dickens, 161–62; meanings of name, 151, 152; vitality of, 159–60, 163 (*see* Boundaries, breaching)
Formalism, 212
Foster, 201
Foucault, Michel, 211, 214
Frank, Lawrence, 28
Frye, Northrop, 26
fusion, 30; deathliness of, 117–18, 120; fantasy of, 43, 54, 84, 127, 174; with mother figure, 15, 33, 38, 40, 88; between self and world, 173; with third-person voice, 103, 113–14

God, 71, 78, 99, 105–6, 111; death of, 13, 30; judgmental, 106, 140; playing, 131
Gowan, 139, 142–43, 155; fictions of, 135–37, 153, 157–58, 161; projections of, 134, 138
Great Expectations, 23–24, 25, 215–16
grotesque, 213; in *Bleak House*, 104–5, 119–20; in *David Copperfield*, 68–69; in *Great Expectations*, 171–72, 182, 188; in *Little Dorrit*, 130–31, 143, 159–60; in *Oliver Twist*, 171–72, 182, 188

Hall, Jasmine Yong, 214
Hard Times, 70
historical documentation, 206–8, 209
Hough, Graham, 88
House, Humphrey, 35
Humanism, 211

identity (Self), 19, 52, 58–59, 98, 156, 191–92, 213; and Dickens, 27–28, 49–50, 201, 203; formation of, 61–62, 88–93, 96, 173, 197, impossibility of generating, 127, 149, 158; loss

of, 15, 46–47, 62, 93, 118, 193; multiple, 76, 159; quest for, 117; split, 21, 198–99
illness, 38–40, 64, 93–96, 113
inheritance: fantasy of, 17, 20–21, 119; as metaphor, 46–47; and nurture, 120–21, 124; and passivity, 32–33, 47–48, 117, 167; rejection of, 55, 185, 197–98

Jackson, T.A., 212
Johnson, J. Edgar, 202, 204

Kaplan, Fred, 202, 203, 204
Kucich, John, 28

Lady Dedlock, 101, 112, 116, 122; death of, 99, 110, 113–14; encounter with, 91, 94, 95; hunting down of, 117, 125, 181, 214; And inheritance, 120; as parent, 122, 177
Language, 34, 73, 80, 136, 152, 160–61, 168; aggression displaced into, 38, 43–44; demonization and mythicization by, 120; Esther Summerson's use of, 85, 88–93; language magic, 105, 190; Pip's use of 189–90; third person narrative voice's use of, 101–7, 215; (*see*, Micawber, Discourse)
Little Dorrit, 22–23, 31, 214; bleakness of, 22, 126, in contrast to *Great Expectations,* 166; and Protestant Ethic, 22
Longmate, 206
loss, 14, 29, 33, 157, 203; and creativity, 187–89; Dickens' identification with, 186; of self, 15, 47, 93, 188–89, 194; and separation, 160, 183
Lukacs, Georg, 27, 29; *Theory of the Novel,* 29

Mackenzie, Jean and Norman, 202
Magwitch, 167, 172–75, 190, 192; and cannibalism, 169–71; and Frankenstein, 178–80; humanization of, 193–95; Pips' relationship to, 197–98; as projection, 181–84; reconciliation with, 176–77, 186
Marcus, Steven, 26, 35
marketplace, 19, 26, 35, 43–46; and coin metaphor, 46–48, 82

Mayhew, 206
Maylies, 25, 36, 45; passivity of, 33, 39, 42, 47, 51–53
McKnight, Natalie, 205
melodrama, 18, 34, 69, 158
Merdles, 135–36, 142–47, 153–54
Micawber, 58, 68, 72, 84; discourse of, 23, 70, 79–80, 85, 97; as double, 77–78, 80–82, 83; and make-believe, 82 (*see* Utopia)
Miller, D. A., 214–15
Miller, J. Hillis, 30, 103, 215; *The Disappearance of God,* 30
Miss Havisham, 130, 169, 184, 187, 190; and cannibalism, 170, 172; and expectations, 178, 197; manipulativeness of, 174, 175, 191; reconciliation with, 176, 177, 186; as victim, 181–82, 193–94
mother, 129–30, 190–91, 205, 209; absence of, 41–42, 117–18, 125, 214; body of, 48; centrality of, 29–30; desire for, 20–21, 33, 40, 88–89; Dickens's, 49–50, 204, 205; fusion with, 15, 84, 127; lost, 16, 40–43, 120–21; surrogate, 52, 59–60, 83, 99, 182, violence towards, 15, 125, 193, 196
Mr. Bucket, 107, 167 (*see* Tulkinghorn and Detection)
Mr. Dick, 58, 64–67
Mrs. Clennam, 143, 146, 148; and Calvinism, 139–40, 185; and death, 130–31; as hostile mother, 129–30, 132, 134, 145, 209; and the past, 156–58; projections of, 138, 139
Musselwhite, David, 27
Mythological figures, 75, 123, 154; Euphrasia, 128, 133, 138, 144, 164

naming, 71–72, 176–77, 197
Nancy, 36, 37, 46, 52–53, 82; and Sikes, 39, 47
narcissism, 90, 96–97, 98, 101, 122
Narrative Voice, 43; characteristics of, 127, 132, 145, 159, 164, (*see* Third person voice)
neo-Marxism, 27, 211–12
New Criticism, 27
New historicism, 28, 211
Newton, Judith, 213
nurture, 38–39, 52, 135, 214; desire

for, 14, 23, 40, 43, 133; failure of, 177, 203; fantasy of, 117–18, 119–20, 135, 153, 170; and passivity, 128,149

nursing, 38–39, 209; in *Bleak House*, 108, 120–21; fictions of, 135, 153, 161; in *Great Expectations*, 176, 177, 182, 195; in *Little Dorrit*, 128–29, 133, 148, 157, (*see* Euphrasia); in psychoanalytic tradition, 120–21

Oliver Twist, 17–18, 25–26, 85, 168; and aggression, 132, 184; in contrast to *David Copperfield*, 55; and fantasy, 14; and the orphan condition, 13, 166

orphan condition, 24, 29–30; in *Bleak House*, 99–100, 111, 117; in *David Copperfield*, 82–83; and Dickens, 11–17, 19, 28, 200; in *Great Expectations*, 166–67, 169, 175–80, 184; in *Little Dorrit*, 127, 148–49, in *Oliver Twist*, 32, 33, 44

orphan imagination, 11–12, 87, 121, 132; and Dickens, 16–17, 20, 176

orphan, in English literature, 12–13, 29–30

Orwell, George, 25–26

Parents: loss of, 13–14, 29, 99 122,; sexuality of, 112; Suit as surrogate 118; surrogate, 40, 66–67, 169, 177

passivity: in *Bleak House*, 117, 122, 125; deathliness of, 35, 125, 127, 133, 141; desire for, 117, 122; of expectations, 176, 185; in *Little Dorrit*, 127–28, 131, 141, 151, 154; in *Oliver Twist*, 18, 33, 35, 38, 53

Pastoral/ Golden Age material, 23, 40, 123, 149, 152–54 (*see* Utopia)

Pinchbeck and Hewitt, 206

Pip, 197–98, 203; and cannibalism, 169–72; and displacement, 18, 191–92; fantasies of, 173–74, 176–77, 179–83; and gender, 195; and guilt, 175; maturation of, 176–78, 186–87, 193–94; narrative of, 166–68, 184, 189–90, 196, 199–200; and orphan condition, 13, 15, 23–24, 169, 185–86

play, 43, 73–76, 97, 215

Plot: paranoid, 17–18, 32, 54, 68, 134; providential, 17–18, 32, 54

Polarization, 16, 50, 51–52, 87, 116; breakdown of, 43, 70, 73–74, 159; of gender, 213; of good and evil, 17–18, 34; of values, 21, 116, 149, 150; (*see* Melodrama, Plot)

Poor Law, 35, 36, 45, 49, 206–7

Poovey, Mary, 213

Postmodernism, 28, 210–11, 212, 215

Preoedipal stage, 122, 174, 202, 204–5

Price, Martin, 116

prison imagery, 29, 134–35, 140–41, 146–47, 154

projection, 35, 134–35; cannibalistic, 37–38; Frankenstein, 179–80; of imagination, 187–89; narrative, 63, 91–92; and Pip, 187, 189, 191–92; of rage, 18, 20, 34; reciprocal, 138–40, 155, 188; renunciation of, 199; self, 63, 138, 139, 148

Protestant Ethic, 19, 22, 56–57, 69–70, 209

redemption, 18, 23, 150–51

repression, 142, 155, 198, 214; in Esther, 88–89, 95, 96, 98–100; in *Oliver Twist*, 32–34, 43; in Victorian culture, 22, 70, 185, 209, 216

retribution, 14–15, 107–9, 182

Richard Carstone, 27, 39, 91, 128; as Bildung figure, 87, 116–19, 124; destruction of, 43, 122, 123; and infantile fantasy, 120–21, 125, 132–33

Rigaud, 134, 138, 142–43, 146; and relation to past, 155–58

Romanticism, British, 29

Rousseau, 209

Satire, 43–44, 66, 104, 136–37

Sedgwick, Eve, 213

sexuality, 26, 45, 48, 89, 107; disembodied, 133; of Nancy and Sikes, 39, 47, 53; and Steerforth, 73, 76; taintedness of, 69, 111–12, 131; treatment of, 213, 216

Sikes, 34, 36, 38, 52; and sexuality, 39, 47, 53

Simpson, Eileen, 207

sleep (liminal state), 34, 39–42, 50–52, 59
society, 134, 136, 146–47, 164; critique of, 12, 24, 154; and the Merdles, 23, 143–45, 153, 161
splitting, 81, 182, 197, 205; and aggression, 18, 34, 198; of narrative, 31, 99–100; of plot, 17
Steerforth, 58, 59, 61, 63; as David's double, 76–77, 115; and Emily, 71; potentialities of, 72–74; and play, 74–76; and sexuality, 73
Stendhal, 28
Stone, Harry, 204
Suit, 135; monstrosity of, 104–5, 119–20; as source of nurture, 117–18, 121, 123, 125–26

The Old Curiosity Shop, 54
Third-Person Voice, 18, 21–22, 160, 163, characteristics of, 100–7; disembodiment of, 160; and Esther, 88–89, 100, 103, 105; explosiveness of, 123, 185–86; expressiveness of, 85, 86–87
Tolstoy, 28
Trezises, S. D., 212
Trilling, Lionel, 151
Tulkinghorn, 22, 107, 111, 116, 125

Uriah Heep, 68–73; biblical analogue, 71–21; as double, 70–71; as grotesque, 69–69; vs. Micawber 81; and writing, 93
Utilitarianism, 44
Utopia, 16, 22–23, 72; impossibility of imagining, 123–25, 152; and Micawber, 78–80, 97

vampirism, 120
Van Ghent, Dorothy, 25, 186
vision, 16, 19, 24, 31; apocalyptic, 23, 104, 140, 150; Dickens', 31, 48; fantasy of, 23, 79–80, 180; impossibility of, 124; of utopia, 22–23, 77; of wasteland, 126, 133–34
vocation, 19, 74, 81, 82, 117–19

Watkins, Gwen, 205
Weissman, Judith, 213
Welsh, Alexander, 202
Wilson, Angus, 208
Wilson, Edmund, 26–27, 201
Wordsworth, William, 20, 29–30,
Writing, as copying, 63, 65–67; and Dickens, 43; Esther's, 91–93; as memoirizing, 63, 65–67, 80, 91, 127 physicality of, 69, 93; Pip's, 194, 199–200

Zwerdling, Alex, 15
Zwynger, Linda, 213